ON A BICYCLE
MADE FOR TWO

ON A BICYCLE MADE FOR TWO

Anna and Howard Green

HODDER AND STOUGHTON
LONDON SYDNEY AUCKLAND TORONTO

British Library Cataloguing in Publication Data

Green, Anna
  On a bicycle made for two.
  1. Europe. Journeys by bicycles.   2. Asia. Journeys by bicycles
  I. Title   II. Green, Howard
  914'.04558

  ISBN 0-340-51359-4

To
John Loudon McAdam
1756 – 1836

'On a Bicycle Made for Two'

Forenote Op. 1

arranged by Howard Green
for two recorders

ACKNOWLEDGMENTS

Those many, many personal donors who gave generously to our work in Nepal on the strength of our cycling there won't mind, we're sure, not being mentioned by name. The following organisations, however, should be mentioned: Ardingly College, Arthur's Mission, Bermondsey Medical Mission, Boots PLC, Charterhouse-in-Southwark, Ciba Geigy Pharmaceuticals, (the staff of) Dulwich Picture Gallery, JJ Promotions – Sealink, The Latimer Trust Fund, 'On Yer Bike' Tower Bridge Road, Phoenix Mountaineering Ltd, St Mary's Church Bermondsey, Sir Charles Jessel Charitable Trust, Southcott's Dental Surgery, Sprayway Ltd, Standard Chartered Bank, Tring Parish Church.

And a huge thank you, too, to our typists, Collette, Janette, and Sarah, who, despite the caprices of the Nepali electricity supply, helped us to get the text to the publishers on time.

Anna and Howard Green

Two are better than one,
because they have a good return for their work:
If one falls down his friend can help him up.
But pity the man who falls and has no one to help him
up!
Also, if two lie together, they will keep warm.
But, how can one keep warm alone?
Though one may be overpowered, two can defend
themselves.

(Eccl 4:9–12)

CONTENTS

Map		10-11
Prologue		13
1	'Vous faites le tour?'	17
2	Ecco Italia!	27
3	A Good Picture	46
4	East Meets West	69
5	Çok Güzel	87
6	Arrested in Arabia	113
7	No East, No West	137
8	Persians and Babylonians	157
9	'Hello Mishter!'	182
10	Paddling Palms and Pinching Fingers	203
11	Inching up the Indus	233
12	Gasping down the Ganges	257
13	'Bye Bye'	274
Epilogue		293
Appendix 1	Personal Effects	298
Appendix 2	For the Bike	301

PROLOGUE

'You may go out into Holborn, without precaution, and be run over.

You may go out into Holborn, with precaution, and never be run over.

Just so in Africa.'

[*Bleak House* Charles Dickens]

'*What* did you say you were going to do?'

'Maybe you could call it . . . cycling to work.'

'But it'll take you months. Whose idea was it, for goodness sake?'

We would look at one another as cold water was thrown upon cold water and try to remember, but we honestly couldn't. The idea had been with us as long as we'd known one another, it seemed – a dream from our courtship. We'd hung on to it after we were married, despite the pressures to take out a mortgage and wait for the patter of tiny feet.

There were a few occasions when we, too, wondered whether we weren't rather reckless and a plane ticket wouldn't have been more desirable: the night wild dogs got wind of us in the northern Greek mountains, for instance, and came baying and barking through the darkness to snap and snarl round our ears as we lay in the tent; or the afternoon in Cappadocia when at zero degrees and pushing against an impending dust storm, the back wheel gave a structural-sounding crack and refused to spin. If we hadn't been so tired, we might also have had the energy to wonder what on earth we were doing when, many miles from tarmac (too close to the Syrian border, we discovered), we woke to find the tent bathed in headlights and military personnel telling us we were under arrest. We had some doubts the night we had our tent knocked down by a demented Sikh at 3.15 a.m. on the border of the Punjab. At times like that, maybe it was lucky that neither of us could remember whose idea it was.

But then, who would have missed the exhilaration of scaling six thousand feet of Alps in a single, clear day and standing in the snow looking back at the road snaking away behind us? We'd never have passed up being hosted with great honour by berobed Arabs outside the town where Abraham lived. And, for cyclists, there can't be much to compare with the sixty-mile downhill run from near the Afghan border into the Indus Valley. We sped down from the mountains to the plain, from barren sands to rich greens, and from spring to high summer, in a single day.

Before we set off, we reckoned the journey would be like the little girl who had a little curl: when it was good it would be very, very good, but when it was bad it would be horrid. We had steeled ourselves to it being fifty per cent miserable and fifty per cent wonderful. It was a wide miscalculation. We weren't seasoned travellers or super-keen cyclists, so we didn't really know what to expect. But as we journeyed on we thought to ourselves, who would prefer a sleepless night on the plane trying not to look at an inferior movie when they could have been on a deserted Italian beach, or watching falling stars from a camel drover's hut in Pakistan, or in a Turkish tangerine grove, or surrounded by peacocks and fireflies on the Ganges plain? Who would exchange even the best air hostess for the hospitality of the village folk in the Greek mountains, or tea and cakes with a Cappadocian troglodyte? If we wanted something more

sophisticated, there was always the kind expatriate in
her unbelievable south Italian villa. Would anyone really
prefer the cellophane meal served, to a diet of French
cheeses, Italian wines, Greek yoghourts, Turkish sweet-
meats, Iranian kebabs, Pakistani guavas, and Indian
parathas? Who might we have sat next to on the plane,
we wondered? We would have been unlikely to have met
our Afghani mujayaddhin, or the Iranian zealot with his
legs shot off who prayed that the Ayatollah would never
die, or the hotelier who used to vomit up all his food
once a fortnight by the Ganges and then swallow a
handkerchief to clean himself out.

Which would be more memorable: a ten-hour wait at
Dacca airport, or the Iraqi cluster bombs we saw coming
down on Isfahan, the taste of almonds fresh from the
trees, the chance to swim naked in the sea at the end of
November, the minaretted skyline of Istanbul, or the
opportunity to visit the throne room of the ancient kings
of Persia? What if we'd been ill on the flight? We
couldn't have sought refuge in a hillside monastery in
Eastern Turkey to recuperate, and have had acolytes
bring up bundles of olive wood every day for the stove
in our cell. Who would prefer the disorientation of jet-
lag to the wholesome tiredness of fit bodies after doing
six hours of exercise in the fresh air? Who, indeed,
would prefer to spend money on an air fare, when
people were willing to sponsor our journey so that we
could give to medical work in a needy country? We had
to be careful that we didn't end up wondering whether
those who went any other way than the one we'd chosen
weren't themselves perhaps the half crazy ones.

Howard was to be Administrator of a programme of
low technology, educative, preventative health care in
the Himalayan kingdom of Nepal, working with Tibetan
refugees as well as the country's hill people. Anna's
official status on her visa entry form was 'undesignated

spouse', which meant that she could choose from a hundred-and-one things to do when she got there. The Christian mission we were members of, the International Nepal Fellowship, didn't take too much exception to our 'cycling to work', all six thousand miles of it, totally in tandem.

1

'VOUS FAITES LE TOUR?'

Monday, October 13th

Howard fought his way through the swigging, smoking press to the counter and managed to catch the barman's eye.

'What'll it be, Sir?' he asked, hand on the pumps.

'Two visas to Iran.' Howard smiled, but anxiously. If the visa broker hadn't managed to get them for us, we had to do some serious replanning, and we were already a day late in setting off because of their non-arrival.

'Two visas . . . ?' The barman paused, and the previous customer's froth spilled over his hand. Then light dawned. 'Oh yeah. You're the ones who couldn't get back to the Visa Shop before they closed, ain't ya?' He reached behind the bottled fruit juices and handed Howard an envelope containing our passports. Howard tore it open, and riffled through the pages. There it was: 'Consular Section of the Embassy of the Islamic Republic of Iran, London. TRANSIT VISA.' The boy who'd obtained the precious documents for us had scribbled 'Have a good trip!' on the envelope before he gave it over to his neighbours at The Welsh Harp, to keep till we picked it up.

Howard turned back to the barman.

'A half – no, make that a pint – of best bitter, please.' He downed it in two, long, satisfied draughts, paid, and

took off at a run beneath the full-faced moon. He nipped
through the London traffic to where Anna stood expectantly with the bike under a street light. We were ready
to go.

* * *

'Cor, you've really got to know one another pretty good
to cycle that.' Schoolboy voices through the Sussex
morning mist panted abreast of us. 'Going somewhere
nice?' They eyed the bulging panniers and water bottles
with the shrewdness of twelve-year-olds. When the
answer came they looked at us sideways: 'Go on! Pull
the other one,' and cycled off scornfully, Puma bags
bouncing on skinny backs. Just out of reach they struck
up: 'Daisy, Daisy, give me your answer do . . .' We
refrained from giving chase, conserving our energy for
the next six thousand miles, knowing that over the
channel we'd be plagued by the familiar ditty no longer
and guessing, too, that it would be the first of many
times we wouldn't be believed.

We were right. The next questioner was an old
Frenchman. We'd just bought two more litre water
bottles that had been totally unavailable in London
before we left. He tapped the wheels experimentally
with his walking stick and demanded,

'Vous faites le tour?'

When we said no, we were going to Nepal, he simply
fixed us disbelievingly with his rheumy gaze for a few
seconds, then straightened his beret without another
word and hobbled off. We were too elated to take
exception to these responses. After the preceding fran-
tic months of preparation and winding up affairs, it was
just a blessed relief to be on the saddle and away, free at
last.

What rooted lives we lead that it should have been
such a performance preparing to leave! There had been

some complications, it's true: like Anna's terrible anaphylactic reaction to her cholera and typhoid jab, for instance. Within half an hour of getting home she was doubled up in bed, vomiting and blacking out by turns, freezing cold, heaving with great shudders from the shoulders down. Then she'd had to have a pair of premature operations on wisdom teeth that were fine at the time, but might have caused trouble on the way. Out East, there'd have been no facilities for such fancy operations. She sat in bed with jowls like a hamster, transcribing all our required addresses into the smallest possible address book and reading up on Islamic architecture. Deciding what to pack took an age, despite Jerome K. Jerome's helpful advice: 'We must not think of the things we could do with, but only the things we can't do without.' The previous year we'd pared our luggage down every time we did a cycling trip. All the 'essentials' had to be submitted to the acid test of whether we wanted to carry them everywhere, every day, for six months. We were all too familiar with Anna's need for warmth – she suffers from Raynaud's disease – and went for the theory of 'layers' to achieve this, plus ski wear on hands and feet. We chose to start in autumn because of the need to be finished before the Indian subcontinental summer, banking also on balmy Mediterranean winters; and came really to appreciate travelling out of the tourist season. The list looks quite long (see Appendix 1) but whenever we came across pairs of cyclists we always proudly noted that, with two extra wheels between them, they invariably took twice the amount of luggage.

Planning our route began as a delightful appetite whetter, poring over the atlas to work out a route via river valleys for flatness. The Saône, the Po, the Meander, the Indus, the Ganges – just the names were exciting enough. If we did a thousand miles a month – a mere thirty-five miles a day, we'd be able to do all our sightseeing and still get to Nepal on time. The planning ended up, though, a mini expedition itself: making repeated, kafkaesque assaults on the Passport Office to get 'Letters of No Objection' and cycling round from embassy to embassy to see which countries, despite hostilities, would let two mad cyclists through.

Indeed, difficulties of communication in the embassies led us to anticipate the same in the host country, and we prepared an ideogram, laminated in plastic for the beating it would presumably get, with a map of our route and a little tandem, on one side. On the other – for camping – was a picture of the moon over our tent, alongside another picture of the sun rising, the cock crowing, and Howard and Anna setting off good and early. Until the Syrian desert, where the map of the world meant nothing to the villagers, it was invaluable.

Shortly before leaving, Howard was signing the forty-five travellers' cheques he was going to carry round his neck for the next six months. It seemed a risky way to organise our finances. It was bad enough being uninsured (the companies had refused to touch us except to the tune of the airfare we were avoiding by going by bike), but there was no banking system or credit card that would operate throughout our route except travellers' cheques. Tyre depots, though, were provided by Standard Chartered Bank, who helped sponsor us. When we made our preposterous suggestion in their very swish City office, they smilingly agreed that we could send spare tyres in advance to their branches across the world.

The next day, in our tiny Rotherhithe Post Office, the Indian Post Master was utterly mystified at having to despatch six pairs of tyres tied up with string and sealing wax (how else do you 'wrap' a tyre?) with bin/back-pannier liners stowed inside. When we explained he gave us addresses of family in Delhi, while impatient customers grumbled in the queue. We promised to write to him.

One night shortly before pedal-off we had a famous tour cyclist and writer round for supper just 'to talk things over' and her specialist vocabulary left us feeling very inexperienced. We knew this much, though; that tandems are quite a different engineering proposition from single bikes. The basics of tyre, rim, spokes, and frame have to withstand double the weight and cope with double the pedal pushing. We pampered the bike much more than ourselves when it came to packing (see Appendix 2) and we never regretted taking the amount we did. In the event, we were only once at a loss for how to repair or fine-tune anything. Howard had stripped the bike right down to find out how it all worked, while Anna stood by trying to make a connection between one part and another. Then we returned it to its maker, Chas Roberts for a final, professional going over.

We had to consider the possibility of returning to our own Maker as we got our wills witnessed, executors decided upon, and parents to agree that, in the event, it wasn't worth flying our bodies back. There wasn't even time to comfort them properly as we packed and stored our belongings, arranged for proxy signatories to our UK bank account, sewed a reflective strip on our tent bag, wrote to donors, got the gasman to come and read the meter, bought the ferry tickets, wrote to a Christian we'd heard about in Southern Turkey to ask if we could pop by for a shower (it turned out to be much more than that), sewed together a passport pouch (with material from an old blind from Anna's sister's house for strength and sentimental value), and had a farewell drink with a friend who'd had Delhi Belly ever since her honeymoon there six months before. All this, but kept going by the expectation that once on the saddle everything would calm down – and then *la tempête!*

Looking back on it, we dealt with what was undoubtedly the longest period of protracted misfortune with remarkable fortitude. A terrific storm blew over us before our first week was up. People used to cars and trains cannot readily imagine just how exposed one is on a cycle, miles from habitation, at the mercy of furious weather. The rain beat on our raincoat hoods so loudly we literally couldn't hear one another shout. The rain having seeped past our raincoats, they served chiefly as wind-traps blowing us to a halt or into the kerb at any moment. Our shoes squelched as we strained on the pedals, passing vehicles sprayed grit up our trousers which chapped as we rode, headlights (on from 4.30 p.m. because of the cloud) glistened blindingly off the roadsurface. Finally a combination of a sudden gust and the air pocket produced by a passing juggernaut had us in genuine fear for our lives. There was nothing for it but to turn off into the mud and put the tent up in the bog right there and then. Not long past tea time we were in one another's arms, in dampish sleeping bags that zipped together, marooned on our Karrimats with everything else we possessed soaked and grimy, and the tent like a drum skin over us, pounded by the rain. That was only the first day. By the fourth, Howard had incurred a bruise which was to last until Istanbul in the heel of his hand from trying to control the bike.

The *tempête*, however, finally blew itself out and left us to bask in the delights of mid and southern France: the lovely Norman architecture, the wonderful autumn colours, a local cheese to be tried in every region, and fresh baguettes for breakfast. Because this was familiar cycling territory we still had niggles of apprehension about what was to come, but we never once doubted that we were doing the right thing, even during the worst of the storm. During the months leading up to our departure, Anna had stumbled across the same verse in Psalm 27 over and again:

'The LORD is my light and my salvation – whom
shall I fear?'

It came in her reading, in sermons, in chance conversa-
tions, in a greetings card, even at a funeral. It just kept
popping up as if God really was trying to reassure her
that He was behind us. On the journey this psalm was to
prove a great source of comfort. In fact, we'd felt so sure
about the trip that we'd been emboldened to do something we'd never really had the faith or the occasion to
do before: to pray with others specifically for physical
healing. Twice since we'd been married Howard's left
leg had inexplicably and very painfully given out so
completely that he'd been unable to walk without a stick.
It had been a watershed for us to get to the point where
we really believed God would heal, so it was very
confusing when the tell-tale twinges came back in the
arch of the foot and the back of the knee. Did we push
on in belief in God the Healer, or were we forced to say
that our prayers hadn't 'worked'? So we prayed again –
very forthrightly – and the pain left, for good.

We had chosen to read the Exodus story on our trip,
dividing it up so that we would reach our promised land
at the same time as Joshua. We expected the Israelites'
journey somehow to give insights into our own. In fact,
our insights proved to be mostly basic, even earthy. Our
experience of 'modern' life was progressively replaced,
from as early as Italy, with a much more primitive one,
which brought the hitherto dry and quaint practices in
the Pentateuch – the sheer practicalities of living –
vividly alive for us.

We slept in some funny places those first few days:
irrigation ditches, village greens, and once beside a
public swimming pool, though we didn't realise that as
we pitched camp after dark. It seemed such a secluded
spot that Anna got dressed outside in the morning. Just
as she pulled on her leggings, a disembodied voice

boomed out something about 'getting dressed *now*' and she nearly jumped out of her skin. Then she realised that the instructions weren't for her, but for the school-children using the pool.

By Grenoble, the mountains were visible and we felt that the journey was beginning in earnest. We stayed with friends who drove us up thousands of feet between snow-laden pines, to spy on the solitary monastery of La Grande Chartreuse where the monks spend mute weeks in prayer and distillation of their delicious liqueur. This was Howard's first real experience of the mountains. He'd been a little dismissive of Anna's mild warnings about the differences between the kind of cycling we were familiar with and the Alpine climb that lay ahead, but this convinced him. He scurried off to get a more detailed map, and to check sugar supplies (still, in France, a plentiful supply of English Mars Bars) and worked out exactly what time we had to leave to get to the *col* by nightfall.

We were usually quick at our regular morning busi-ness: one inside the tent rolling up the sleeping bags and Karrimats, the other outside and unchaining the *vélo à deux* from the guy ropes and opening up the bags, which had sat under the flap all night, to repack. When the tent was empty, we'd both dismantle it, one spread-eagled on it to squash out the air (not a pleasant job when the tent was frosty wet) then roll it into its bag and clip all our luggage into its particular place on the bike. The morning we were to tackle the Alps we didn't even bother toothbrushing into the hedgerow with our water bottles, but went into the *boulangerie* for fortification without delay.

We had learned, however, that it was very important not to rush our meals, even when we were in a hurry. If we didn't chew our food properly, and leave five minutes before getting on the bike, our stomachs simply couldn't cope with digestion and energetic cycling. So, having washed our breakfast down with a large coffee, we champed at the bit for the requisite five minutes, clicked into fifteenth gear and began to mount, reducing conversation to bare necessities. Once we'd left the granite villages seemingly cut out of the rock, the grim electricity plants and factories straddling the boulder-filled river beds, the snowy views were indescribable. We filled our water bottles with sweet water gushing out from springs; village women chattered as they soaped the clothes at communal washhouses; the bells of Alpine herds clunked in the pastures; the tiniest flowers crowded along the verges; and the dwellings – scarcer and scarcer as we mounted – were covered with corrugated iron, easier for the snow to slide off.

The truth was, the road was so beautifully engineered, the gradient so even, the cool sunshine so perfect that, though we were down to five kilometres an hour at times, our only nasty moment was when Howard appeared to be dehydrated. We hadn't expected to have to use our rehydration tablets so soon. Still, anything to lighten the load. Howard dropped a couple into a water bottle and the mixture of salts and sugar cured the cramps and weakness remarkably quickly.

Drinking lots of water could be very uncomfortable when we were exerting ourselves, but as we panted up the winding road we got very dry. Often we weren't really thirsty – it was just our tongues and lips. We took to holding a mouthful of water in for as long as possible, allowing minute amounts to slip periodically down our throats. As with the food, 'little and often' was the ideal. We learned, too, that the best way to cope with the steep bends as they turned back and back on each other as we went up, was to tack across them at the most shallow gradient; from the outside of the right hand lane to the inside of the left lane – if there was no traffic coming! These tricks stood us in good stead in the months to come.

We made it from Grenoble, on its sheer plain the flattest city in Europe, up over the alpine barrier and down to near Briançon – at nearly five thousand feet the highest city in Europe – in a single day. We felt like real cyclists then, in training for the final Himalayan climb six months later, and flattered by the hands-off-the-wheel amazement of the occasional passing motorist. Our journey had well and truly begun.

2

ECCO ITALIA!

Thursday, October 30th

The dapper Italian guard sitting at the border post, soaking up the bright mountain sunshine, sprang to delighted attention as we came into view. It wasn't that he'd never seen a *tandem bici* before – the Italians are experienced cyclists – it was just that at this time of year there was very little traffic of any kind.

We'd thought it was only in comic strips that Italians waved their arms, rolled their eyes and cried 'Mamma mia', but it proved to be a predictable response when we turned up, and it could be very endearing. Indeed, what better to do (or perhaps, what else can one do?) after a meal of home made pasta, fresh bread, and at least two more courses, than sit in the midday sun which blesses this land even in winter, and comment on the world passing by?

We'd also thought that national differences would be more gradual than they proved to be. In fact, just as our 'Mother's Pride' sandwiches had become a delicacy once we crossed the Channel, so our French *baguette* had only distant cousins after the *col*. We sat outside the customs office some way down the road from the friendly guard and tucked into what they call, funnily enough, *pane francese*. It's flatter and chewier than a French loaf, and twice the price, though the same size. Italy, we were to

discover, is not cheap. Living on bread and water alone
in north Italy for a week would have come to about
twenty pounds for the pair of us. When, several countries hence, we were forced to do just that, we were
grateful it wasn't at these prices.

That lunch-time, however, we were too stimulated by
the novelty to notice how much we'd paid for our
delicious meal. When we got back on the bike and
coursed the forty kilometres down, what was a dramatic
descent was nonetheless retarded by the condition of the
road – markedly poorer than in France generally – and
by having to put on more clothes. The sweat up to the *col*
in the sun had made us forget that freewheeling down
in freezing air temperatures was going to reduce our
body heat substantially, despite the sunshine.

The mountains stretched their long arms either side
of us till well along the road to Turin. Finally, their
purple mistiness dissipated into nothing, and we were
coasting along beside terraces of grapes and autumn
apples which gave off a rich cidery smell as we crushed
the windfalls under our wheels. We stocked up on the
good pieces, and persimmons – the first of many 'exotic'
fruits to come. The laden boughs of the persimmon
trees contrasted markedly with the barely foliated pop-
lars planted in evenly spaced rows to form perfectly
square woods. They were grown for paper, and the
marshy ground they need and their openness meant
they were no good for camping.

Evening was going to be falling earlier and earlier
now and we weren't yet adaptable enough to kip down
at six o'clock. We established a new pattern to kill time
before bed: putting up the tent under cover of dark,
getting everything ready inside for sleep, then leaving it
whilst we walked along to the nearest bar, munching our
sandwiches. (Slices from a block of solid Nutella was a
luxurious new filler in Italy.) We always combed our
hair before we went in, but sometimes our boots were

evidence that we'd been tramping through muddy fields and undergrowth. We weren't sure what the village barmen made of us, nursing our drinks as close to the radiator as possible, looking over the map, writing the diary, reading our Bible, and, at the end of the evening, disappearing into the cloakroom for what must have seemed an oddly long time, armed with our shared toothbrush and emerging with newly scrubbed faces.

Italian bars were a constant pleasure. As they also served hot drinks and sometimes pastries, we spent a good deal of our spare time in them. Indeed we spent an enormous amount of time in drinking establishments – alcoholic and others – on our journey. Where else is there to go from sunset to bedtime? In the mornings we'd sit up at the gleaming stainless steel counters, bottles and taps and *cappuccino* machine winking with well polished daily care, and sip our frothing coffee with the occasional treat of a sweet croissant or a plum jam tart with almond pastry.

In the evenings we'd either go for one of the vast array of apéritifs which were things that could be ridiculously cheap in Italy, or warm ourselves with a steaming hot chocolate in which you could virtually stand up your spoon. *Ecco Italia!* Then we'd stumble along in the dark to the tent. If possible one would undress outside because both inside the cramped space too often resulted in elbows in faces and impossible contortions. We'd get into our sleeping bag as quickly as possible and make pillows of our discarded clothes, though we left on more and more as the November days wore by.

It was after one such night that we cycled into the town of Vigevano, through low lying rice fields divided by spindly breaks of aspens. The town square with doves nestling in its elegant arcading is a delightful extension of the slumbrous serenity of the outlying countryside. It's closed to traffic and, thanks to the time of year we were visiting, there was total silence save the click of our heels echoing off the walls.

This seeming tranquillity gives the lie to the circumstances in which the square was designed: by a duke who'd recently conquered the city and wanted to make quite sure everyone knew who was in charge. The triumphal arches, the antique decoration, and the meaning of a laudatory inscription in front of the adjoining castle, subtly indicate that Duke Ludovico Maria Sforza II Moro (the name is enough to show he meant business) intended to rule as mightily as the Roman conquerors of yore. It was here that we began to realise that the thing which made Italian towns so special for us were the arches everywhere: something infinitely varied about the view through one, or a series, as it is gradually revealed and framed.

That night we stayed near one of the extraordinarily ornate cemeteries that are as much a part of Italian life, and as well tended, as the roadside shrines. Both are lovingly bedecked with flowers and candles, and faithfully visited. Flower-sellers do a roaring trade outside the cemetery gates on saints' days. There is, however, something disquieting about the way in which, long after the village lights have gone out, the looming walls of the cemetery are alive with the flickering of hundreds of candles which make the swags and mouldings distort and gyrate.

Lest the proximity of our tent to a burial ground should cause offence, and because of alarmingly close dawn shooting by farmers in the surrounding woods, we rose early the next morning and sped off to Milan, noting sadly how many dead domestic animals there were in the already rubbish-choked verges. We noticed too, how much of the wayside litter comprised sodden, hard-core pornography torn from magazines. When we came across God's warning to the Israelites that, because of the Canaanites' corrupt ways even their land was defiled, it fitted uncannily.

The frequency of it, and the indiscriminate, lurid way any and every passer-by was exposed to it left us at a loss as to how to reconcile this side of Italian life with its cultural past, so fabulous and so evident.

In Milan, we browsed amongst the Tintorettos in the Brera and gazed at the forest of pinnacles on the cathedral roof. Last but not least, we went to pay homage to the basilica where Ambrose had baptised St Augustine in the fourth century.

Augustine explains in his *Confessions*: 'In Milan, I found your devoted servant, the bishop Ambrose . . . I listened attentively to his sermons . . . to see whether the reports of his powers as a speaker were accurate.' Ambrose's skeleton still lies in the church where he did that preaching, splendidly bedecked in episcopal attire and visible to all. We looked at the jawbone which spoke the words that convinced Augustine, not only of Ambrose's powers of speech, but of the Truth, exactly 1,600 years before, to the year.

We went on to Cremona, whose cathedral square boasted the best public toilets we came across on the journey and therefore had an even longer visit than the cathedral. We washed our clothes and safety-pinned them to the basket and tent bag to dry whilst we explored Stradivarius's workshop: paper patterns for the ideal placing of sound holes, stencils for embellishing, half-finished violins. Anna's violinist fingers itched to take them out of their glass cases.

A weather pattern had established itself now; misty mornings, dissipated by a reliable sun, warm lunchtimes, then very soon we'd had our heat for the day. Whenever we stopped for lunch we'd look up and try and work out a comfortable spot that would still be in the sun in twenty minutes' time. It was doing its rounds so low in the sky now that it kept swinging us into the shade while we were sitting there, penknife in hand, crumbs everywhere, and little packets of cold meat and cheese all over our laps. There was nothing for it. It was too chilly in the shade, so we'd pick everything up and stagger across with all the bits and pieces to where it was still warm.

Soon after two-thirty, the sun would give up, white in the remnants of the morning's mist – or was it the following night's already coming up? The Po valley is flat like the fens where we'd been to university and first met and there was something homely for us about the thin white layer one or two feet above the newly ploughed fields as the afternoon drew on. At five-thirty sharp the sun was over the horizon. Within fifteen minutes it would be getting hard to see the ground perfectly enough to be sure of a comfortable mattress for the night.

The night before we got to Mantua, we got caught out. We didn't like either of the first two places we'd poked around in. One proved to be poorly drained, and there were rather a lot of scuffling sounds in the other. It's no use trying to sleep if you're expecting a water rat to have a go at your pâté in the night. We had to go back through the village and plump for somewhere we'd rejected first time through. We'd go silent at times like this; it meant that what was never a particularly entertaining task had become a grind. No simple, deciding 'pillar of cloud' (Ex 13:21) for us.

After our evening in the village bar we got back to the tent to find that the zip had frozen for the first time. It was only nine o'clock and we felt intimidated. It was nothing compared with what was to come, but it was new. The next morning shocked us too, because Anna's watch said that the sun should have been up for ages, but from inside it looked as though dawn was only just breaking. Outside, the frozen fog was so thick we couldn't see more than ten yards across the field. It was the first night our water bottles had frozen, and by the time we were up and going we were both suggesting tentatively to one another that we might be able to splash out on extra large hot chocolates in Mantua.

A remarkably short time after we'd huddled over them we were taking off all our outer layers in the entrance courtyard of the Palazzo del Te. It's a wonderful suntrap, as well as a cheeky masterpiece: designed in the 1530s it's an optical illusion from start to finish. It comes after a long period in Italian architecture in which the most fabulous successes had been achieved in harmony between parts, symmetry in design, order, monumentality – the grand effects of Classical forms. In this palace the architect 'puns' with the architectural vocabulary that had become so familiar and he upsets your expectations at every turn.

There are the central paths cutting the courtyard into four quarters, the grand entrance doors at the head of each path, but . . . as you look you get the suspicion that the doors aren't quite central. 'Ah,' you think, 'but there are the same number of windows each side of the door, so it must be central. But no. It still doesn't look it. Maybe the spaces between the windows are slightly different? No, there are the same number of big rusticated blocks between them. Are the windows the same size? Yes, the same number of panes.'

We left it, foxed, to go inside the rooms where there were more, but more obvious, tricks. Either the walls were painted with such convincing outdoor scenes that you thought you were looking out of the window to the garden, or there were painted giants up in the roof about to pull great boulders down on your head. It was delightful.

But we still hadn't solved that door and we didn't want to leave until we had. Maybe the frieze at the top had a clue? It was no help at all; its divisions stretching and contracting along the length of the building with absolutely no relation to anything below. It was subtle: unless you stood there to scrutinise it you could easily go straight past and think it was 'just another Classical building'. It took Howard to go up to the wall and measure the size of the bricks with the span of his hand to begin to find out the deception. The bricks weren't an even length, so they made the windows look symmetrical, even though they weren't. The big blocks down at flower bed level had been played around with in the same way to mask the discrepancies between the windows. As if to distract you, you would suddenly notice that the central block above one of them had slipped out of position and had a crack down the middle of it. No, the building wasn't collapsing with age; it had been built to look that way.

If the building wasn't completely wrong, then the ground it stood on had to be. It was brilliant. It was indeed the ground. Howard paced along the edge of the grass quadrangles and discovered that they were out by one and a half paces. From six feet off the ground, the eye cannot hope to notice the difference and immediately blames the building which it can scrutinise much more accurately. The architect brings you into the courtyard a few feet off centre, and compensates for it in every way possible by fiddling the building. If you're deceived in the first three seconds, you'll puzzle away until you start distrusting the very ground you stand on – and there you have it!

The next day we began an unwitting second honeymoon, quite ruining our weekly mileage rate, and surprised remote Italian farmers on wiggly minor roads with our requests for directions. This was Palladio country. By the time we'd left Venice, we'd seen more than three-quarters of all he built, and had thumbed the Penguin *Palladio* till the page edges were black. Particularly heart-warming was the way most of the villas were in use as they had been designed to be. Under the cleanly dentilled cornice there would frequently be a functioning grain store in the roof, avoiding the damp of the reclaimed land. Sometimes we'd see a tractor lumbering out of the sweep of the drive under the noses of the Roman goddesses adorning the gateposts, or returning from the nearby vines to deposit its load in the barns, beautifully integrated with the living quarters. Hours of poring over Palladio textbooks at college couldn't have paid off better for us than this.

Those vines, as well as providing soft, sparkling wines that occasionally found their way into our water bottles, also provided us with the pleasantest tent cover. We'd wheel the bike through the tunnels of leafy trellises. The overhead cover would give us a warmer night – and sometimes a free breakfast in the morning. We only gleaned if the crop had already been harvested and a bunch here and there missed out. 'When you harvest your grapes in your vineyard,' we read in Deuteronomy (24:21), 'do not go over the vines again. Leave what remains for the alien.' That was just what it felt like when the farmers, early tramping the fields, would turn a kindly blind eye to our presence. How different they were to prove to be from the Punjabi farmers who actually came and unzipped our tent at dawn to see what was inside.

In Vicenza we saw the extremest example of Italy's outlandish cycling habits. On our first day in Italy we had honestly wondered whether Italian law required cyclists to cycle on the opposite side of the road to the motorised traffic, we'd seen so many doing so. We watched two amorous cyclists wend their way – on a single bike, not on a tandem – across the supposedly sacred pedestrian precinct round the medieval town hall which Palladio had ingeniously revamped. Blissfully unaware of the architectural triumphs around them, Juliet sat on the handlebars, feet on the crossbar, facing Romeo, who narrowly missed overturning the pair of them as he tried to snatch a quick kiss and forgot he also had to do the steering.

Indeed, the natives' cycling habits in general made us

look pitifully staid. It was nothing to see one person on
the saddle and another standing, not sitting, in the back
basket, hands placed lightly on the other's shoulders for
stability. Even if they didn't get as many people on one
frame as the Subcontinentals, the Italians won the prize
for inventiveness.

In Padua we had a nasty sense of *déjà vu* when, turning
up at the address of Standard Chartered for a new set of
tyres, we found that the branch had moved to Milan as
the one in Lyon had done to Paris. There was nothing we
could do, for it was too far to cycle back. We made for the
Giottos instead. In Padua there are a fabulous thirty-
eight frescoes in one chapel. The wonderful thing about
them is the way he manages to convey the emotion of the
people not only by the expression on their faces but also
by the attitude of the body. As Christ receives Judas's kiss
(it is evident he is not kissing Judas back) the way he
inclines towards him somehow echoes the terrible sorrow
in his face. Giotto's not all serious though. In the
Adoration of the Magi the wise men are rapturously making
obeisances to the infant king while their servant scrupulously adjusts a camel's bridle.

With Giotto's lovely shepherd's delight pinks and blues
irradiating our minds' eye, we took the beautiful canal-
side road to Venice, literally lined with palaces. We were
brought down to reality with a bump, as we negotiated
the suburban sprawl of Mestre. Between them, Mestre
and Venice must comprise one of the greatest juxta-
positions in Europe; Mestre a caricature of industrial
sprawl and wasteland, Venice the unparalleled fairy,
floating city. It was Remembrance Day. As Britain stood
still for two minutes at eleven o'clock, we were negotiating
mini spaghetti junctions and having the living daylights
honked out of us for not moving fast enough at the
green light. By the time Britain was sitting down to
Sunday lunch, we were wandering the canal banks to the
sound of lapping water. We had been assured by people,

none of whom were able to give us any firm reason why, that we couldn't wheel the bike into the city. But we went ahead and did just that, lifting it over the little stone bridges without anyone stopping us, till we found a reasonable hotel.

Who can describe the magic of Venice? We shan't try. We'll go back one day, for three weeks instead of three days, armed with John Julius Norwich and an umbrella. We certainly wouldn't visit any other time than November when across the water Palladio's church of Il Redentore disappears quite from view in the fog and there's not a soul to share the sober interior with you once you've disembarked from the *vaporetto* at its steps. We shall remember not to visit St Mark's after 6.00 a.m. either, when the salmon-pink light of dawn is beginning to reflect off the wavelets on to the stone, and there are only sleepy pigeons for company. All this contrasting it has to be said, with the constant short-changing and queue barging of the Venetians themselves, for whom the tourist, perhaps understandably if not excusably, is to be despised then rooked. 'Alien': it's a word that comes up frequently in the Exodus story. Until our own Exodus it had sounded strange, indeed comic, to our ears. Suddenly, however, we were able to shuffle off associations of outer space and the film industry, and identify with it. Usually, though, our alien status won for us far more privileges and kindnesses than abuse.

Before we left Venice, we had two strokes of practical luck. We met a couple of British cyclists on their way back from Turkey and North Africa. Besides helping us to feel we weren't such weirdos after all, they also gave us lots of useful information about the countries we were going to cross. The Turks sounded amazingly hospitable. The other stroke of luck was when we went to get the rabies jabs we hadn't had time for in London. With many a 'Mamma mia' and tongue-clicking at the unfamiliar doses the British nurses had given us at six pounds apiece at British Airways, they finally inoculated us – for free. We came out feeling quite pro the EEC.

Coming back to the world of motors was a nasty shock: the perpetual white noise of engines and unpleasant petrol smells. Little did we think there was to come a time, many miles hence, when the sound of a car was to be the sweetest thing our ears could hear. We noticed how easy it was to begin to dread discomfort, after the proper room in Venice – the possibility of rain, painful frost, or the uncertainty of where we'd wash. Anna was to have to work against a mild resentment, of a cold evening, against those with warm houses and hot food. Ironically, when her fantasies came true and these were put unremittingly at our disposal in Greece and Turkey, we sometimes even turned the offers down, so we could have a bit of peace!

We took what we hoped would be the warmer coast road to Ravenna, with its churches and tombs dating from the fifth century. There were marvellous frescos here and mosaics surpassing those of St Mark's. There was a foretaste in Ravenna's church of San Vitale with its *matronae* – overhead galleries for women – of the separation of the sexes we were to experience in church in Pakistan and Nepal. Ravenna's sights were some of the high points of the journey, but that evening was also one of the low points.

Where they occurred, our downs were usually as a result of a string of bad pieces of luck, and frequently featured the wet or cold. It was just so in Ravenna, taking two hours to find a tent site in the beginnings of rain, newly aware in the city traffic that our back light wasn't working, being attacked by the first dog of the night in a public park, and being shouted at by farmers when we looked hopefully in the direction of their hedge. When we came off the bike, having taken a bend too sharply, that was it. *Faute de mieux* we plumped for the shelter of Ravenna Tourist Office. We were far too visible unless we put our tent right up against the wall but ... there proved to be a pavement sticking out two feet from it.

It seemed like the end, but that night we learned how to put the tent up on concrete. Despite the ravenous Alsatian dog next door who snarled on his leash as we tried our darnedest to be as quiet as possible, we put pegs in on the side of the tent abutting the grass and tied the guys on the other side to protrusions from the wall. The final stabiliser was our bungy which we passed round the pole and attached to the grille of the toilet window. Sleeping on concrete didn't induce the sweetest of slumbers.

In a nearby bar, bruised, damp, and exhausted, we came to the conclusion that the trip did sometimes produce special areas of testing and endurance where we owed it to one another to try even harder than usual to be tolerant of each other's bad moods and strict with our own. We don't remember arguing on the journey. We'd learned how easy it was to cause a bad situation to deteriorate rapidly by mishearing one another through the rustle of leaves or past the noise of overtaking lorries, so for both our sakes we'd enunciate extra specially clearly at potential friction points. Maybe, even, it was answered prayer: when our church asked whether we had any specific prayer requests for the journey, Anna said she was most afraid of being a whinger when things got uncomfortable. However, sipping *caffè corretti* (coffee 'corrected' with a dash of liqueur!) and nibbling at a hazelnut chocolate apiece, we also had to conclude that our times of trial had so far been extremely few and far between.

The coast road down to Rimini reminded Anna of the Côte d'Azur out of season, where she'd worked as an au pair, with its boarded and shuttered resorts. There were the same alluring night club signs gathering cobwebs, the same smart restaurants, coloured lights now forlorn necklaces of dead bulbs, the same vast barbed wired campsites. We were glad to be experiencing them in winter and had lunch on the empty beach more often than not.

Rimini opened up the possibility of a short detour inland to the independent state of San Marino, and thus sneakily adding a ninth country to our overall total. Founded in AD 885 this is one of the oldest and tiniest states in the world, striking its own coinage, with its own police force and army. They're friendly enough with Italy not to make you show your passports though. It's a veritable *nid d'aigle*, perched atop the three peaks of Monte Titano and, because of its extreme height, start-led us with the first mist-free night since the Alps. It was the anniversary of our departure, and full-faced above us stood the moon. We pitched the tent on the edge of one of the concentric rocky terraces with magnificent views over the sheer cliff. Owing to the intervening clouds, the towns and villages in the abyss looked like great ships floating at anchor. We had the balmiest sleep imaginable and rose in the morning to explore the medieval fortress and landscaped slopes before the hawkers opened their booths to sell, amongst other more expected tourist tat, fluffy Pink Panthers! The town subsists almost entirely on its tourist trade, profit-ing particularly from its stamps and alcohol. We plunged giddily back down to the sea mist before the first tour bus had disgorged its passengers.

It was sad to see so much on our journey how, from the visitors' point of view, 'travel' and 'tourism' can be antagonistic to one another. Well managed, the antagon-ism can be disguised, and in rare cases they can merge to mutual benefit. Overall, however, our prejudices were confirmed again and again: tourism, in the pejorative sense of the word, devalues the quality of relationships between visitor and host, causes the host to adapt to the visitor more than the other way round, and thus distorts and makes unreal the very thing that draws the visitor in the first place. Real travel, on the other hand, can produce the most memorable and touching relationships, maintains the honour of 'host' and 'guest', changes the outlook and understanding of the traveller, and leaves the life style of the host unspoiled enough for the next traveller to appreciate. 'Unspoilt'; hasn't the word now got a new and specific meaning – not visited by hordes of people? We were probably pretty snobbish about it too: we had the time, the independent transport, the winter, and the necessity of traversing remote places on our side.

As we made our way down to Bari, that balmy night became the norm. The landscape was transformed into a drier, rockier, cacti-sprouting land. The deep aquamarine of the sea was rivalled only by cloudless azure skies. The people were industrious, laying nets under the trees to catch the olives, making honey, and culling the figs that had become an important part of our bread-heavy diet. The cost of living got noticeably lower, and we stuffed ourselves on fresh pizzas. It was 'a good land – a land with . . . vines and fig trees, pomegranates, olive oil and honey; a land where bread will not be scarce.' (Deut 8:8).

Bari, the birthplace of that same St Nicholas who resuscitated the pickled boys of Britten's cantata, and where Virgil breathed his last, provided another rude contrast to the preceding coastline. If we thought the Italian queueing and traffic habits were bad elsewhere, Bari was worse. A splendid policeman in a spanking white hat presided proudly over the mayhem from his platform, not taking any notice of the cars parked five deep on the pavements and others driving round at racetrack speeds. In the post office, they simply refused to make any effort to find a large parcel we knew had been sent poste restante from our parents; the first of several missives to go astray, each producing the same homesick disappointment.

We fled the crush of central Bari as soon as we could disentangle our pedals from the surrounding traffic and mend our first blow-out, and made our way to an outlying village where we made one of the really special friendships of the trip. We'd been given this woman's address as 'the representative of the Diocese of Gibraltar' in southern Italy, but there was nothing grandiose about her, despite her title. She was simply a displaced Anglican like ourselves, a Cambridge woman, married to an Italian architect and town planner. They live with their golden haired daughters in a spacious villa they'd bought for a song and gradually done up in the most tasteful, gracious style imaginable.

We had our own cool rooms below the main part of the house, giving on to the citrus trees and swimming pool of the colonnaded garden. They scolded us roundly for pitching our tent the previous night in a grove of palm trees on Bari sea front, for fear of disturbing them at too late an hour. Then they spoilt us rotten on cream cheeses, pomegranates, wild *funghi*, and Palladio talk with Antonio over gin and tonics. We wondered why we'd ever got on the bicycle seat if studies and diligence could buy this kind of comfort. Ours weren't the only moist eyes when we left the Villa Squicciarini. That night though, we found an unforgettable moon-silvered beach on which to pitch the tent and, comforted, fell peacefully asleep to the gentle lapping of the waves.

The next morning we kept to the smaller coast road we always preferred to the main one, and hoped for a bank. Travellers' cheque time in Italy was always a despondent one. Not only did we lose track of our money faster here than any other country, but we lost track of our tempers in the banks too. In France you get an element of consumer relations' overkill as you walk in: high-tech laminates, and the oh-so-casual clothes to make you feel at home. In Italy you can't even get in without snarling up in the security system. You beg the doorman behind the bullet-proof sheeting to help you through the pressure pads on the floor, the green buttons, red flashing lights, and double locking systems. When you do finally get in, you get studied, corporate indifference. Italian xenophobia reaches its height at the foreign currency counters. In a place called Monopoli, of all things, where you might expect to find a good banker, it came to a head. If it had been the end of August and tetchy tourists had been flocking through all season it might have been understandable, but it was the middle of November and to be honest, Monopoli is unlikely to be flush with tourists at the best of times.

It was pretty big hearted of us to call it the 'foreign currency counter' because it's unlikely to be marked and probably moves according to where the appropriate person is sitting on the day. The close bunches of people around each cashier don't look very inviting and it appears that the employees are deliberately trying to avoid catching your eye. You find the smallest huddle and wait for a very long time till the fellow glances up and tells you to go 'over there', waving his hand in a Mediterranean manner calculated to convey more exasperation than direction. Someone else is already being served before you have the chance to ask for clarification. You press him and now both he and the other customer are angry. You go off and can't believe your luck when you find the fellow free – and he is the foreign currency counter – but no . . . 'You have to come with forms filled out first, and they're available over there'. He points meticulously and unmistakably to a large huddle of shoulders at a particularly popular counter. You smile with gritted teeth and join the throng.

You even get to feel sorry for this next cashier perhaps, because of the intrusive interruptions he's got to put up with. You may even study the group dynamics and have a bash at copying some successful moves. Being a well brought-up English child though, you soon lose heart when someone firmly elbows you out of the position you've stealthily inched your way into. You take to practising your Italian phrase quietly to yourself instead so that you don't get outmanoeuvred by split second indecisiveness. Finally you're at the front: you've got there by fair means and not foul, he looks you squarely in the eye, you open your mouth, and he picks up the sheaf of paper that's just been pushed forward over your right shoulder.

Rats! When you finally get the forms, they're enormous; you wonder what on earth they're going to do with all this information they request, and there's no carbon paper, so you've got to do it all twice, but you're chuffed, because you remembered to bring a biro, didn't you? You tell them everything they want to know about which town you were born in, sign with a flourish, and look back to the 'foreign cash counter'. He's not there, and you've got to catch someone's eye to ask where he's gone . . .

Further down the coast, we came across the Roman road that Horace had travelled on during his journey from Brindisi to Rome. The rutted paving stones are still visible. By contrast, in Brindisi itself it's hard to conjure up much of the atmosphere of the historic sailing for the Battle of Actium which most probably took place from there. On the surface it's just another busy port. Killing time in the harbour before we could board the overnight ferry to Greece we fell talking with a bright eyed Canadian who looked at our luggage with a professional: 'Going far?'

If any pride did betray itself in our voices when we stated the truth, he unwittingly erased it with his own gently told story. He'd been on the road for eight years, he said, on a bicycle, till last New Year when he'd given it away. He preferred to walk, he explained, for just as we

gauged the pace of cycling to be infinitely more con-
ducive to observation than a car ('so much television' he
called that) in the same way did he compare a good pair
of feet to a cycle. 'I haven't plumbed the depths of
Europe yet,' he said, and of course he hadn't. The only
thing he regretted about the change was that, with the
bike, so had gone his respectability and credibility in the
eyes of the police. A man on foot, it would seem, neatly
but not pristinely dressed from whatever he could find,
getting a picking job here and there to maintain himself,
suddenly became an object of suspicion to the authorities in a way that a cyclist, perhaps doing exactly the
same thing, did not.

From our point of view, it seemed a pity to be so
confined to non-Communist Europe west of Italy: the
only countries which would tolerate his wanderings.
From his, he said, it gave him the time he needed to
concentrate. The one thing he missed was reading
matter. What was most striking about this man,
however, was not his stories nor his precarious closeness
to the breadline (though only with the utmost pressing
would he share the smallest part of our food, assuring us
that he wasn't starving, and trying, in turn, to share his
own comestibles). The striking thing was his normality.
By any standards he was courteous, cultured, self-
possessed, slightly wry perhaps, but totally acceptable
and indeed unexceptional, except in the walking he'd
been doing. 'This is the life I've elected to live' he stated,
simply and without any pretension. The truth is, you
can still be normal and do unusual things.

3

A GOOD PICTURE

Thursday, November 20th

We'd been warned again and again about culture shock when we got to Asia, but nobody had told us about Greece. Perhaps it had to do with the fact that Igoumenitsa was a port and a resort out of season, which always confers a certain forlorn shabbiness; this in contrast to the prosperity of Brindisi which we'd left the night before, and the luxurious hot showers we'd taken on the half-empty ferry. Ridiculous as it may seem the drab, dated clothing of the people, and the general unavailability of goods in the small dusty shops that morning were more of a surprise to us than the pavement dwellers in Delhi. We were probably also affected by the general non-comprehension that first hits one in a foreign country. Anna felt particularly at sea not so much because she didn't understand the language, but because, not having Classical Greek as Howard had, she couldn't even make head or tail of the script. In Italy we'd usually made out pretty well deciphering the shop signs and drawing links with the languages we knew.

We disconsolately trudged up and down grey streets, some with, some without pavements, past old women on their way to mass, dressed in black, heads covered. Grubby-faced children in old rayon sweaters peeked at us from unlit shops. Finally Howard laboriously spelled

out b-r-e-a-d painted on a window and we went inside
the bakery. Things began to look up. There wasn't
much to choose from – mostly white loaves like over-
sized bloomers you could buy all, or half, or quarter of –
but they were coming out hot before our very eyes. It
was a nice change after Italy to be able to buy a loaf
which lasted the whole day and cost the equivalent of
30p. We ate puffs too, full of piping hot goat's cheese
and herbs, as we sat on the sea wall looking out at the
spits of land fading into the distance. We washed down
the last morsel with tiny cups of Greek coffee which are
best swallowed in one go, to avoid mixing the bitter half
inch of grains at the bottom with the good, strong, black
liquid. Perhaps Greece wasn't so daunting.

We left the port and began to climb. This northern
area of Greece is really very mountainous. It took us
some days to grow to see the beauty of the dry, thorny
terrain, accustomed as we were to the rolling verdure of
the south of England. When we saw a dead donkey on
the road, its guts and last meal all spewed out over the
tarmac, our revolted pity gave way to reflecting how
much it cost to buy a new donkey, and how did you pull
your vegetables to market or get around without one? It
brought Exodus right into the New Testament for us: 'If
you see the donkey of someone who hates you fallen
down under its load, do not leave it there; be sure you
help him with it.' (Ex 23:5)

Before us reared the Pindos mountains, the first real
climb since the Alps, now in considerable heat. Having
stripped off to the last layer (which still couldn't solve
the problem of Anna's fur-lined ski boots) we thought
how strange it was to be getting hotter as November
drew on. Instead of being able to climb steadily up, as
the beautiful French road had enabled us to do, Greek
mountain roads, we found, go up and a little down, up
and a little down. We couldn't simply click into fifteenth

gear and apply ourselves concertedly which is, in the
end, much less tiring.

Our Bible study that first day on the Greek road was
the account of the Israelites asking the King of Edom for
permission to go through his territory if they promise to
stick to the main road. The image the story gives of a
highway slicing impersonally through the country was
apposite. Our road wove through the mountains, never
touching the real life of the villages and towns. It was
virtually empty except for us and the occasional delivery
van shattering the crisp mountain stillness with a
megaphone proclaiming its wares – a disturbance we'd
resented in Italy. There were very few private cars. If we
did see any local traffic, before long it would turn (or
trot) off down one of the little concrete side roads which
led to the villages. Pausing at the top of a hill for a
breather and looking through a break in the mountains
to our left, a thought suddenly crossed our minds. We
got out our map to check and there, sure enough, in
large letters was printed ALBANIA. It only served to
reinforce our sense of isolation. We were grateful at
least that our aloneness would ensure we'd have no
problem with a tent spot. We didn't. There was never
any problem in Greece, though it was often rather
prickly under the Karrimats. There was plenty of free
land and people left us alone.

The sun began to sink, but we decided we'd try to get
within hailing distance of the next village before we
stopped. The day's climb had been really stiff and we
didn't fancy starting off the next morning without
breakfast – if it could be obtained. We heard shouts from
over the fields and made out two figures waving vigor-
ously. We waved back, remarking how friendly these
Greeks were. Five minutes later we heard 'Hey stop!'
from behind and a young man came panting up beside us
on a very nice British bike. His companion had stayed
behind to look after their tent. John and Vicky were

cycling to China for War on Want, taking a different route from ours after Greece but planning to arrive in Pokhara about the same time as us, before going on to the Chinese border. We said goodbye in the falling dusk, and arranged to meet again in five months' time which, sure enough, we did. It was a nice meeting, one of those strange encounters the traveller seems to fall prey to; even stranger when we discovered months later that Vicky's Mum and Howard's had a mutual friend.

We were lucky that night. We happed upon the only roadside *taverna* for many miles. We pitched the tent under an oak tree and went to sit on a dry stone wall nearby to eat our sandwiches in silence. We'd been rather shaken up by John and Vicky's itinerary. They were avoiding Iran and the troubled Punjabi zone of India altogether, by flying. Had we planned something impossible? Our worries were cut short by the *taverna* proprietress addressing us from her chicken coop. 'Oh dear, we'd better get off her wall,' said Howard, hastily beginning to wrap up our olives and tomatoes. But she was smiling widely and when she realised we didn't understand she made shivering motions, drawing her black shawl closer about her and pointing first to us and then to the door. We tried to say that we'd finish our food and then come in for a drink, but no, that wasn't her meaning either. We must come in and eat our sandwiches by the fire. We felt pretty awkward. Howard said the sign meant this was a place selling both food and drink. We couldn't even have eaten our sandwiches on a British pub wall, let alone inside, but she was joined by her husband and a couple of friends all enjoining us to come in. This was the evening we felt we really graduated from being tourists to travellers. They just treated us like honoured guests.

Inside it was very simple – stone floor, basic wooden furniture – but it couldn't have been cosier or cleaner. The central stove was basically a metal cylinder, with a pipe that went up through the ceiling. The kettle sat and hissed on top and its various lids and doors were periodically opened to pack in more wood, to check the coal level, or to fan the embers. Chairs were drawn up right beside the stove for us and great interest taken in our ideogram. When they saw the picture of the tent, they shook their heads sorrowfully and urged us to sleep by the heat. We protested that a drink would be enough to warm us, so they offered us Retsina or Ouzo – the standard choice. When we tried to pay and found to our embarrassment that we didn't have small enough denominations, they waved away our notes and brought out tasty little plates of cheese and something like bubble-and-squeak, in filo pastry. Greek Special, they aptly called it, and then they left us to write and read and watch TV with them – a British detective serial from the 1970s which reminded us incongruously of our teens.

This kind of warm but thoroughly discreet hospitality was to become the norm in northern Greece. There was the woman in the village shop one evening, who overheard us explaining our trip to the grocer. We were sat on a bench a little way down the road when she came past and quickly thrust a little packet of cold meat on us before hurrying off without a word. There was the *taverna* where someone came in selling bunches of luscious grapes. Before we knew where we were, three huge clusters were on our table, the landlady was offering to wash them and put them in a plastic bag for us, and whoever had paid for them was keeping mum while everyone else grinned and winked and wished us well. Occasionally the donor had a link with Britain: one man brushed away our thanks, saying his son had been well treated there. He couldn't, he protested, holding out two pints of lager, do anything but treat British children likewise. Another fellow told us he'd formed a 'good picture' of the Brits from the army of liberation. This, or admiration for our venture, was only ever a very partial explanation for what was, at root, the milk of human kindness, proffered with a consistency and an openness that made us question our famous British reserve. The old man's phrase, 'good picture' stuck in our minds. It made us realise how important our role as ambassadors was: as the British attaché in Teheran was to describe it, 'to maintain relations between peoples, irrespective of governments'.

The one bad experience we had, where we were wilfully misunderstood and barefacedly rooked only seemed to clinch this evaluation. It was on the coast road where rural Greece was being transformed into the same tourist trap as Corfu and the islands down south. We'd been tantalised occasionally, of an evening, by the skewered lamb barbecuing outside the village taverns, and one night decided to have some. Probably this *taverna* owner had received a thoroughly 'bad picture' from affluent holidaymakers, unable to speak his language, but intent on taking possession of his beaches. How easy in such a framework to 'take advantage of . . . an alien' (Deut 24:14). The hurt went surprisingly deep though, as the sniggers went round the room when the barman announced how much he'd charged us before we were even quite out of the door. It wasn't just that we'd been let down in the place that was treating us so exceptionally well, but that we'd become personally implicated through others' bad witness. We were to find a similar legacy waiting for us on the hippy trail out East.

It was the same with the TV. Those first kind *taverna* owners away from the port and off the beaten track probably owned the only set in the village and got most of their ideas about the affluent West from it. No wonder we sometimes get a bad press. To an unsophisticated villager and his farmer neighbours the scarcely clad blonde astride the bar of soap she's advertising is not only crude but probably rather baffling, because it is so far from their own experience. We possibly wouldn't have turned a hair at the soap advertisement at home, but after observing their simple way of life, we began to receive the innuendoes a little bit as they might, without sensibilities dulled by over familiarity, and we were angered by the demeaning 'picture' we saw. It contrasted conspicuously with their own attempts to produce an advert that was 'modern' and 'attractive': their 'Tasty Crisps' one, for instance, with poor shots of little boys on BMX bikes. They had no background or context but just cycled on to the screen from nowhere, did their wheelies silhouetted in front of an orange backdrop, then cycled off, still with the same manic grins on their faces. For all their clumsiness, there was something clean cut about their advertisements that we felt indicted us.

We felt that for Christians there was even a further dimension to this 'good picture' business. One night we tumbled down the goat's trail from the hillside copse in which we'd put our tent, to a quiet little village *taverna* run by a middle-aged woman. She had no English but, like many Greeks, because they send a sizeable workforce to Germany and themselves receive a goodly proportion of German tourists, had a substantial grasp of German. Anna had done two years of German at school, ten years ago, but when this woman came curiously to compare her Greek Bible with ours and began to question us closely, Anna was unnaturally capable, despite her rustiness, to convey the deepest reasons for going to Nepal. The woman's daughter was as intelligent and pretty as she was depressed by the employment situation which forced her to work, not as the potter she was trained to be, but as a garage mechanic. She forgot to chain smoke and drew closer and closer as Anna spoke of the Gospel in German. The next morning we came down for breakfast. When we'd eaten, Madam wouldn't let us pay. She hugged us, weeping silently as she waved us out of sight. 'We are . . . Christ's ambassadors' St Paul reminds us, rather awesomely. Funnily enough we were on the very road he had once taken to spread the Gospel.

It was a pity, simply to have to pass through like that but we pressed up into the mountains again and made our first bad, if understandable mistake. We'd got within ten kilometres of the summit. It was nearly time to kip down, but it was too tempting to get to the top and simply coast down in the morning. It was a beautiful evening, if a little chilly as the sun sank redly behind the pines fringing the road. With sign language and our map, we asked a goatherd whether there was a village at the summit where we might spend the evening in comfort. He nodded, pointing at the map and giving us a name, so we put on a last, end of the day spurt.

Mountain weather seldom does anything by halves. It was getting markedly colder. We began to see glistening patches of snow and ice on the road, but the exertion was keeping us warm and the height was intoxicating. We kept our heads down – a piece of advice Anna's music teacher had once given her. 'That way you don't know how far or near the top is. You just keep climbing and it comes to meet you rather than vice versa,' he'd said. At long last the ground levelled and we lifted our heads, expecting to see a friendly shop or some houses. There was a large, unlit building marking the pass and not a soul around, though we banged at the doors, dislodging some of the icicles hanging from the eaves. There was nothing for it. It was impossible to sleep here, with sharp drops on one side of us, and bare rock face on the other. We had to descend, despite the moonless night. Plunging down the ice-silvered road, skidding at the hairpin bends on gravel we could only feel, the cold bringing tears to our eyes and locking our fingers to the handlebars, it was a fine time to find out something new about one another.

Howard, despite his glasses, had night eyes Anna's excellent vision couldn't match. If she'd thought getting on the back of the tandem had been a test of faith, this was

infinitely worse. The steering and gears were exclusively
in Howard's control. Anna was like the House of Lords:
with the powerful hub brake she had the right of veto
but not much more. There was no question either, of
her taking a turn on the front. We'd tried it when we'd
first got the bike and had wobbled hopelessly all over the
road. The heaviest person has to take the front seat on a
tandem. 'Darling, are you *sure* you can see the white
line?' she shouted as we swerved and twisted in a way
that left her stomach round the last bend, though her
eyes were straining hopelessly ahead. 'What?' Howard
shouted as the rising wind took her words and tossed
them over the precipice. 'Can't we go slower?' she yelled.
'Not unless you want to be out here all night,' he
screamed back, and then, 'There'll be a village soon, my
love. Just release your brake a little.'

The natural impulse when one feels oneself skidding
is to jam on the brakes but it's the most dangerous thing
to do. It was another horrible lesson to have to learn in
such circumstances, as we careered on in the blackness
with still not a building in sight. We made only two stops.
The first was when we were forced to pause to pull on
every single item of extra clothing in our panniers,
including rainwear, with excruciatingly numb fingers
that refused to do up precious, heat-preserving buttons
and zips. The second was when the white line marking
the edge of the road gave out on us, and by some fluke it
was Anna this time who saw the edge of the road, and
the drop below just before our front wheel reached it.
Neither of us know quite how long we were on that road
until we saw the lights of a village twinkling blessedly
down to our right. It must have been hours, for we
didn't get to bed till nearly midnight having trudged
and poked round in the dark outskirts of the village in
vain for a good tent site. In the end we gave up and
pitched the tent on the next piece of ground that would

take pegs, not knowing whether we were in someone's garden, about to fall over another precipice, or what.

We soon got the idea that this was someone's patch, though, for a dog, and then another, and then another, growled and dared each other to close in on us as we listened, shivering with frost and fear. One dog was all right: between us we could take it on if we really had to. Two were probably okay, but our penknife wasn't going to be much good against three or four or more. It was typical. Our real weapon in case of emergencies, the hulking great chain we locked the bike up with, was doing just that. It would mean braving the pack first to get it. As the assault wore on into the early hours, all we could guess was that rival packs were vying over the spot we were on, for the nearest dog would seem to break off when another came in. We lay there, praying that their private quarrel would keep them from us and just hoping one wouldn't puncture the skin of the tent . . .

Though they kept it up all night, the dogs, thankfully, were too cowardly to do anything but bark. Outside Western Europe there are far more untethered and roaming, if not wild dogs. We were amazed at how many Greek villages put up with packs of hounds barking for hours on end in the middle of the night. It was to be the same all the way to Nepal. We got up the next morning fearful of where we might find ourselves, but we were only between a barn and a dung heap.

The trip gave us ample opportunity to reflect on the knotty problem of God's protection and what to expect from it. We were in no doubt that our Father would fulfil His promises to protect His children; promises so clearly expressed in the Exodus story we were enjoying:

'See, I am sending an angel ahead of you to guard you along the way and to bring you to the place I have prepared.' (Ex 23:20)

But common sense also told us that God's children wind up in plenty of sticky situations and Job's predicament was proof enough of that. How, then, should we claim this protection that is ours, yet also face facts? How did we respond to people earnestly praying for our protection? Some, we knew, believed that their prayers worked on a very pragmatic and physical level.

That same psalm – Psalm 27 – which had been laid on Anna's heart so many times before we set out, gave us a clue. It suggested to us that it's not the fact of God's protection that is variable but the type. Doesn't the psalmist change his mind or, at least, encompass many ambiguities within the given of his Lord's protection?

> 'The LORD is my light and my salvation – whom shall I fear?' (Ps 27:1)

could be read as assurance of God's physical protection, particularly in view of:

> 'when my enemies and my foes attack me, they will stumble and fall.' (Ps 27:2)

But the very fact of the enemies and foes attacking indicates that God hasn't removed the physical threat entirely. And when the writer then considers the possibility of an army besieging him and war breaking out against him he appears to make a subtle shift. He doesn't address the outward circumstances; instead he points inward: 'My heart will not fear . . . even then will I be confident.' But then he seems suddenly to veer off:

> 'One thing I ask of the LORD,
>   this is what I seek:
>   that I may dwell in the house of the LORD
>   all the days of my life,
>   to gaze upon the beauty of the LORD' (Ps 27:4)

What has this to do with protection? Isn't David suggesting here that if the believer dwells in the presence of God; if he actively seeks the beauty of His face, when 'the day of trouble' comes – and he says it will – that beauty and that sanctuary will abide with him over and above whatever terrible things may happen?

We trusted, then, that He would protect, but we didn't always know whether that protection would manifest itself as physical deliverance or something subtler – the internal assurance that even in disaster our Lord has the best for us. Sometimes our prayers encompassed a direct plea for physical help. More often, it was for protection in whatever guise He would graciously give it. We were very grateful for other people's prayers, believing that they were praying according to their own measure of faith. Our meditations on Psalm 27 didn't exclude fear – that would have been superhuman – but they did help a great deal.

After our night plunge the mountain road descended less steeply and was of the most beautiful gradient for the bike. Too steep and you have to clutch the brakes all the time; too shallow and you can't enjoy the exhilarating wind in your face. Just right – as this was – and you have the sensation of gliding: dipping, and tacking at the corners, contributing nothing to the glorious descent.

The traffic never really troubled us in Greece. It was both lighter and much safer than in Italy. There was less rubbish on the verges probably because there was noticeably much less packaging to dispose of than hitherto – a phenomenon that was to increase the further East we went. The Greeks also had their roadside shrines – frequently, here, glass-sided boxes with an icon and the Host inside. When we heard a tongue-clucking, then variations on a whistle – trilling, swooping and fluttering – we knew, even before the pungent smell rounded the corner ahead of the animals themselves, that a goatherd was coaxing his flock along. Something that was to diminish markedly as we left Europe was fences, which in turn said something about ownership of land and meant stock had to be cared for by herders instead of just leaving it to graze in safety in one's own field: 'If you come across your enemy's ox or donkey wandering off, be sure to take it back to him.' (Ex 23:4)

Something totally new to us was seeing cotton growing in the fields. We saw it at all its stages: first a prickly closed pod; then popping open into four segments revealing four buds of close-packed cotton wool round a hard seed which would have to be removed in the ginning; and then a gradual fluffing out of the cotton wool. The Greek word for cotton is *sindon* after the Pakistani province of Sind, from where the Greeks first imported it, and through which we were to travel. Until we knew what was in the sacks, the swaying cotton lorries piled sometimes twenty feet high presented fearsome road companions.

Gradually we dipped down on to the east coast road and the weather took a turn for the worse. We were in striking distance of Mount Olympus, the very House of the Gods, and there was too much cloud even to know there was a mountain there. It was one of the big disappointments of the trip. There was evidently a storm above it – we could hear the distant thunder up to our left; but Howard's suggestion that the gods were angry sounded distinctly limp.

A little inland, at the foot of the mountain, we came across the newly excavated remains of the city of Dion. Alexander the Great visited here in 334 BC. He'd come to seek the Olympians' blessing on his trip to revenge himself against the Persians who'd overrun Macedonia and the Greek mainland generations before. Our route to India was going to coincide with his a number of times so it was good to be able to visit his starting point. We were well rewarded. The drizzle stopped, the archaeological site is too recent to be touristy, the villagers were friendly, and the little museum informative. The immaculately preserved row of public loos dating from Classical times was one of the remains which reveal a town which lived largely on the proceeds of pilgrims who came from far and near to the many shrines dedicated to whichever of the pantheon they sought. The proximity of the town to the Mount gave it special significance. Mosaic floors and a particularly beautiful temple courtyard with the goddess's statue still standing in an ornamental pool of water remain as a link between Alexander's legendary journey and our less earth shattering one.

Having now traversed the ground under our own steam, the enormity of his endeavour is all the clearer to us. Between Dion and the Indus Valley, which was the furthest point he reached, there is now a considerable amount of tarmac, places where you can buy new tyres, quite a few tea shops, and where there are warring tribesmen they weren't interested in warring against us. It's also easier to travel when there are two of you than when there's a ravenous great army in your command who are having to walk every step of the way. Alexander's historians tell of what a hard job he had persuading his men to press on further and further from home. He was sure that if he went far enough, he would reach the end of the world and there were rumours of a great sea that represented it. His personal charisma must have been formidable to get them as far as the Indus.

From Dion we took a little inland road for a while before rejoining the sea, passing the battlefield of Pydna where the expanding Roman Empire finally superseded that of Greece.

By the outskirts of Thessalonica we were in the first big traffic and the first incomprehensible one way system since north Italy, trying to get to the bank. Travellers' cheque time. In Italian banks you just get the run around. In the Greek banks we went to, you can walk through the door like any ordinary door; you were directed to the foreign currency counter in four languages; the person behind it didn't finger your cheque disdainfully; they filled in the form; you signed it; and they gave you a little slip as if you'd just popped into the corner shop back home for some butter and shortcake. 'What's wrong?' asked Anna when Howard came out after two or three minutes . . .

One of the best parts of the journey was being able to read our Bible in the locations it covered. Every time we came to a town that had had a letter written to it by Paul for instance, we'd make a point of reading it in one go, which is, of course, how they were designed to be read, instead of only dwelling on tiny segments, as we are wont to do.

We sat down on the harbour front and began to read – not 'and here beginneth the first epistle of Paul the Apostle to the Thessalonians' – but a relieved, 'so you're still okay' kind of letter. Paul had been sneaked out of the city at night after a mob from the market place, which is still visible today, had rioted at his preaching. He hadn't had any reliable news of the remaining believers until at long last he was able to write, 'Timothy has now come to us from you and brought good news'. (1 Thess 3:6) Thereupon he set about tying up some of the loose ends left by his hasty departure.

We wondered whether Timothy had seen the way the sea and the sky could dissolve into one another in the November sun when he had been here. The white, misty waters lapped along the pavement's edge, inches from our feet. Far out to sea the sky was as white and misty as the water, and we weren't sure whether there was a horizon today or not. The long, black oil tankers out there could have been floating or hovering for all we knew.

The first Thessalonian converts probably didn't have a church building of any note in which to worship.

If they did, it's not there now to our knowledge, but locals swear there are two buildings remaining that Paul spoke in. Whether that's true or not is difficult to say as Thessalonica today has many very early Christian churches still standing of seminal architectural importance. That generally means one of two things: either that a building is very beautiful, or that no one in all the history of all the world had ever thought of building one like it before. Thessalonica's early churches certainly aren't photogenic but they are unique. It was a thrill to stand inside a church called Hagia Sophia and know that, after 700 years of building churches the shape of shoe boxes, here was the first whose groundplan was like a cross – and much more interesting inside for it.

We had great fun exploring the city and interspersing our sightseeing with the practicalities of maintenance that any longish stop offered us: finding some excellent string in a pile of rubbish, sandpapering our strong but rusting needle to resew the zips which had come away on our luggage, darning Anna's sweater, cleaning and retaping the front mudguard that had ripped, adjusting the saddle, giving the chains a good clean, and finally taking the front wheel to a bike shop to have the spokes re-trued. Mr Mario, the Italian wheelwright, had a very proud assistant who told us that his boss was the best wheelwright to be had in all Greece and he did do an excellent job. He'd performed similar services for all sorts of transcontinental cyclists on just such trips as ours, we were told. We felt suitably cut down to size. We were also pretty disheartened that we'd unwittingly managed to damage a wheel that badly – and on European roads. What did that forecast for Asia?

On the steep climb out of Thessalonica to a place aptly called Panorama ('seeing everything') Anna's stomach began to trouble her. She reckoned it was something in our water. This was nothing like the upsets we were to have in Pakistan, when we lost so much weight so quickly we nearly lost our wedding rings as well, but cycling on a bad stomach is hard whatever the degree of nausea: the motion seems to exacerbate the pain. From the panorama on the other side of the hill, over two beautiful lakes whose names we shan't divulge lest their shimmering, wooded serenity be spoiled by lots of visitors before we next go back(!), we could see little villages down in the valley where we guessed we should be able to get some Dettol to swill out our bottles.

When we asked the villagers however, they looked at us blankly, then kindly offered toothbrushes, honey, exercise books – whatever they had to sell. Finally someone cottoned on and directed us to the pharmacy in Apollonia where we were astounded at the expense of what to us was such a basic product, but gratified that our search had culminated in yet another of the places that Paul had passed through as part of his Macedonian journey. Only a small village now, with whitewashed walls and a little bench in the square where we ate our lunch in the sun, it had been important enough to be singled out in Acts as a town through which Paul and Silas had passed on their way to Thessalonica.

Down on the lakeside road we regretted that we didn't have the means to cook fresh fish, for lone roadside vendors held it out as we passed. To our as yet uninitiated eyes, such a form of trade seemed pitiful. Each man had never more than a score of fish to sell as he sat patiently on the stony verge waiting for the infrequent traffic to slow down. In the Subcontinent such people would have been regarded as the lucky ones, for at least they had something to sell.

The next day, pains quelled, bottles purified, water tasting horribly antiseptic, we eased our way out of a rocky chine to the sea and couldn't resist a dip. We hadn't packed costumes in our sparse luggage, but it didn't matter. The place was deserted. Then, refreshed as much by the fun of knowing that we were swimming on

November 29th as by the swim itself, we stopped off for lunch at Amphipoli. Paul had passed through here, too, and Howard had slogged through pages of Thucydides describing the siege of Amphipoli during the Peloponnesian War for his Greek 'A' level. He swore he recognised the broad lie of the land from his painfully extracted translation.

Up the steep river valley and on to the promontory, we got inside the walls. We unpacked our sandwiches on a sarcophagus, scratched over with crosses to prove that this had been a Roman place of worship before it was a Christian-Roman one, and afterwards we paced out the Hellenic temple which had been built before the Roman one but over the pre-Classical one. Coming back down the hill we gathered fresh, wind-scattered almonds into our front basket. We also surprised a tortoise creeping along at a speed worthy of this ancient place. Thanks to the Greeks' name for our tandem, we felt we could identify with it. We were now nothing as suave and speedy as a *tandem bici*, but a distinctly plodding sounding *diplopodilato* – literally a 'double foot carrier'.

There was marble blasting on the road to Philippi. They were bringing out the beautiful white stone from the quarries and cutting it into great slabs for transportation on lorries which inched along like the tortoise under their weight. It was good to think that the lucid marble that Ancient Greek statuary was so famous for was still being produced. Ancient Greece is also famous, of course, as the cradle of democracy. That too, funnily enough, had prominent place on this road in the number of small, shopfront premises in villages housing the local offices of 'Neo Democratica' or 'PASOK', the vying political parties. Local debate seemed alive and well.

On the northerly approach, the first thing one sees of Philippi are the three remaining piers of a late Roman church, built probably by the children of the first believers, and standing massive among the ruins of the elegant and ordered city Paul encountered. The well preserved remains substantiate Luke's description of the city as 'a Roman colony and the leading city of that district of Macedonia'. It was where soldiers from the Roman armies were pensioned off with free land and a new start in life. Paul came here as a result of a vision in which he described seeing 'a man of Macedonia standing and begging him, "Come over to Macedonia and help us."' (Acts 16:9) He came up from the Turkish coast and walked in the opposite direction along the road we were cycling on. All the guide books mention Philippi, but not so many mention the small river which runs to the very edge of the ancient walls, a little way up the road, where Paul and his companions went one Sabbath to pray. They began speaking to some of the women who happened to be there. Among them, one Lydia accepted the Truth and was baptised with some members of her household, very likely at the site where the small church called Lydia's Baptistry now stands. They've constructed a little platform and steps down into the water for today's new believers. After her conversion Lydia extended the same uncluttered hospitality as we, nearly two thousand years on, were daily receiving from her countrymen. '"If you consider me a believer in the Lord," she said, "come and stay at my house."' (Acts 16:15).

Staying with Lydia was probably the most peaceful part of Paul's otherwise eventful few days in Philippi. The thanks they got for delivering a demon-possessed girl was to be thrown into prison. However, as they sang hymns and prayed in front of the other prisoners, the tremors of an earthquake broke their chains. Archaeologists have discovered evidence of an earthquake here which would coincide with Paul's visit. Their witness to the jailer was to refuse to escape, for which he was so grateful that he and his household listened to the word of God and were saved. Rather late in the day the authorities realised that they'd imprisoned two Roman citizens and Paul capitalised on their blunder by actually making them escort him from the prison. In fear of further ado, the officials requested them to leave the city, which they did for Thessalonica.

We too left Philippi, but in the opposite direction, through some of the most beautiful countryside of the journey. Macedonia in the autumn is as memorable as a New England fall and we relished every minute of our cycle to Alexandroupoli. (There were countless Alexandroupolis, Alexandrias, and Alexandropolises from here to Pakistan. The conquerer was not so subtle in the way he founded cities.) There we slept on the beach a stone's throw away from a particularly nice *baklava* parlour where, leisurely sampling some shredded wheat, as we irreverently called it, which we particularly enjoyed dipped in cream yoghourt, we suddenly realised that the last thing we should be doing was kicking our heels. We'd arranged to meet a friend coming back overland from Australia, outside the eastern door of the Blue Mosque in Istanbul at 12.00 noon on December 2nd. We'd not been looking at our map carefully enough, and we weren't going to make it on time – not on two wheels at least.

Our resolution was to cycle whenever humanly possible so we didn't enjoy having to make the decision to take the overnight train from a town up the road, straight through to Istanbul – or Konstantinoupoli as the Greeks still called it. We made the most of the last day's cycling through the easternmost military zone where one is strictly forbidden to take photographs. Being good law-abiding folk, we resisted the temptation to cut over the fields and simply hop across into Turkey and continued instead up the nearly deserted road. At times we'd pass a train, wheezing its way up a one in twelve at a weary fifteen miles an hour. Overtaking it, we wondered about the Istanbul train; was it going to be such a time-saver after all?

As things transpired, had our train been on time, we'd have missed it anyway for, at the loneliest imaginable spot between villages, with rolling arable land to either side of us, Anna's energy suddenly totally gave way. We'd learned to cope with the hypoglycemia we were both susceptible to in Britain by quickly devouring a Mars Bar. It was quite incredible how effective that concentrated burst of sugar had been. Here, the most available and suitable thing was *halva* which would have been a pleasant medicine indeed if we'd had enough in our panniers. We didn't and though she slowly demolished all the food we had, sitting in a little shack used to dry tobacco, there just wasn't enough sugar to do the job. We set off for the next hamlet, oh so slowly, labouring up hills with the train's departure time creeping up on us, Howard trying to compensate for her weakness. The shopkeeper looked at us wide-eyed, as we burst into his shop in a remote corner of Macedonia in a great hurry, late on a Saturday afternoon, and bought up vast quantities of sesame snaps. He watched us from the shop door as Anna wolfed them down in the street. Restored, we sped off again in the darkness and arrived at Soufli Station in a chill mist quarter of an hour after it should have been through.

'Oh don't worry it's bound to be at least an hour and three-quarters late,' the guards said as they watered the geraniums in square seventeen kilogramme tins that originally contained olive oil, and serve, when empty, for anything and everything in Greece. They weren't in the least perturbed: 'We're at the end of the line almost, and it gets progressively later and later as it goes up.' We were prepared to believe them for we'd read somewhere that the train time from Athens to Istanbul was the same now as it had been during the Ottoman Empire. 'Come into the warm.' By now the frost was well down, and we were glad to get into the tiny ticket office with a roaring tin stove in the middle.

There was no place to sit for honoured passengers who were let into the tiny nerve centre. It was an office for two. Three other people were also in there to get out of the cold, and we made seven. The excitement created in that room as the train approached, was certainly a match for the heat generated by seven bodies and fierce stove in the confined space. Calls were made up and down the line from those kind of phones you have to spin the handle on. Messages were pouring back and forth, and every so often there'd be an urgent glance at the station clock and we'd be informed that it would be in so many and a half minutes.

It transpired that this was the telegraph as well as the ticket office, and the two officials would break off suddenly to pore over the message that had just come in over the ticker. Then there'd be total silence save the tick-tock of the clock and the occasional rustle of newspaper from one of the other Greeks. All of a sudden, the phone would tinkle, the silence would get even more intense for a moment, and then the jubilant news would be relayed that the train had left . . . Likofos. We tried to look as if we'd heard of the place. Estimated time of arrival would be collectively re-calculated, and we'd fall back into silence again and raise eyebrows at the howling of the wind outside the steamed up windows. As if to break the agony, one of the guards suddenly stood up, put on his coat and official hat, and went outside. We all shivered as he closed the door behind him and his assistant picked up the papers that had blown down. We could hear him pacing back and forth along the platform. Suddenly he burst back in with the command that it was time to get ready.

We zipped up, put on gloves, braced ourselves, wheeled the tandem across the line to the spot where the luggage van would be drawing up, and the guard heaved at the signals with his strong arms. We peered up the line into the blackness for a minute or so till the lines themselves began to sing and then clunk to the arrival of the great beast. Next came pinpricks of light, and finally, in solemn dignity, the engine itself, hissing and dripping. We were engulfed in quantities of steam that disorientated us, till a shout from above told us we were alongside the guard's van. There was a hustle bustle of torch flashing and general man-handling to get the tandem in. We scaled the ladder to get into the carriage, and half fell inside. And then we just sat and gazed, at the leather (very much the worse for wear), at the wooden fittings, at the tarnished, etched-glass mirrors, and the curly-stemmed light fittings. It was superb – straight out of a film; not such a bad way to travel to Istanbul after all.

The ensuing bureaucracy was straight out of a comedy. Getting over the Turkish border between 11.00 p.m. and 12.30 a.m. necessitated a string of visits into our private compartment: twice to examine passports, three times to examine tickets, twice for changing money, once for registering the bike in our passports so that we couldn't sell it in Turkey, once more for registering it as luggage, and once more to make us buy a luggage ticket. Each time we'd turn the lights off again in the hope of deterring further visitors. Each time we had to get up again and do business. Well into the small hours the activity ceased. We dozed the remainder of the night away, luggage tied to our wrists for fear of thieves, and rattled towards our first glimpse of the only city to stand astride two continents.

4

EAST MEETS WEST

Monday, 1st December

We got off the train in Europe, pedalled over the
Bosphorus, and had our morning tea in Asia. At 7.00
a.m. Istanbul was very grey, and, despite its magnificent
minaretted skyline, puzzlingly un-oriental. There is
much in it that is still familiar, and it's exactly that
mixture of East and West that its position might lead
you to expect. It is subtle and engaging and absolutely
reflective of Turkey as a whole: mosques cheek-by-jowl
with buildings in the Classical style; women fully veiled
in black, or tight skirted and displaying the latest perm;
thoroughly Western looking businessmen in tastefully
cut suits beside rag-clad beggars; coal delivered in piles
outside clapboard houses; not quite skyscraper banks
with misted glass frontages and a squatter settlement in
the lee of the city's greatest tourist attraction, Hagia
Sophia; flamboyant American cars from the 1950s, and
colour newspapers available on all the stalls.

Barrow boys push or pedal through the streets, their
glass-sided cabinets all steamed up from the hot *simits*
(sesame bread rings), or icing-sugared suet pastry inside.
Men holding aloft tin trays of delicate glasses filled with
black, sweetened tea (*çai*) vie for custom in the colder
weather with the purveyors of *salep* – a heart-warming
concoction made of sweetened milk, cinnamon, and

tapioca (some even say iris) root. Turkish coffee has
largely been replaced by Nescafé. Everywhere is absolutely teeming with activity, and the town is still divided,
as Dickens would have known London, into areas or
streets exclusively devoted to one trade or another: one
section specialising in industrial chains and wire mesh,
another selling only door handles and padlocks. We
found it appealing to find so many businesses in restor-
ing, repairing, refurbishing, or in some way reusing old
items which our own society would simply throw away.
Labour is cheap and there's always someone in Istanbul
who'd like you to help him make his meagre living by
letting him polish your shoes, fry your cockles on a stick,
refill your cigarette lighter, clean your windscreen as
you wait at the traffic lights, tell you your weight from a
rusty pair of bathroom scales on the pavement, or sell
you alarm clocks, carpets, tweezers, or his service as a
guide. But Istanbul is struggling with decline. As often
as not the stray cobbles on the steep streets barely give a
foothold in the mud. The abandoned holes for work-
men are yawningly unshielded. Street lighting is largely
absent which made for a strange experience after 5.30
p.m. (All Greece's villages had been lit.) While we were
there the happy news broke that the Dutch Government
were donating so many hundred thousand tulip bulbs to
be planted as part of a general face lift to the banks of
the once famous Golden Horn, now in rather a sorry
state. The Dutch had first bought bulbs from the Istanbul market hundreds of years ago, and this gift was
conceived as giving back to Turkey what it had given to
Holland initially.

Our hosts in Istanbul were the kind of soulmates you
meet once in a blue moon on your travels and almost
wish you hadn't, for the separation that must come.
They let us use them as a base from which we explored
the legendary Covered Bazaar and wonderfully aromatic
spice market, the Ottoman Sultans' Topkapi Palace with

its incomparable needlework and the very sword and
mantle of Mohammet; Hagia Sophia, still loftily breathtaking all these years after the Emperor Justinian built
it, and the vivid tile work of the superb Blue Mosque.
(We waited outside for our friend but he never came.)
Stepping inside in our socks, on to the many carpeted
floor, Howard was suddenly overawed by a totally unexpected uncertainty as to what reaction there might be to
his infidel presence in this place of worship. In a way
that hadn't struck him outside, he realised that we were
out of Christendom.

A handful of men knelt in a line towards the front,
facing the *mihrab*, the niche pointing towards Mecca,
which is how Moslems always orientate their prayers.
Together they recited the first chapter of the *Koran*
beginning: 'In the name of Allah, the Gracious, the
Merciful. All praise belongs to Allah, Lord of all the
worlds. The Gracious, The Merciful, Master of the Day
of Judgment'. Then the *imam* said, 'God is great' and
bent down until his forehead touched the ground. The
men did the same after him. In this position they said,
'Glory be to God the Lord of the Universe'. After this
they stood, declaiming, 'God hears those who praise
him'. Three times they prostrated themselves saying,
'Glory to God the Lord most high'. Kneeling and raising
their heads they cried, 'God is great'. Then they recited,
'O God, forgive me, have pity upon me, direct me
aright, preserve me and make me great. Strengthen my
faith and enrich me . . . ' Finally the prayer finished.
Each man turned his head, first to the right, then to the
left, and greeted the angels with the ancient formula:
'Peace be unto you. Peace be unto you.'

We were so ignorant: smug, Christian, sensibilities
bringing the Holy Wars and very little else to mind when
'Islam' was mentioned. We even, foolishly, half expected
intolerance and aggressiveness. Instead most were far
more intent on their worship than on taking any notice

of us and it was evident that for many these words represented a genuine and deep yearning for God. Less impressive was the railed off section at the back where the women sat mutely clicking *tesbihs* – something like rosaries, with each of the ninety-nine beads standing for a different epithet for Allah. Women are forbidden to worship in the body of the building – one better than Pakistan, where women are discouraged from coming in at all.

As well as the mosques, we also had to visit the bank. Yes, it was travellers' cheque time again. In Greek banks it feels like home; in Turkey you get your first inkling of the East. Our initial bank was an uncharacteristic one, it's true. We were in Standard Chartered's swish new Istanbul branch looking, not only for cash, but also for new tyres. In fact, the office was so new that the address we'd used from Rotherhithe post office was now out of date and the tyres were . . . 'Well, we'll have to speak to the manager about that sir – madam.' We had enjoyed the same irreproachable politeness in London. By the end of the journey, we felt it must have been something of a house style for them. Unlike London, though, there was a man discreetly walking about taking orders for tea or coffee from everyone. The silver tray, the tulip-shaped tea glasses, the china coffee cups, felt positively neo-colonial, but the truth is that every institution, from the humble to the haughty has a troupe of lackeys – a system which elsewhere we sometimes saw abused.

We couldn't believe our luck: settled into plush chairs, complimented on our cycling feat, then ushered into the manager's office. He was a very Scottish Scot, as efficient as they come, and on the phone to the right person in London in a matter of minutes. It was strange suddenly to think of Billingsgate, just over the river from where we used to live. The tyres may well have got to the old branch, but they had not got to the new. Without hesitating he undertook to have replacement ones bought, asked where they should be delivered to, and gave us his card to phone him to confirm that they were all right. Howard wondered for a moment whether he shouldn't have tried for a job in international banking rather than out of the way missionary administration, and then was offered another tulipful of tea while they processed the travellers' cheques. Now that's the way to do business. The tyres were delivered to the house where we were staying. They were nylon and took a bit of cajoling to get on the rims, but proved to be extremely durable and took us even further than we'd calculated for the rubber ones.

Istanbul is a city with a history as long and lavish as any in the world and its past is impossible to avoid as you walk round. It's similar for Turkey as a country. The history of the modern state is very short, but more than most places we know, it wears its history on its sleeve. After the First World War, Atatürk, meaning literally 'the Father of the Turks', by all accounts plucked the country out of near extinction following the collapse of the Ottoman Empire. He repulsed the Greek armies who had almost taken over, defined the modern boundaries, and set about transforming the complacent, cleric-bound country into a modern state capable of religious tolerance and democracy. He Latinised the Arabic alphabet and ordered every householder to choose a surname to last for posterity. Up until then, Mehmet who lived beside Topkapi Palace was distinguished exactly so from Mehmet who lived down by Galata Bridge.

A clear decision to move away from Arabia and towards Europe at that time has been largely followed ever since. We never came across anyone who dissented from heartfelt hero worship of Atatürk. His face adorns the bank notes still, and the posters the children have up in school of the history of the world don't break at the BC/AD divide, but instead mark Atatürk's birthday in

1881 with a picture of him as radiantly nimbed as ever was the Christ child.

Whatever the truth of Atatürk's achievements, this much is certain: the Turks are proud and happy to be Turkish. They're politically thoughtful and still in a very malleable stage. Muslim fundamentalism is almost as much a political possibility as EEC membership. Public debate on the status of women, and industry, and Islam, is lively, and the people were the loveliest of the journey. We spent most of our time in Turkey turning down unsolicited offers of lifts, tea, meals, beds, and chats.

* * *

From more than a mile away we puzzled over the billows of smoke on the horizon. When we hit them we realised that it wasn't smoke at all but dust; our first non-metalled road of the journey. We jolted our way along in the white stones and chippings, eyes streaming, trying to keep to one rut, gasping and spluttering every time a bus went past. At speed it raised enough dust to make it pretty dangerous, for neither party can see the other nor, for that matter, anything else on the road. That afternoon of no tarmac seemed extremely long. When, shaken and grimy, we reached the black road again, even this poor surface felt unbelievably smooth. Up until Turkey the rule of thumb for testing the trueness of the bike was how silently it ran. If it wasn't quite right we'd always know it by a ticking or a rubbing, however faint. It was a bit like that still centre we aim for inside ourselves. After Turkey, with ever deteriorating roads, the test no longer held good. We were always a-rattling.

The poor state of the roads and a progressively drier climate meant that dust became an unavoidable fact of our lives. 'Shake the dust off your feet when you leave . . . home or town' (Matt 10:14) had never really made sense to us – until now. Later that evening, Howard, doing his best to wash off the peppering that always lodged most indelibly at our hair lines and in our tear ducts, and ears, said rashly, 'Well, at least that's probably the worst road we'll have to deal with on this trip'. Anna, naturally the more pessimistic, promised to remind him of his claim when the time came that we encountered something infinitely worse.

Because of the road, we didn't make much headway on our first full day of cycling in Turkey, which rather jaded us. All in all we were a bit down. Leaving our friends had been pretty hard. Anna was on edge – as usual far ahead of time – because it promised to be a frosty night. In addition, we had the niggle of disquiet that usually accompanied us in a new country – nothing that familiarity wouldn't brush away, but prompted by the awareness that we knew neither language nor people in a land we were going to have to rely on to supply all our needs. We didn't yet know how lovely the Turks were for we'd been staying with Americans in Istanbul. Later into the trip, we got over this feeling, as we passed repeatedly 'without let or hindrance' as the passport puts it, from one place to the next and realised that it wasn't the land at all to which we needed to look for provision.

We set up the tent in a hedgerow, and made uncertainly for the nearest village to sniff out the local tea house. The *çai* shop was full to bursting with men. There wasn't a single woman in sight. This had begun to be a pattern back in Greece, but Istanbul had been more even-handed. If it hadn't been so early Anna would have turned back to the tent but the thought of lying there, as it got colder and colder, until sleep overtook us, was about as unappealing as the scenario before us.

We pushed open the door. The card playing, newspaper reading, TV watching, general uproar, subsided in a second. There was complete silence as all heads turned towards us. Unlike the Greeks, who'd resumed their chat after a minute or so, the silence continued. We looked for a seat. There was none. We stood there, not knowing what to do. 'Smile,' Anna hissed at Howard: 'It's probably not my place to as a woman but it may be yours.' Howard falteringly turned up the corners of his mouth. Instantly the ice broke and there was an effusive welcome. Chairs were found; tea came. It doesn't cross every language barrier, but a smile, the trip taught us, was pretty much international currency. When we told them what we were doing the teas came thick and fast in thunderstruck admiration. Because they're not a cycling nation, it was in Turkey that our journey began to take on the aspect of a mammoth feat in the eyes of the nationals that it never really lost after that.

It was here too that our education regarding Eastern attitudes to women began. Indeed it was Anna's presence on the tandem that constituted much of their disbelief in what we were up to. In the really big cities (which in Turkey can be counted on the fingers of one hand) one might see a woman on a bicycle. Elsewhere, such a thing wouldn't only be inconceivable, but the sight of a woman was more than likely to be that of a veiled one. Purdah, though banned in universities and in government jobs, is still very much apparent, whether in the form of a mere headscarf, or – usually in the more rural areas – in the all-over black robe that constitutes the traditional *çaddr*. The word is the same as that for tent, a lexical slippage that well suits the garment itself, which we examined closely in someone's house the next night, where it was hanging on the back of our bedroom door. (Incidentally it's pronounced *ch*addr as with every ç in Turkish.) It's basically a floor length dress with a huge collar, so big that it forms a scarf that goes right round the neck and head and hangs down the back.

The significance of the veil is vastly complicated by the effect of the media. Every evening, all over Turkey, men flock to the *çai* bar to watch totally Western-dressed

female newsreaders, belly dancers and soft porn Western films on the one screen the village possesses. It's the
same in the newspapers which, again due to the high
priority Atatürk gave to the need for country-wide
communication, now reach most corners of the country.
The Father of the Turks probably didn't intend that his
press should put the down-market tabloids of the West
into the shade, but that is what they do. So the unveiling
of woman is associated with the West which inevitably
affects attitudes to Western women generally; the same
kind of association we'd come across in Greece and were
to find until our journey's end.

Anna did feel sexually pressurised at times in Turkey,
though usually, as on that first night, rather fulsome
gallantry was all it ran to. Rather late on she realised that
it was her cycling leggings which contributed to the
problem, associated in their minds with the almost
identical woollen undergarments both men and women
wear in Turkey. '*Jamshir, jamshir*' ('laundry, laundry') she
heard one man mutter disbelievingly, looking at her
legs. She couldn't work out what he was on about till she
discovered that the word also meant 'underwear'. When
she donned a pair of *sholvars*, the skirted trousers men
wear in Eastern Turkey, she felt much more comfortable than with the interim measure of tying a shawl
round her waist.

The next day we were up early, eager to make up
some of the mileage we'd lost along with the asphalt the
previous day. We cycled for twenty-five miles in blazing
sunshine that melted the hoar in no time and then
realised we'd misplaced the case that contained not only
both our sunglasses, but also Howard's spare pair of
glasses.

We made the decision to retrace our steps, seemingly
in the middle of nowhere. As far as the eye could see
there were deserted fields separated from the road by a
deep, overgrown trench. We concealed the tandem in

this and put a pink plastic bag over a post to mark the place. The very next lorry stopped for us, the driver obligingly making room in a cramped cab and dropping us, not without a few puzzled questions, at our camping spot. The glasses were there, and in no time at all, we were flagging down the next lorry to take us back as far as he was going. At his turn-off the driver leapt out into the road to stop a bus hard on our tail, to take us the rest of the way.

The stares as we climbed on, two Anglo Saxons appearing out of the blue, and weighed down with luggage, were redoubled when, twenty-five miles up the road, we indicated that we were getting out at a spot even more remote than where we'd alighted. 'No, no,' the driver said, making one of their expressive 'What in Allah's name do you think you're doing?' gestures we came to expect from our fellow road users in Turkey. He went right on driving up the road and repeating the name of the next village. 'Stop here,' we insisted frantic-ally, 'right *here*,' which, some half a mile up he finally did, with the entire bus gawking as we trudged off into the dusty nowhere.

Barely had we stepped out of the bus when a car with two men in it halted to offer us a lift. We had a hard job persuading them we didn't need one. We tried to explain that we were about to get on our bicycle, but it must have seemed a bit far-fetched. They drove off looking, we thought, rather put out. We'd just retrieved the bike when the same men came back down the road, motioning to us to stop once more. We weren't quite sure what was going on. To be on the safe side, we veered into the middle of the road, so that we couldn't be pushed off into the verge and mugged, Howard muttering over his shoulder something about 'bandits'. We turned to face our attackers and two hot doughnuts were thrust out of the car window. They had been expressly procured for us from the nearby village.

When they heard where we were cycling to and from,
they were dismayed they hadn't bought more. 'I'd be
kaputt if I'd got on a bike at Istanbul, never mind
London,' the fatter of the two commented cheerily.
When they really couldn't persuade us to give up this
cycling lark for the day and stay the night with them,
they departed, leaning out of the window with waves
and grins for as long as we were in sight.

If the day's events hitherto hadn't been enough to
suggest that there was something rather special about
Turkish hospitality, its close clinched it. Cycling into a
small village at sundown to stock up on provisions, the
one and only shopkeeper, having been called out from
his house to open up, wouldn't hear of us sleeping in the
çaddr. We were ushered into his spare bedroom and,
purchases of a moment ago notwithstanding – served
tea, cheese, and frostbitten tomatoes to go with our
bread. He discreetly closed the door on us as the last
plastic plate was laid down, so that we could enjoy our
meal in private.

It was nothing to what we would experience but at this
point in our trip the standard of living at *Bay* (Mr)
Ibrahim's gave us pause for thought. There was the
sheer scantness of furniture, utensils – everything.
There were the stone floors and the lack of a hot tap.
There were the rats in the kitchen that didn't bother to
wait till we'd closed the door behind us, to get back to
the waist high hessian sack of soft biscuits that was
presumably waiting to replace the others – also soft –
that we'd bought in the shop.

One thing that was plentiful were soft furnishings –
rugs, carpets, quilts, blankets, cushions. This was often
true of Turkish homes we went into. The things that
made for basic comfort and could be produced by home
industry, including food, weren't in short supply. In
truth, there was something very appealing about this
satisfied simplicity which didn't go as far as 'want' but

was just contentment with what was available. 'As goods increase, so do those who consume them,' says the writer of Ecclesiastes some two and a half thousand years before Marx, and when he's finished reducing all men's activities to nothing, he concludes tersely:

'There is nothing better for men than to be happy and do good while they live. This is the gift of God.' (Ecc 3: 12,13)

It was a helpful view when, not many miles further on, overwhelmed by the countless hand to mouth, hand to soil, peasant existences, Anna was reduced to a rather mystified 'What's the point?'

After supper Howard was hauled out by our host to the three village tea houses, one after the other, to show our ideogram and explain over and over, with the village schoolteacher as interpreter, what we were up to. Anna wasn't invited. She had to stay at home with the women: the shopkeeper's wife, mother, and their cronies, similarly abandoned by their spouses. They sat and span beside the only stove in the house, refilling the teapot from it periodically. In this colder weather, the other rooms were closed off (except to passing tandemists!) and they did everything, including sleeping, in the parlour.

The next morning after a breakfast similar to supper, though with the addition of hardboiled eggs and granulated honey, Ibrahim took us to see the village mosque. Howard was famous after his night out with the boys, and there were smiles and hellos at every door. The mosque, built this century, presented the strange mixture of kitsch and what our eyes constitutes 'tasteful', with which we became familiar out East. It has something to do with the assumption in developing countries that whatever is modern is good. There were shoddy, mass-produced pictures on the walls which were covered to chest height with tiles that we'd only call 'bathroom'. There were garish, synthetic rugs, but also ones in the rich glowing colours we'd seen in the bazaars and a couple of real 'Turkish carpets', not to mention the exquisitely crocheted white caps the men were supposed to don on entering. Ibrahim picked up the *molvi's* notes from the lectern and said he thought they were for a sermon. He wasn't exactly sure though for he didn't come very often, and he admitted that, when he did, he didn't pay too much attention. Regular attendance at the mosque was more a thing of older times, he said.

We took a road that got increasingly, hauntingly, more beautiful, as the sea narrowed into the Straits, and the Gallipoli peninsula lay purple-grey across the haze of the Hellespont. The place had a melancholy loveliness as we gazed over the many tinted browns of the fields, to the spot which had witnessed such terrible slaughter in the First World War. Apart from the occasional farmer tilling the gently undulating land with oxen and wooden plough, black-veiled wife trudging in their wake, there was little to disturb our sad reflections until we turned the corner with the coastline, and our thoughts also turned to the battleground that lay ahead.

People's reaction to visiting Troy is very mixed. Caesar is said to have been disappointed all that time ago, and we'd been warned not to expect too much by people who'd been more recently. Howard had worked us both up into quite a fervour of anticipation, though, by pushing and pushing up the hilly coast road to get to the city by dusk so that we could say we had camped on the Plain of Ilium, the field outside the citadel where the great battles between the troops of Agamemnon and Priam had been fought. The truth was that we slept on the floor of a restaurant closed until the start of the new season. We'd got to the site just too late to get the lie of the land and plan our hideout; had been immediately spotted bumbling around in the dusk; had been hauled in under the electric light and told to sit down with some tea and spend the night inside.

This little village off the main road has been revolutionised by the foreigner's interest in the old stones down the hill and the Turks are still visibly amazed by it all. We spent a long time talking to our host, not quite sure whether to believe he was being ingenuous when he said how pleased he was to be able to help us because in this world there was only one brotherhood. All nations were brothers and sisters really, were they not? There must have been some novelty value in our arrival at the beginning of December and on a tandem but that wasn't it. It was undoubtedly true that his life style had been transformed from the peasant farming that would have been his lot, but that wasn't it either. There was certainly an element of pleasure at having conspirators who would drink alcohol with him (we didn't realise, but though it's legal to sell it to tourists, you can't drink it yourself under Turkish law – an interesting reflection on the ambivalence in the mind of modern Turkey). Nor was that, however, important enough to him to explain his pleasure at having us. We don't know what, two years into the routine of having busloads of wealthy foreigners breeze in and out of his village for an hour or so, made him and some of his friends so genuinely hospitable to us, supplying us liberally from their flock, their threshing-floor and their winepress, as Deuteronomy has it.

We don't want to vouch for what kind of time you'll have at Troy if you go in the peak season and have to fight your way past postcard stalls, Kodak adverts, and ice cream men. But from 7.30 a.m., when we unlocked ourselves from the restaurant, wrapped well up against the buffeting cold (Homer warns that this is 'windy Ilium') with not a soul to be seen, it was magical. Howard had struggled through the *Iliad* at school, so it was very special for him to be at the legendary spot. By far the most memorable part of being at Troy is not the city itself however, but the plain below. It's sad that the discipline of archaeology was born in such a haphazard manner at the site of this city. The damage caused was almost as extensive as the finds themselves. The sea must have receded some miles since the days when the jealous Greeks drew up their beaked ships to shore, but the battlefield with the Scemander river snaking across it is still laid out below you, visible from a rocky promontory high up in the town. Was it not from just such a spot as this that the Trojan men would have looked in helpless horror as Achilles drove his chariot round the base of the walls, dragging Hector's corpse by its ankles, while his head tossed in the dust?

Alexander came here too, regarding Troy's conquest by the Ancient Greeks as a prototype of his own impending conquest of Asia. Sultan Mehmet II also visited after he'd conquered Constantinople in 1453 as a symbolic gesture to prove that, at last, European incursion into Asia was at an end. An eternal emblem, then, of the dissent between East and West, it reminded us of generations of misunderstanding and warned us to take care in the coming months.

As we left the site we were met by Ahmet. He'd promised in furtive whispers the night before, to show us his 'museum'. We'd hoped to be on the road before he could delay us with a few unrecognisable shards but there was no deflecting him now he'd caught us. First there was Ahmet's wife to meet and the vegetable garden to admire. Then we had coffee in the room with the stove. The place reeked of yeast, nowhere more strongly than the exact spot where we were sitting, on a long, low, wooden box. We asked Ahmet about the smell. 'Get up,' he said, with a twinkle in his eye and he lifted up the cushioned lid and revealed seven neat little compartments inside our seat, each with a kilo of dough

proving in it. 'One for each day of the week,' he said
proudly, and he took us out into the garden once more
to show us the beehive shaped oven they baked it all in.
He treated us to a piece of today's bread – rather stale
because it was Day Seven, but still recognisably superior,
as he said, to factory made.

Laying his finger alongside his nose at us, Ahmet sent
his missus on an errand into the village. He locked the
front door, spent some time rustling and scrabbling in an
adjoining room, came in with a large, torn, plastic carrier,
closed the connecting door, and drew the curtains. He
dipped into the bag and began to draw out grimy
newspaper and rag bundles, laying them down with such
tender care that even before we saw Ahmet's museum in
all its glory, we knew we were in for more than some old
shards. There were Trojan coins, silver bracelets, and
gold ankle rings, tiny marble votive statues and terracotta
images, semi-precious and precious stones. As they
glowed and glistened in the yeasty gloom, *Bay* Ahmet
explained. The best time to find such things was when the
fields had just been ploughed and a shower washed the
mud from what was turned up. Caressing the chiselled
deities and necklaces, he made us promise not to tell the
authorities. 'Who would love these things as I do in the
state museum?' he asked. 'The tourists, they leave four or
five minutes. They say they saw the spoils of Troy. They
dust become and nobody loves them as I do.'

From Troy the road left the coast for a while. The first
night we slept in a resinous forest upon a bed of pine
needles which scented the tent fragrantly for days to
come. We were woken by the soughing of a balmy wind
among the sheltering trees, accompanied by the fluting
of goatherds, weaving their way in and out of the furze.
One goat-girl – she must have been in her late teens –
took such a fright when she saw us wheeling our strange
steed down to the road that she scuttled off the path and
up a rabbit track, rather than meet us.

Today was the day we were expecting to see some acquaintances from England who were driving back to UK. They'd taken replacement parts out for us, to Izmir further up the road. Turkey's roads are few and bare enough for a meeting 'somewhere' on the scores of miles of coast to be able to be counted on. Ten miles down the road, there they were, and we had a matey 'Brits abroad' cup of tea from their Boots Thermos flask. They took snaps of us to send to our parents. With our healthy December suntans, we couldn't think of a better Christmas present to allay their fears. As it turned out we'd left the old province of Asia (now Turkey) before the photographs reached their destination and this was the letter we received, miles further on, from Anna's mum, scolding us for not communicating at that very time:

I am sometimes quite beside myself with anxiety, every external situation causes me to react like a litmus paper. We had bitterly cold weather (the coldest I have ever known). This made me decide you were suffering from hypothermia in the desert. Then with the trouble in Lebanon I decide this unrest is bound to affect things in Iran too . . . The Bible isn't much help. I pick up Corinthians and read, 'We should like you, our brothers, to know what we went through in Asia. At that time we were completely overwhelmed; the burden was more than we could bear; in fact, we told ourselves this was the end.' Thanks very much Saint Paul.

So much for trying to be dutiful children.

The road dipped down again to the sea, at points so close that the road was the strand and an error of judgment would have landed us in the water. This, the Gulf of Edremit, was surely one of the most beautiful stretches yet, its slopes clustered with cypresses, its islands floating in iridescent waters. They're actually Greek islands, though not more than ten miles from the Turkish shoreline in places, a fact which the usually peaceable Turks acknowledged with something approaching a snarl. We hadn't anticipated serious antagonism in the heart of NATO territory but we heard on the news the very next day that three soldiers had just been killed on the border.

5

ÇOK GÜZEL

Tuesday, December 9th

When you're travelling, particularly in countries you're
unfamiliar with or whose language you don't speak,
there'll almost inevitably be occurrences which defy
explanation. The whys and wherefores are so wholly
beyond your ken, the protagonists unfathomable partly
because of the speed with which they exit from your life,
that these experiences remain forever in the elusive
category of what we came to call 'imponderables'. One
such episode was with the restaurateur in the town
'where Satan lives'.

Pergamum of Revelation comprises a citadel whose
library became such a serious rival to that of the Ptol-
emies that Egypt stopped sending papyrus to stock it.
(Later Mark Anthony was to end the rivalry with Alex-
andria forever, by giving the Pergamum library to
Cleopatra.) The search for a substitute resulted in the
discovery of 'Pergamum paper' or parchment skins
treated with lime and dried – too thick to roll up like
papyrus into a scroll and therefore giving birth to the
codex or modern paged book.

The city, now the upper town of Bergama and whose
Altar of Zeus may be the 'throne of Satan' Saint John
refers to, perches vertiginously on a sheer crag overlooking the mid town where the church Paul preached

in and John wrote to still stands. It's a vast red brick structure surrounded by carpet sellers and purveyors of brass and leather ware, originally a Roman temple to Egyptian deities. The lower and modern town proper sits well and truly on the plain – a location which provided unobstructed passage for the bitingly cold wind which greeted us as we cycled in.

Here was a new situation. We felt so indignant at the possibility of having to abandon our tent and take a hotel after the mild nights we'd experienced – after all it was 'only' December – that we put the decision off, warming ourselves with a steaming cup of *salep*. Then we departed our separate ways, Howard to the barbers, and Anna to sniff out a restaurant to celebrate the fact that we'd just crossed another thousand mile mark. (Though we'd celebrated it already with the statutory kiss we'd instituted to mark every hundred miles.) In the bus station was just the thing: a clean little café where the smiling owner was only too pleased to practise his English.

'My daughter see you come into town on bicycle. She say it is a . . . ' – his English failed him – 'an *iki kishilik bisiklet* (two person bicycle). One man, one woman. Is he your husband?' Anna answered in the affirmative, smiling at the by now familiar questions. The next one would be, 'Do you have any children?' then 'How long have you been married?', then 'Why no children if two and a half years married?' Out they came, then: 'Where will you sleep tonight?'

'We don't know. Probably in our tent.'

'It's very cold tonight.'

'Yes. Perhaps we'll take a hotel, but it may be too expensive.'

'If you like you can camp in my garden.'

'Thank you, how kind', genuinely relieved at the thought of a windbreak; 'I'll go and collect my husband from the barber's. He'll be very grateful.'

'If you like you can sleep in my house.'

'Oh . . . surely not. We can go in the garden. That's very kind as it is.'

'No no, you must sleep in my house.'

'Well . . . ' resolve weakening as the wind whistled between the buses.

'Please sleep in my house, really.'

Anna didn't take much persuading. British reserve had been gradually eroded since Greece by the constant kindness. As she was leaving however, he asked: 'Where are you going?'

'To fetch my husband.' She thought she'd just explained that.

'Oh. Where will you sleep tonight?'

'I thought . . . that's to say . . . ' quickly rethinking: 'we don't know.'

'Oh.'

She went off to find Howard, who'd been gone a mighty long time for a simple trim. His delay had been occasioned by the barber's insistence that a short back and sides included two hairwashes, pomade, beard and moustache trim and eau de cologne – at no extra charge. Anna filled Howard in on the way back as to what had happened so that he shouldn't let his hopes be raised if the invitation came again. Back at the café we paid all of one pound seventy (we'd have thought it daylight robbery if we'd been asked that much only a couple of countries further on) for a delicious meal served by the pretty, bright-eyed, five-year-old daughter. Tongue between her teeth, holding her breath, she'd carefully balance plates of rice and beans and meat in steaming spicy sauce from counter to table, holding them away from her school uniform and fetching more soft white bread without prompting.

As we finished our meal the father began to quiz us:

'Where will you sleep tonight?' This time we were ready.

'We don't know. Probably in our tent.'

'It's very cold tonight.'

'Yes.'

'If you like, you can camp in my garden.'

'Oh thank you. How kind', trying hard neither to giggle nor to wish that he'd offered his house instead. He began to lock up and we to prepare for an icy ride, we knew not where. Then, smiling brightly as if the thought had just struck him, he offered: 'If you like you can sleep in my house.' We did sleep in our baffling host's house that night, though until we had our heads on the pillow we didn't dare count on it.

The following day we cycled just down the coast to latter day Izmir. Previously called Smyrna, it is the site of another of the churches of Revelation. We'd told the kind Anglican pastor of our arrival in advance, and he'd lit the British Consulate church so that we wouldn't miss it. With its mock Victorian gargoyles and 'Pre-Raphaelite' stained glass, so incongruous against a background of minarets and palm trees, there wasn't much chance of that. Our tandem was taken care of by two consulate guards armed with machine guns and we were set up on camp beds on the stage of the church hall with a calor gas fire and stacks of blankets to supplement our sleeping bags. Thoughtful members of the congregation donated all sorts of comestibles and we were given the run of the kitchen.

That first evening Howard made straight for the bookshelf and Anna for the sink. The first all over soaping was just a bio pre-wash and the real business only about to start with pans of hot water on the stove and Howard patiently scrubbing her back twice over ('But darling, there's nothing more to get off . . . ') She had to admit however, that though many Turks seemed to have only cold water and limited facilities there was nothing dirty about them. They were just not Western clean, and Western clean as we know it is actually only a fairly recent phenomenon.

We found a garage near the harbour and put on the

new block that had been waiting for us when we arrived
in Izmir. We were supplied with rags and petrol, a
wrench, a spare pair of hands and tea, all free. As we
produced cigarettes and chocolate biscuits in thanks,
there were the same amused, even slightly confused
smiles our other various Turkish benefactors had shown
when we tried to repay them for a fraction of their
kindness. It was the same with the hide dealer round the
corner who'd refused to let us pay for a strip of leather to
sew round Howard's handlebar in place of a cork sheath
which had worked loose and got lost. Over time it became
clear to us that Eastern hospitality at its best – and in
Turkey it was definitely best – expects no reward. For
them it's truly more blessed to give than to receive.

   Their kindness in fact was so predictable that we had to
work quite hard against not presuming upon it, when the
night promised to be a little nippy, for instance, or we
needed some sustenance but there was no food immediately available. We had to remind ourselves at times like
this that the (marginally) more restrained goodwill of the
rural Greeks had been ample at the time. Actually, when
all was said and done, it was never hard to find a place to
put up the tent in Turkey (though it was often difficult to
persuade the locals that we had everything we needed)
and it always felt safe when we'd left it there. 'No stranger
had to spend the night in the street, for my door was
always open to the traveller'; 'You will know that your
tent is secure; you will take stock of your property and
find nothing missing' (Job 31:32; 5:24).

   Ephesus is the first church St John addresses in
Revelation and the recipient of that mighty letter from
Paul. The town's silversmiths 'who made silver shrines
of Artemis' (Acts 19:24) were incited to a great fury by
one Demetrius who feared that Paul's message spelt the
end of their trade in idols (Acts 19:25). 'You know we
receive a good income from this business. And you see

and hear how this fellow Paul has convinced and led astray large numbers of people,' he said to them.

We visited the splendid theatre where the crowd 'shouted in unison for about two hours: "Great is Artemis of the Ephesians!"' (Acts 19:28) and as we came out, stood on the very paving stones on which Paul had been dissuaded from addressing them any more by other disciples, frightened at what might happen to him if he did. We noticed for the first time as we re-read the story under the single forlorn pillar that remains of Artemis's once resplendent temple, that there's another, usually overlooked, hero in the account – a shrewd city clerk who 'quietened the crowd and said: "Men of Ephesus, doesn't all the world know that the city of Ephesus is the guardian of the temple of the great Artemis . . . If there is anything further you want to bring up, it must be settled in a legal assembly. As it is, we are in danger of being charged with rioting because of today's events. In that case we would not be able to account for this commotion, since there is no reason for it." After he had said this, he dismissed the assembly.' (Acts 19: 35–40).

From Ephesus, instead of continuing on the coastal road as we'd planned for warmth's sake, our attention was caught in our guide book by the promise of camel wrestling, hot springs, and whirling dervishes, if we were to take the inland road. (Anna wasn't totally sure she wanted to see the first until we found out that the camels were separated before they did one another any harm.) We made a quick detour at Nyssa to see the library in which Strabo studied and to look down from the amphitheatre on to the giddy gorge the city spans. The Romans had simply thrown over a viaduct, doubtless in a spare moment. There was something quite mind-boggling – humbling – about these great feats of manual engineering we came across so often. The seats in the theatre were in the same league, raked for drainage, each one gently lipped and beautifully preserved, despite the casual way in which olive trees were sprouting out of the stalls. *Çok güzel* is the all purpose Turkish term of approbation. We found ourselves using it more and more to express our appreciation of Turkey itself.

Turkey has been described as 'a Third World country with a First World past' in respect of its attitude to its antiquities. The Turks themselves argue that it's not a change of attitude that's needed, but simply money to maintain its heritage. Whatever the truth of the matter, and it has to be said that present-day deterioration and misuse are sometimes painfully evident, there's something highly appealing about being able to enjoy some of these treasures quite alone and with free access.

It was tangerine harvest time. We ate them, and oranges the size of grapefruits, as if they were grapes, all through Turkey. The orchards were spectacular at any hour of the day, but towards evening the fruits glowed like lit lamps against their dark green leaves. One night we tried to set up camp in among them but the farmer wouldn't hear of it – not because we might steal the produce – but because we couldn't possibly be outside while he had an outhouse with a bed in it. We'd given up trying to protest too long in these instances. The Turks had a peculiar way of saying 'No' that covered the whole range from mild disfavour to decided prohibition, but we could never quite interpret it as anything but absolutely mortified denial. One palm would go up, like a British 'wait a minute', the other hand would touch the heart, and the head would jerk up with what in Britain would be the most scornful of eyes-raised 'tuts'. '*Lütfen, lütfen*' (please, please) they'd remonstrate, and we'd end up the mortified ones at having, we thought, caused so much displeasure.

We were beginning to eat our sandwiches in the outhouse when there was a knock at the door. They would be mortally offended if we weren't to take *çai* with them; *çai* which turned out to be a full scale meal. It culminated in the most delicious combination of fresh walnuts and almonds, and figs as big and as juicy as the satsumas.

Third World they possibly are when it comes to restoration but, as far as sheer natural plenty went, Turkey was quite unrivalled in our experience. Meat, fish, vegetables and dairy products are the plenteous and fresh basics of a delectable and healthy diet. Every meal is accompanied by bread (*ekmek*) usually white and seven or eight pence a kilo, and there are plenty of variations: fried and sweetened dough, for instance, or rings tasting like croissants. There's *ayran*: spring water mixed with yoghourt – as refreshing a drink as the juices pressed on the spot from mountains of fruit in the bazaars. Dried fruit and nuts of every conceivable type spill out of shops also selling honeycomb and Turkish Delight. One of the best things of all is *börek*, a cross between puff and noodle pastry, packaging wonderful mixtures of egg, herbs, goat's cheese, spinach, or minced meat. *Çok güzel.*

In all respects Turkey seems to be blessed

> with the best the sun brings forth
> and the finest the moon can yield;
> with the choicest gifts of the ancient mountains
> and the fruitfulness of the everlasting hills;
> with the best gifts of the earth and its fulness.
> (Deut 33:14–16)

So luxuriant is the land that the restriction on imports (to foster indigenous industry) appears to have no adverse effects whatsoever and the two resources that still need improvement – electricity and water – are being seen to. Seven thousand labourers have been building a vast dam across the Euphrates since 1982. When it's built, Turkey will be thoroughly self-sufficient, to the annoyance of the Russians who currently supply Turkey with power. To judge by the features of some of the people we saw, the influence of the Russian Tartars had been a powerful one, as had that of the Mongols and the Chinese; nowhere so evident as in the faces of our host's little boys. They sat quiet as awestruck mice among their mother's capacious skirts, their tracksuit bottoms and pyjama tops extending from beneath the charming black shirt tunic with white Peter Pan collar that comprises school uniform countrywide. (Schoolgirls wear an even more charming little black dress with the same collar and similarly supplemented according to the weather and the time of day.) Their slanting eyes creased up with silent mirth at our halting Turkish and they'd bury their wide yellow faces into their mother's ample folds. Unlike the willowy Iranian women we were to meet, buxom is beautiful in Turkey.

Adults in general didn't find our *merhabas* and *tesekkurs* (hellos and thank yous) so much comic as flattering that we'd taken the trouble to learn them. For some reason Turkish came easier to us than any other language on the trip – at the very basic level at which we tried to pick them up as we crossed each border from Italy onwards. We'd glean the necessaries from whatever sources available: a guidebook, street signs, the people themselves. We'd transliterate as best we could 'How are you?', 'How much please?', 'Where's the toilet?' and so forth, on to lists that Anna produced from her pocket on quiet stretches of road and tested us on. Biscuit packet cardboard was the best for these because it didn't disintegrate as quickly as paper wedged up against a handlebar at sixteen miles an hour.

For Anna the system was also ideal for getting snatches of Bible off by heart then having lovely long times of meditation on the back seat. Howard couldn't do this; he had to keep his attention on the road. It was on the saddle, funnily enough, that Anna learnt something of

what it meant 'to gaze upon the beauty of the LORD and
to seek him in his temple.' (Ps 27:4).

We never got to see the camel wrestling. We arrived a
puncture late to see the bedraggled conqueror being
paraded in triumph round the village, with bells round
his ankles and ribbons round his neck. Of the vanquished
there was no sign. We weren't too sorry when we saw how
prodigiously the victor was foaming at the mouth.

We made for Pamukkale then, the aquamarine
streams along the side of the road giving a steaming
foretaste of what was to come. The approach to Pamukkale looks as if it is permanently covered in a fresh fall of
snow. It all originates in the hot springs that do to the
countryside basically what happens to the inside of your
kettle when it furs up. Solidified limestone cascades
down the hillside and the villagers do their washing in
outdoor canals – in hot water. As night fell we clam-
bered round the crystalline falls. It was the second
(lunar) anniversary of our setting out and we were set on
another bathe, this time under the full-faced moon, but
there was no free water to be had. All the swimmable
pools have had hotels built over them. We held the
vulgar tourist (which of course didn't include ourselves!)
directly responsible.

Down the hill is Laodicea, another of the seven
churches of Revelation. As we read the letter we wondered if there was any connection between the springs
nearby and the charge: 'because you are lukewarm –
neither hot nor cold – I am about to spit you out of my
mouth.' (Rev 3:16) Then we set off for Konya, pushing
to reach the city by the anniversary of the beatified
Mevlâna: poet, teacher, and mystic, and founder of the
order of the whirling dervishes. We were told that if we
could get a ticket for this, the final night of week-long
celebrations in his name, we'd have an evening we'd
never forget. We never will.

Celaleddin Rumi, or the Mevlâna as he is better

known, was one of the Sufis who are the mystics of
Islam. Sufism grew up in opposition to hard core
Moslem fundamentalism, partly as a search for a more
personal god than the Koran would seem to present. It
also however, gave rise to heresies whose prime perpet-
rators were seen to be the monklike *shaikhs* whose
garments of wool (*suf*) gave the movement its name.
Faqirs or dervishes (poor brothers) attached themselves
to the *shaikhs* as disciples and as in the case of Mevlâna
hagiolatry was the almost inevitable result.

The dervishes are alive and whirling. About forty of
them filed into Konya stadium making obeisances to one
another and the *shaikh*. They circled the hall three times,
shedding their black cloaks (the fetters of the grave) but
retaining their tall 'gravestone' hats. They were left in
white costumes which signify their winding sheets, their
heavy ankle length skirts made from a full circle of
material. Following the lead of the dance-master they
began, one after the other, to rotate, counterclockwise
both on their own axes and round the room, slowly at
first, then faster with the music till the room was
spinning with *faqirs* symbolically enacting the revolution
of the cosmos and the soul's search for God. Their skirts
swung out into ever-fuller discs as the motion increased.
Their arms were outstretched: right palm facing up, left
down 'taking from God and giving to men, keeping
nothing for themselves'. Despite the symbolism it was
not a dance of death for though the Mevlâna died on
this night back in the thirteenth century, it's called his
wedding night because it was in death that he was
wedded with his lord.

The music was very hard for us to make sense of:
viols, flutes, lutes, drums and zithers played entirely in
unison all evening. We realised that our ears and intel-
lects were accustomed to harmony – layers of music
going on at the same time. The craft in this music,
however, was all linear and needed to be appreciated

section against section over time – something we were
quite unused to. It's amazing what culturally specific
skills you pick up without realising it.

The end of the *sema* is marked by all the participants
sounding the word 'Hu', which was the signal for the
audience to jump up – before the echo had died away –
and push and shove their way out. Their behaviour
made Boston's Symphony Hall audiences (the worst
we'd ever known) seem virtuous. They burped into their
cokes, rustled their sweet papers, ripped open their
biscuit packets, stood up to take snaps, hissed at us when
something new was about to happen and agreed in
sorrowful wonderment that the spectacle they'd just
seen was really *çok güzel*.

The sumptuous mosques and tombs of Konya (Icon-
ium of Paul's missionary journeys) are brimming with
ardent Mevlâna worshippers. At intervals during the
day the ululations of the *muezzini* (criers) would soar
above the plain below and over the hubbub of the
crowds. Giving out from slender minarets silhouetted
against the skyline, they are one of our most abiding
memories of Turkey. In the mosque where Celaleddin
Rumi had himself worshipped (horrid-smelling and
very bare, ironically) we met three earnest students of
English from the local campus most desirous of some
language practice. They were proficient and thoughtful.
'What would you say is the key to all this pilgrimage?' we
asked. They furrowed their brows: 'Fear of God.'

'Fear, not love?' Again more thought. 'No, fear; is that
not more proper to Allah?'

It was odd how we often slept best in the most unlikely
spots. It may well have been to do with the relaxation
that sometimes comes when you've resigned yourself to
having a terrible night. In a frosty little park bounded
on one side by the city bus station, on the other by one of
Konya's main arteries, we slept as soundly as if it had
been we, not the dervishes, who'd abandoned our souls

to the infinite. Not even the *muezzini* woke us with the dawn call to prayer ('prayer is better than sleep' is one of the exhortations as they rouse the faithful) and we were fairly sensitive still to loudspeakers ever since the one by the swimming pool in France. They'd be sure to start up the daytime calls to prayer just as we were squatting in the bushes to go to the loo. We'd each been caught out this way, jumping guiltily and scrabbling to put our clothes to rights as the loudhailer intoned across the slumbrous fields.

Their microphones proved to be not the only ones in sometimes rather intrusive regular use. The police – particularly traffic police – employed them extensively, and caught us on the hop more than once. 'Come here' would suddenly boom into the stillness as we cycled along and we'd take a split second to disassociate it from the voice of Allah and trace it to a cheery cop snugly ensconced in a lay-by. We'd obediently begin to make for his car but then he'd start to flap his hand out of the window in a downward motion our Western upbringing told us meant 'that's enough', or maybe 'stop there'. We'd halt uncertainly, discussing in undertones: 'Does he want us to go or stay?' and the hand flapping would become more and more agitated. '*Merhaba, merhaba,*' he'd beam encouragingly, 'Just wanted to say hello. Where're you from?' In time we managed to divest ourselves of enough cultural baggage to interpret these 'Come here' gestures aright. After a few such interchanges with 'The Law', none of which amounted to anything more than an inoffensively nosey chat, we began to be a bit reluctant to stop, even for the police. If we had braked every time someone waved a welcoming hand down at us in Turkey we'd have averaged about ten miles a day. It felt a bit mean, though; people looked so very excited when we approached and so very perplexedly rejected when we sped past, albeit smiling.

We took the north-easterly road out of Konya over

plains which currently hold the earliest archaeological
evidence of human habitation in the world. Traffic was
practically non-existent and when it came, domestic
animals seemed to have developed no road sense at all to
deal with it. It was nothing but a seemingly unending
wasteland, but on the other side of the plain was the lure
of cave cities.

For outright weirdness the Goreme Valley probably
ranks highest in our expedition. Thirty million years ago
three volcanoes dropped ash over the landscape to form
the vast outcrops of Uchisar, Ortahisar, and Goreme.
Tufa, the erupted substance, is soft and easy to work; so
much so that the locals resourcefully tunnelled and dug
their houses out of it. To this day, despite prosperous
lower towns that have now struck up round their bases –
these great warrened masses rearing up from the surrounding plain like Brueghel's *Tower Of Babel*, provide
eminently cosy dwellings and storehouses.

The night we reached Uchisar the snow lay thickly on
the fields and there was a biting wind. Leaving the bike
chained to the metal hasp of a hefty door hinged into
the cliff face we teetered and clawed our way along half-
eroded, spiralling paths and staircases. We laid out our
sleeping bags in an abandoned chamber with carved
ledges and scooped out windows. The wind howled
round the porticoes and towers and balconies all night
long, but inside we were as snug as troglodytes in a rug.

In the morning a bareheaded woman with bright
flouncy skirts and gypsy features came and invited us in
to her cave for a cup of *çiçek* (flower tea) and tiny, mouth-
watering, honey cakes made on the stove with its pipe
disappearing up into the tufa, her husband all the while
trying to mend the skylight embedded in the same. It had
cracked in last night's gale. Despite this, on cushions and
quilts specially plumped up for us on the two bedsteads,
we were roasting in this warmest of little dens. When she
brought out exquisitely crocheted table mats, miniature

knitted gloves, and rag dolls, asking us to name a price (the only other piece of furniture in the room apart from the beds and the stove was a Singer sewing machine) it seemed the most civilised way of doing business we could imagine, apart, perhaps, from the bank in Istanbul. She transacted in broken French thanks to the proximity of the Cappadocian Club Med. Others were just as inventive in their use of the environs: storing and drying fruits in the chambers, parking their cars in those accessible enough to use as garages, using the darkest, most concealed ones as illegal stills.

It was just this same property of concealment that attracted those fleeing persecution during the iconoclastic conflict of the eighth and ninth centuries. In the valley we hunted and scrambled our way up fissures and crevices, bent double along tufa shutes to emerge breathless into perfectly cross-shaped churches, covered with frescoes. The eyes of the Father, right hand raised in a gesture of blessing typical of Byzantine illuminations, slant blackly in his olive skin, boring into the soul of the visitor as he looks up into the dome of one of these secret churches. Mary, in the apse, holding the Child to robes of pure sapphire blue, bears him with a tender, stiff, gracefulness worthy of the madonnas of St Mark's. There's another completely, almost laughably, different style of decoration in some of the churches. In its crude, stumbling abstraction, it looks just like what comes out when you give a six-year-old child a pencil and tell him or her to take a line for a walk.

Tufa, being so soft, is also easily eroded, a factor which gives rise to the third marvel of the valley. When the volcano created this landscape of tufa hills it also threw out lumps of harder basalt. They were the thing to remain sitting atop when the hills were reduced on all sides by wind and rain to mere needles. The result is the fabled 'faery chimneys' of Goreme: slender pillars of volcanic ash with basalt hats on.

But central Cappadocia hadn't shown us quite all its cards yet. There were still the underground cities. At a place called Derinkuyu we plunged into the bowels of the earth, or so it seemed. The cave cities of Goreme are dateable and quite well documented. The underground cities, by contrast, partly because of a complete absence of historical or travellers' records are quite undateable, though with a Hittite-style grain mill found in one and a Roman sarcophagus in another, it's likely they're pretty old. Investigation is further confused by the actual design. They have miles and miles of low tunnels connecting windowed and niched chambers, which can be completely sealed off at various junctures and at the drop of a hat by rolling a giant millstone right across the passageway from its slot in the wall. This nifty device renders them perhaps the most impregnable urban sites in the world.

Therein lies the puzzle, for there is no evidence of invasion or internecine strife in the region at any time to warrant such total fortification. It has been jokingly suggested that the Cappadocians simply had a bad case of paranoia. They certainly must have had claustrophobia, despite the relative spaciousness of the caves, the points at which the narrow corridors widen to form the equivalent of a market square with benches all around, and the highly sophisticated ventilation shafts. Still, with 'grain from the threshing floor and juice from the wine press' life can't have been too grim (Num 18:27). One large chamber was given over totally to wine-making, vats and basins and treading floors all cut out of the rock. The communal bakery is similarly ingeniously equipped.

Emerging slightly dazed to the light of day after all this, we might have been forgiven for thinking that the excitement was over for a while. In reality it had only just begun. The sky was beginning to fill with a sinister yellowy-purple light as we left town. After half an hour there was grit in our eyes, ears, socks, and hoods. We were in for our first dust storm. We strained on doggedly and then suddenly there was an awful grinding noise from behind and the back wheel locked, stopping us dead. Our hearts missed a beat as we jumped off, unloaded, and turned the bike upside down with the speed of dread, knowing as we did so that there was something horribly wrong. We had the presence of mind to look back for anything that might have come off, and in the swirling dirt of the road were rewarded by a tiny screw which we wrapped in cloth for safety.

There was only one part of the bike Howard wasn't entirely sure how to mend – the hub brake. It's essentially the same principle as a motorbike's, required for the double strain on a tandem. He knew the principle of it but had never actually got inside the sealing metal plates. The problem, of course, was inside the hub brake. Howard quickly got to the stage where he feared going further in case he broke something irreparably. As we straightened up from squinting through dust-stung eyes at the offending part two huge dogs came bounding and snarling across the fields from the only house in sight, to see what was for supper. By crouching right down at their level we could keep them at bay but every time we tried to stand they leapt forward, fangs bared.

Banking on the reliability of Turkish goodwill, we decided the best plan was to leave our bags and the bike, minus the back wheel, at the house. We'd hot foot it back into the tiny town with the wheel and try to find a mechanic, and, even more of a long shot, one who understood about hub brakes on tandems. This particular brake was a fairly new thing in Britain, so what a small town mechanic in one of the remoter parts of Turkey was going to make of it we couldn't – didn't want to – imagine. To make matters worse it was four-thirty on a Saturday afternoon. The shops would shortly be closing and would remain so for the whole of the next day.

Hot foot it was just what the dogs were determined we

shouldn't do. Only by frequent bendings double and
surreptitious inchings forward, hailing them with stones
and thwacking them with a large stick when they
dodged the onslaught to get close enough to snap, did
we finally reach the house. Howard kept them off while
Anna banged at the locked door. There was no answer.
She banged with all her might. Still no answer. As she
turned to Howard in defeat, two faces quickly slid away
from the adjoining window. We coaxed and wheedled
those children – obviously alone with strict instructions
not to open the door until Ma and Pa returned – at least
to call off the dogs so that we could have an audible
conversation. They brought the animals to heel, more or
less, but as for a reasonable interchange, with our lack of
Turkish and their age, there was no possibility.

We couldn't waste any more time. There was an
empty outhouse nearby to which we transferred the
bike, then staggered back on to the road with the wheel
and all our bags. A lift was thankfully not long in coming
and we were soon back in the town. With only part of
the bike – the wheel – with which to explain our case, we
couldn't make the urgency of it clear. 'Come and drink
çai' was alternated with vague mutterings about the
wheelwright having gone to visit his Mum in Ankara for
the weekend. We were getting nowhere fast. We'd
committed ourselves to spending Christmas in Tarsus
with a contact from Britain and we just didn't have a day
to spare with the climb that lay between us and there.
More importantly, the spectre of those Iranian visas was
beginning to take flesh. From now on we had to be
pretty concerted about sticking to a timetable if we
hoped to reach the border by January 12th, our last
possible date for entering Iran.

As we fretted and tried to communicate a young man
edged his way through the crowd which had gathered.
He was the only English speaker in town – the schoolteacher. Whatever we needed, he'd do his best to provide,

'but out here in the sticks . . . ' There was no time to hug Aydin for there were decisions to be made, fast. *Bay* Wheelwright was definitely out of town for a week it now transpired. Was there somewhere we could make an international telephone call? Miraculously, or perhaps thanks to Atatürk, the post office could do that. In this vast country where the idea of a private phone outside of the main cities was unthinkable, the PTTs stayed open all night – the only means of getting vital messages in and out of the remoter areas. There didn't seem to be any other option except to phone the bike builder in London (could we catch him before he went off work late on a Saturday afternoon just before Christmas?) and ask him how to get the plate off.

We didn't have his number; that's to say, we had his old number. The post office were very sorry, Aydin interpreted, but they didn't have access to International Directory Enquiries. We tried Howard's mother, then one brother, then the next, for them to get Chas Roberts' number and phone back. Each attempt meant going via the staff and the Istanbul operator, and waiting for a call back. None of them were in. We plumped for some London-based friends. 'Hey, good to hear from you. How're things?' they began, and feeling horrible, we had to cut them short and issue orders lest our money ran out.

They acted like lightning once they understood but that still meant another hour's wait as they found the number, phoned him, asked him to phone us, and his call seeped through the system. Howard squeezed into the booth with the wheel, dismantling it on his lap as the instructions came over the line. When we finally put the phone down, we just laughed weakly with relief at one another. Now we hugged Aydin who'd patiently stayed with us right up until the last phone call. 'You must come and spend the night with me,' he said. It was dark outside. Our bike was five miles away. We didn't know

whether this town had a hotel or not. We'd seen no
obvious tent spots. Being British we protested but probably not very strongly, and he being Turkish, protested
very strongly. When, at the end of the evening, pushing
open the door to go to the outhouse we were confronted
with six inches of snow which had fallen unperceived as
we'd whiled the evening away, we were mighty glad we'd
been persuaded. Theoretically our tent could stand up
to such rigours without letting in the wet, but could we?

Aydın's isolated location was entirely typical of two
branches of public service in *Türkiye Cumhuriyeti* (The
Turkish Republic): teaching and the military police.
Often the most remote postings devolve on young
unmarrieds, and in the military, on those on national
service. Many schoolteachers, like Aydın, find themselves in one breeze block room with no running water
for living quarters, and no one approaching their intel-
lectual level to enliven the years before another, more
congenial situation arises.

If we thought Aydın's pupillage was hard though, in a
town which at least saw a proportion of tourists in the
summer, we were to come across even more isolated
existences near the Syrian border. They were as much
'missionary' situations as anything we were going to be
in. One young man from Izmir had been posted to a
desert hamlet which had lacked a teacher for half a year.
Without electricity or the most basic of supplies (it was a
day's jeep ride away from tarmac) his father, a retired
general, had come with him in the first few months to
help him settle. They instituted an all-round haircut for
cleanliness' sake and mediated between the 'new' ways of
Atatürk and the old traditions of the village. Their
cheerful fortitude was as remarkable as that of the
police we also met out in these parts – obviously dying to
get back to 'civilisation' but recognising, too, the necessity for everyone to take their turn.

The next day, the time it took us to hike back out to

the bike and mend it was about the same as it took the snow ploughs to clear enough snow for us to be able to cycle. The family of yesterday's immured children were fascinated by the proceedings and had obviously given the bike the once over but everything was intact – and it was their shed, after all. By lunch-time we were ready for the slush the brilliant sunshine was creating out of the remaining snow on the road. We started out fine but when we tried to change gear we ran up against an insurmountable problem. Slush on the road was melting easily; slush thrown up on to the chain and travelling at seventeen miles per hour through the cold air refroze solid and before we knew it we were frozen out of fourteen of our fifteen gears. Luckily we were locked into a manageable one and we made it to Nigde with frequent tea stops to restore our extremities, in snowy villages where interested observers totalled up to fifty in one audience.

The snowy, mountainous landscape was dazzlingly beautiful. It was also too much for the eyes even with sunglasses on. Xenophon's men, somewhere in these parts, had got snow blindness. Progress was slow that day and tiring. We took a very cheap, very cold, truckers' hotel in Nigde, where travellers' cheque time came round again. In Istanbul's Standard Chartered, we'd got the swish treatment you'd expect from a multinational based in London. Elsewhere we got what we'd come to expect from the rest of Turkey: nothing strikingly efficient but everything peppered with a liberal dose of good heartedness and washed down with tiny glasses of tea. The paperwork isn't hidden away on computer files or even cash register rolls; the whole paper chain of a modern provincial bank is there somewhere behind the counter for you to see.

Someone is employed expressly to be ready to catch the eye of any of the clerks and move paper to the next official's desk. This man worked with great dignity, drawing attention away from himself, moving with speed but not obsequiousness from table to table, and responding graciously to all he came into contact with. It reinforced what we had come to realise again and again as we cycled East: namely that for the vast majority of the world's history, the vast majority of people have had to eke a meagre living from long hours of menial work. Ecclesiastes reads to us now, as a result of the trip, much less like the work of a melancholic than a realist.

The next day should have been ideal for our long-awaited challenge: getting over the Silician Gates in Alexander's footsteps. The snow had been entirely cleared from the near-deserted road and the sun was shining. We bowled out of Nigde and began to climb. A farmhand spotted us at one bend. He dropped his churns with excitement, beckoning with one hand, making eating and drinking motions with the other. We couldn't stop if we were to do the Gates and get to Tarsus by Christmas. We tried to make 'thank you but sorry' smiles and then we saw The Dog.

It came tearing out of the barn, straight past its master and straight for us. It was the biggest either of us have ever seen, ears and tail clipped, we were later told, so that the bands of foraging mountain wolves it was employed to deter couldn't get a purchase on it. If we'd been standing its head would probably have reached our chests. Too late the farmhand began to whistle for it. In seconds it was at us, lunging at the bike from every angle. We were going so slowly because of the gradient, it was only a matter of time before it would sink in its teeth. Mountain dogs mercifully, are not only ferocious protectors however, they're also trained to be totally obedient. For a few horrible moments we thought its master was too hurt by our refusal of his invitation to bother to call off the beast, and its single-mindedness made it evident that we were in for big trouble if he didn't. The dog reluctantly — painfully slowly — submitted to the long whistles and retreated.

The next dog that came at us was on a fifty-yard chain. The next was on the flat where we could just keep abreast of it. After a mile or so, when we were flagging, but the dog, red-eyed with fury, seemed to be redoubling its energies, some boys saw our plight and ran out and cornered it. We were fearful for them but it seemed that it was the pedals moving in unison (tandem pedals don't operate independently as so many people seem to think!) which frenzied them so much, not simply strangers. They must have signified flight which, translated into mountain dog language, means target practice.

After three attempts on our lives even Howard, who likes dogs in the normal run of things, was white-faced and busy working out what our line of attack would be in the event of another such encounter. We dismounted and took long breaths, standing long enough to get some strength back into our legs. We decided to try and keep cycling if at all possible in an attempt, not to outstrip — that would have been impossible with such speedy creatures and on such retarding terrain — but to keep moving just fast enough for them not to be able to fasten their jaws on us. If that didn't work, Howard would try and club them with the padlock and chain.

With the next though, there was no chance of escape or defence for they were a pair. Anna was pretty hyped up by now for she heard and saw them coming from a mile away across the fields where they'd picked up our scent. At first we didn't believe they were coming for us at that distance, but as the yelps grew louder and they loped across the snow at a pace that reminded us of a speeded up sequence of *Call of the Wild* it was evident we were the prey.

There wasn't a soul or a house in sight. Lorries had been passing us about once every quarter hour. This quarter hour wasn't even half way through. The dogs had reached the road now, and were pelting along on the unobstructed ground, easily closing the gap between us. Anna was beginning to whimper. Howard said afterwards that if she applied herself to the pedals in that way regularly we'd be at the Iranian border with time to spare. They were almost upon us. Then two lorries – not just one – came into view, one from each direction of the road. They cut across the path of the dogs, slowing them, and pushing them off the road into the ditch. The drivers jumped out and pelted them with stones as we put as great a distance between us and them as our adrenalin enabled us to. Five minutes later one lorry caught us up. 'Want a lift?' they asked kindly; '*çok güzel* bisiclet'. We forgot Alexander and the Silician Gates; we forgot our resolution to cycle every inch of the way unless absolutely forced not to (perhaps indeed this counted as being forced?); the bike and the luggage were up in the back, and we safely in the cab.

We were both too shaken now to do anything but sit tight, shell pistachios, and answer questions for the rest of the afternoon. If we had got out and continued further along the road we'd have been in exactly the same predicament for every homestead, or group of them up here had its watchdog and every one seemed bent on man-eating, judging by the sallies made even on the lorry. We were livid: one of the best ascents yet and all seen from the window of a lorry. Howard, who'd been the one who'd started us on this Alexander idea in the first place, glowered at the snowy pinewoods in pure disgust and any chance mention of Silician Gates over the next few days was enough to throw him into a brown study.

They dropped us just outside Tarsus as night – and rain – began to fall. Perhaps our rescue had been timely in another sense for the ensuing night's downpour and the drizzle of the days up until Christmas would have been positively dangerous up in the mountains. We arrived at our English contact distinctly damp and splattered with mud from the undrained roads. 'No mean city' was how Paul had boasted about his home town (and, incidentally the place where Anthony met Cleopatra). To us it seemed just that – a mean old town, like a sprawling, muddy building site.

If Tarsus itself was unwelcoming, Frances, our English teacher at Tarsus College and her American colleagues couldn't have provided more of a contrast. She swore it was we who'd made her Christmas rather than vice versa as we sat around reading her books with the eagerness that came from having had only our Bible for the last two and a half months and used gallons of her hot water on very frequent showers.

The weight of the past falls heavily at any Christmas time. Abroad, and as guests at another's celebration, we felt it all the more. As the time drew near we discovered that we'd each been thinking what present we could possibly give the other considering we had zero luggage space. Comestibles seemed the answer, but the *lisesi* (school) was overflowing with them. Everyone was charming to us, easy and considerate, but there was no pretending we weren't thinking of home and we went to bed quiet and early on Christmas Eve.

On Christmas morning we had a private time of tea in bed with mail that we'd restrained ourselves from opening since picking it up from the post office the day we'd arrived, and one present. Somehow Anna's younger sister had got through with German chocolates, and much needed underwear to replace what had been taking a hammering on the saddle. (We felt rather inferior when we read Moses' reminder to the Israelites: 'Your clothes did not wear out . . . during these forty years.' (Deut 8:4)). It was funny: that one present made all the difference. We wanted nothing more. It was enough that someone who loved us had made contact.

Then it was out into town to phone home; into the

bustle of an ordinary Moslem working day and past a bank of typists sitting in the sun outside the PTT doing any and everybody's official business. After lots of waiting but also lots of post office tea, a great deal of talk to Ankara and Howard shouting down the line to sleepy Mum in Surrey, poor Anna only got a wrong number in Australia where the rest of her family were spending Christmas with her older sister. When they saw her crestfallen face the Turks behaved typically, rallying round to comfort and refusing to let her pay for the call. On the way back Howard had his shoes polished on the side of the road in honour of the day (there being no smart clothes to get into) and we came back to Frances's to enjoy a familiar accent and some British humour. We didn't need to say anything but we knew we were all three remembering the Queen's speech at the appointed time and, without even meaning to, were reaching round the walnut cookies for the mince pies. When the Gospel was read in a Texas accent we tried very hard to remember we were going to live in Nepal and must be tolerant. Then we felt heels, noticing how all the Americans were automatically reaching round the mince pies for the walnut cookies.

6

ARRESTED IN ARABIA

Saturday, December 27th

Laden with banana bread cooked by the principal's wife
we headed due East for the first time in a long while.
After all our winding and weaving from Izmir it felt
once more as if we were actually going to Nepal – and
Iran. We'd followed the advice of an experienced Iranian traveller in Tarsus by concocting a very official
looking but actually totally spoof medical certificate with
all our medicines itemised on it, which we had signed by a
doctor to say that they weren't narcotics. An Iranian
pupil's father had translated all the unintelligible squiggles on our visa for us. These two moves served somewhat
to allay for us the rather infectious panic that was
increasingly greeting our admission that we intended to
cycle through Iran. 'Boom, boom, zap, kaputt' the
nationals tried to dissuade us, with graphic accompanying gestures and invitations that we just stay with them –
indefinitely.

We fair ate up the miles that first day back on the road
– eighty by dusk and not with a particularly early start or
ill effects. We put it down to the roast turkey and our
new tyres, picked up in Tarsus. They were the first of
the six sets sent ahead to reach their destination. The
only other pair to survive the journey got through to
Pakistan which, from what we saw of subcontinental

post offices, was a sheer miracle. The sun was blazing down after the intermittent rain of our time at the *Lisesi* but there were storm clouds ahead. Like Canute we pushed them ahead of us all that day, hoping that the law of averages might mean that we'd had our rain for a while. At a place called Toprakkale the road forked decisively with a fortress castle from Crusader days perched high up on the hillside overlooking the breach. There was something about the junction that made us get out our map. Sure enough, if we'd taken the southern road we would have ended up in Israel. It was the crossroads between old Asia and the Holy Land.

The wind, forcing open the door of the disused shop we slept in that night and pushing over the bike we'd leaned up against it, should have warned us of what was in store. We aren't weather buffs though and we were just annoyed at having to get out of our warm cocoon to set things to rights. At least it wasn't the intruder we'd first feared. We had a hefty 990-metre pass to overcome ahead of us and after our disappointment with the Silician Gates we were determined to make the ascent ourselves. Since we'd got the bike we'd noticed that we did actually take pleasure in attaining physical goals. The pleasure often lay more in the freewheeling down the other side than the arduous slog up and it probably had something too, to do with making it in tandem. Also, the fitter we got, the easier the achievements became.

The rain didn't begin till we were half way up and even then it felt more as if we were *in* it rather than that it was falling on us. It was a seeping damp which permeated our seams, our cuffs, our shoes. It hadn't seemed worth putting our waterproofs on at first but it had us thoroughly sodden by the time the first trucker leant out of his cab. Usually not a day went by on this kind of terrain without our being offered a lift. The drivers could hardly restrain themselves from forcibly plucking us off the saddle, installing us in their nice warm cab and slinging the bike in the back. One fellow, delivering concrete reinforcer bars to Iran, had followed us, grindingly slowly (for long stretches here we were actually going as fast as the lorries) for three or four miles, positively imploring us to jump in. He lifted his hands alternately to Allah, and to all the spare space he had at our disposal. When this didn't elicit from us the desired response he cast around desperately for a way of persuading us. His eye lighted on the *Mas'Allah* (it's up to Allah) slogan emblazoned, typically, across the top of his windscreen and he gestured towards it expressively as if to say: 'Look, Allah's provided you with a way out. Why don't you take it?'

We stubbornly refused, even when the rain began in earnest, slashing through the mountain fog and swirling in great billows along the road. We couldn't see a hand in front of our faces and were upon the sign that marked the summit before we were aware of having reached the top. The descent, with the torrents lashing our faces, was horribly slippery and slow after all our expectations. Even the offers of lifts decreased as visibility got poorer and poorer. We passed a shepherd herding his flock to shelter with an umbrella up but were too cold and wet even to laugh though we perked up momentarily as we crossed 'the great river, the Euphrates' (Deut 1:7) into Mesopotamia. Like the turning off to the Holy Land, there was something so illustrious about the very names of such landmarks, that they thrilled us with an admittedly rather nebulous sense of 'History'.

We never really dried out after that day and night long downpour till we reached Urfa, some days cycling further on and hung our clothes up in a warm hotel room. Still, we couldn't really complain: it was the first time we'd actually had to cycle in rain since France – nine weeks previously – and this was winter time. Our

black plastic inner bags – not regular bin liners which
aren't durable enough for this kind of journey we'd
discovered, but super strong ones – had withstood this
harsh test brilliantly. We'd not fared so well in other
respects. Somehow, somewhere, in the haste and discomfort of doing things in the pouring rain, we'd lost
our padlock and chain. Buying a new one wasn't as
difficult as we'd anticipated. Instead of going to a bike
shop (there were none) or purchasing one of the flimsy
ones from a general store, we stumbled across a man
who sold only chains and padlocks, wire and plastic
piping. Typical Middle Eastern specialisation, this.
Nothing could have been more ideal or fancy-tickling
than choosing exactly the thickness of chain we wanted
from the swags on the wall, specifying the length, and
watching as an assistant laid it on a metal disc on the
concrete floor and hammered a wedge shaped metal
blade into it for about ten minutes to sever it.

As he banged and we shared jokes and *çai* with the
shopkeeper our eye was caught by the reels of plastic
hose. It's almost impossible to feed a chain through the
spokes of a bike unless there's some kind of sheath to
hold it right. The Turks are always game for a challenge
and they never charged for that kind of labour – at least,
not us. It was a tight squeeze but by dint of pulling the
oiled chain through the heat softened hose by an
attached piece of wire, we had just the thing. The chain
was sold by the kilo, the pipe by the metre, and we
selected the trustiest looking padlock, sufficient in their
eyes for a barn door.

Back at the hotel the bicycle came into its own. By our
standards it was a reasonably pricey place but we had to
dry off and we got a good deal because of coming out of
season. The chief was immaculately suited and scented in
a way that was quite unusual for a region where Western
dress took a noticeable back seat in favour of *sholvars*. He
spoke tolerable English and was most gracious about

bringing the bike inside and upstairs as we'd had nothing to lock it with when we'd checked in. He impressed us with his scrupulous devotions as well: on a portable carpet square in a Mecca facing corner of the wide hall which ran right the way round the rooms. He was most diligent about getting someone to provide some pliers to mend our front basket, like us the worse for wear after the storm, and was only sorry we insisted on doing the job ourselves.

He eased his conscience by inviting us to watch TV with him in his private parlour behind Reception. Konya was quite unrecognisable under snowdrifts metres deep and there was an entirely justifiable national pride in the efficiency of the Turkish snowploughs. If Britain had been visited by such weather the country would have been at a standstill. With our toes up against the radiator and Anna's boots on the hot pipes we watched the devastation the floods of the last forty-eight hours had caused elsewhere.

Halfway through the News the hotelier's journalist brother walked in and asked for an article. When the interview was over, mug shots cleverly disguising the fact that though on the saddle we were actually inside, the chief, still in his pin stripes, suddenly expressed a desire to have a go on the tandem. He was transformed in an instant from a discreetly elegant businessman to a giggling schoolboy, shrieking and whooping along the hall as Howard and he careered along, and not a jot abashed by the presence of his underlings. Indeed, they were essential for breaking his fall when the ride came to an end.

The fun in Urfa wasn't only to be found in the hotel. We'd suspected we were in for something special when, on visiting the tourist office the literature informed us that Urfa was in a region 'Alexander the Groap' had traversed and there were 'half animated castles valuable to be visited'. We set off for Job's Cave and Abraham's

Pool, appetites whetted all the more by the assertion that besides these two illustrious personages, Adam and Eve had also lived here. There was Urfa's twelfth century *Ulu Jami* – the 'big mosque' every self-respecting Turkish town boasts – whose clock tower is the only one in the country, it being the *muezzin's* job to tell the time to the people. There were the exceptionally clean, flagged residential streets. Their houses seemed to be turned inside out with unfenestrated backs to the street and zigzag decorations kept for the delectation of those inside concealed courtyards.

We bought cakes, honey-drenched and studded with pistachios, from one of the many barrow boys negotiating the mire of the unpaved main street. It was interesting how very regional Turkey was. In each town there were any number of street vendors and over the country as a whole great variety in what they sold. Excepting Istanbul however, the range within any one town was extremely limited. There were only two types of *ekmek* to be had in Urfa, something called *yufka* and a new, oval-shaped flat bread about six inches long. We didn't know it then but it was almost identical to the leavened chapattis we were sometimes to get in Pakistan.

These *pide* were wonderful hot and wrapped round kebabs and salad. The *yufka* – two foot diameter circles, so paper-thin they could be folded into quarters for storage or transportation – was best with something like, but infinitely better than, scrambled eggs. The trick was to tear off little portions and roll them into a scoop instead of using cutlery – again something we'd be familiar with by the time we'd got through Pakistan. Strength of tea was another regional denoter. Availability of food seemed to depend on time of day, which was why, presumably, almost everything in Turkey was so mouth-wateringly fresh. 'Sorry, no *pides* now' the place where we'd had them for lunch told us, 'lots of *lamaçun* though', and sure enough young boys would be bringing in steaming stacks of the spiced ground meat on thin circles of dough from the twilit streets.

Nothing, however, in Urfa could rival the covered bazaar. Even more than Istanbul's it was a real Aladdin's cave, a lamplit maze of narrow walkways, and mysterious dens of wealth and craftsmanship. A lot of it was so exotic we couldn't even guess what it was. Still thumbing through references to the region in our Bible, we came across Ezekiel's lament for Tyre where he harks back to when 'Haran . . . and merchants of Sheba, Asshur, and Kilmad traded with you. In your market place . . . beautiful garments, blue fabric, embroidered work, and multi-coloured rugs with cords twisted and tightly knotted' (Ez 27:23–24). His catalogue no longer held the olde-worlde, never-never land quality it had previously had for us; it was all here:

'silver, iron, tin, and lead . . . articles of bronze . . . mules . . . ivory tusks and ebony . . . coral and rubies . . . wheat . . . and confections, honey, oil and balm . . . wine . . . and wool . . . wrought iron, cassia and calamus . . . saddle blankets . . . lambs, rams, and goats . . . spices and precious stones, and gold.'
(Ez 27:12–22)

Perhaps the very best thing about it was that the opulence wasn't laid on for the tourist. The people themselves invest in the beautiful wares – and not just urban consumers but village people too. The thing we most regretted having no space and no money for were black, ankle length coats with a stylishly ample cut that would have placed them among the designer collections back home. They had a curious appliqué descending from the shoulder seams, which met in a V and a loop mid back. They were lined with something very like Astrakhan, which could be casually displayed by folding back the cuffs or letting the hoods dangle. (Since they were Syrian imports the fur lining was probably Syrian lamb.) They quoted us something in the region of a hundred pounds when we asked. When, to our amazement, down the road to Haran we saw shepherds tending their flocks in these garments, we wondered whether they'd really paid that much. Even if they'd paid only half, it was still a substantial outlay which helped to turn on its head our simplistic categorisation of riches – a hi-fi in a nice house; and poverty – no toilet and mud floors.

Back home one of the best moments of our planning sessions had been when we realised that en route we could visit Haran where Abraham lived (definitely this time!) for many years on his way from Ur (not Urfa) to Canaan, as we're told in Genesis 11. The tourist office promised that it was a 'very tidy road' from Urfa. The town of Haran is almost on the point of extinction. Despite its extremely long history, despite the fact that it gave birth to the first Islamic university, it is now almost exclusively an archaeological site. A few apparently broken down farms remain, but here too there was evidently still plenty of wealth – measurable in the gorgeous silks and velvets the women wore just to go to the communal tap, and their jewellery: masses of weighty, wrought gold, semi-precious stones, ivory and ebony. We felt dowdy in our practical, patched, cycling wear beside these flouncy, jingling peacocks, but when they caught sight of Anna's sapphire engagement ring we were redeemed. In fact their eyes gleamed rather fearsomely and in another village the women actually grabbed at her hand suggesting, only half teasingly, that she give it to them. No wonder then that Abraham, seventy-five years old by the time he moves on from Haran, is said to take not only his family and necessities, but 'all the possessions they had accumulated . . . in Haran' (Gen 12:5).

It is very rare for cyclists to feel the wind behind them.

The best way to explain why is with a clock face. Even if the wind is actually coming at you from four o'clock, the chances are that your passage forward is fast enough to make it feel as if it's actually striking you from somewhere around two o'clock. Winds that appear to be coming from the side can easily be a combination of your speed and a breeze from five o'clock. And even if there is one directly behind you, if it's not stronger than the fifteen miles per hour or so you're cycling, it can simply feel like a still day. We'd been blown along the baked mud from Urfa to Haran in blazing sunshine at a cracking pace which falsely caused us to suppose that this kind of riding was always pretty much as 'tidy' as on tarmac. When a shortcut was mentioned which avoided retracing our steps to Urfa but took in an Assyrian city, a thirteenth century caravanserai, and a sun temple, and would bring us out substantially further along the main road in the direction we wanted to go, we didn't think twice about the fact that there was no macadam.

We sped off into our first desert and that evening were put up by our first Arab. There was nothing else to call him, with his flowing robes and *kuffiyah* (Arabic *çaddr*) held in place on his head by the camel hair circlet they call an '*iqal*'. He said there was no way we could get to Der Yakup (the caravanserai) where we'd rather fancied sleeping, by tonight. We were a little confused. 'Back there they told us it was only four miles away.' 'Miles?' he said vaguely, 'Der Yakup? About twelve maybe.' We were mystified. 'Back there' they'd said four miles to Der Yakup; even further back they'd sworn blind to three. And now here was this guy, some miles closer to our destination surely, quoting a dozen. Time, not distance, it gradually became clear was their measurement, gauged according to whether you were going by foot, mule, mule and laden cart, or pick-up. When, later that evening, we showed them our ideogram, there was total puzzlement on all faces, though they perked up a little

when we pointed to Istanbúl and Haran and there were
a few grunts of recognition when we indicated Yunanis-
tan (Greece). From here to journey's end, this proved to
be by far the more usual reaction to our laminated map.

Hasan Ozbay insisted, though with an aloof dignity
that distinguished these people from the warmly impor-
tunate Turks, that we step inside for the night. We
hadn't the heart or the conviction to chain the tandem.
It would have appeared to doubt their honesty. We went
into the front room of one of the four concrete houses
which constituted the village. It was as big as a football
pitch, and there was a Persian carpet covering its entire
length and a stove in the middle. The final, extraordinary item was . . . a large colour TV. That was all, until
fingers were snapped and plush cushions and thick rugs
were produced from back rooms for us to sit on. One by
one the extended family (that meant the whole village)
filed in to encircle us, but again in a restrained, slightly
diffident manner which didn't allay their hospitality but
actually made it less overwhelming to deal with. Men
and children respectfully knocked at the door, removed
their shoes, and divided their attention between us and
– of all things – Russian cartoons beamed from Syria.

Supper was served on a huge brass tray: dishes of
something like pasta mixed with rice and butter. Only
one woman was permitted entry: the grandmother of
the gaggle of tousle-headed, velvet-clad, but barefoot
urchins. She was streaming with 'flu which she mopped
at with a filthy rag that also did for lightning swoops on
the children's snotty upper lips. The 'respect for the
elderly' (Lev 19:32) gave her the place of honour next to
Anna who had been carefully stationed on the other side
of the room from Howard. She sat very close and was
very liberal with where she waved her hankie.

Before she saw the old woman's eyes Anna joked in an
undertone to Howard across the stove: 'Well, when I
come down with 'flu, at least I'll be able to say I've got

Arab 'flu.' When the eyes were turned full upon her they put an end to all levity. There was an awful, nightmarish, emptiness in them. At first Anna thought she was over-reacting, culturally bound by the other strangeness of seeing her tattooed lips and cheeks, but she heard Howard catch his breath when the eyes were fixed vacantly – terrifiedly – on him. We were certain it wasn't we, directly, who were the objects of fear. We'd very occasionally cause rural children concern, but that wasn't it. There was the same, unmistakable, baffled yearning in the eyes of women from other villages in the area we met over the next few days. The men didn't seem to have it. What was it? If we'd have seen it on the London Underground we'd have said 'drugs' without any hesitation. To this day we can only hazard the guess, prompted by a gut reaction and the discovery that the children's tattoos were to ward off 'the evil one', that there was a spiritual component.

It came to bedtime and we were to sleep in the front room. Anna asked for the loo and a young woman, whose arm she'd seen passing dishes through the door earlier, accompanied her to a strangely large stone basin in the middle of a starlit field. She 'flushed' with a jug of water through a hole at the bottom. That was it: a bowl, a hole, and a jug; with no walls it commanded an uninterrupted view for miles around. What they did during the day we couldn't imagine.

When she got back inside there was a tussle going on between Howard and our host. Our high-tech sleeping bags and Karrimats were not doing much for the British image. With looks of pitying superiority after fingering what to them was pathetically flimsy protection, orders were issued for something worth its weight to be brought. First came the mattresses – two apiece; then embroidered bolsters and pillows; then satin feather quilts with sheets tacked on; then pure wool blankets; and lastly – in case we got cold – more fuel for the stove.

As, sweltering, we threw off layer after layer in the
night, we figured that these, the TV, the digital watches
the men had been wearing under their robes, were to
the Ozbays what the jewellery and stuffs had been to the
women down in Haran: wiser items to spend your
money on than things like tastier or more varied food,
when the slog to get that from land to kitchen to mouth
must be considerable. There was no question of a quick
trip to the bazaar out here.

Before leaving we took a photo, which was all people
ever asked of us in return for their kindness, of the
whole clan – about forty of them – and promised to send
it to a PO box number in Urfa. Then we were instructed
to follow two boys in a donkey cart, providentially also
going in the direction of Der Yakup. We raced them up
and down the sandy hummocks in response to their
cheeky offer to give us a tow until, breathless and
laughing, we went our separate ways.

Our caravanserai was visible from at least half a mile
away as a vast mass overshadowing a small settlement
that had subsequently grown up outside its Western
wall. When we drew closer it was evidently the same plan
as some we'd passed on the Konya plains: an imposing
gateway headed by an inscription bisecting one wall, and
a 'porter's lodge' to one side of the gate. The only
substantial difference from a Cambridge Front Court
was the little mosque incorporated into the rooms which
ran all the way round the square.

A caravanserai or *han* is an inn for travellers, in this
case built by the Selçuk rulers of Turkey in the twelfth
century for caravans of merchants on the Eastern trade
routes. It was good to discover that at least someone went
slower than us along these tracks; the laden merchants
are supposed to have travelled at an average of nine
miles a day. Nowadays, with the Turks only just waking
up to the reasons for preserving these curious edifices,
they're certainly not to be found every nine miles along

the old roads as they once were. Those that are left, like Der Yakup, are shells in various stages of decay, which the locals use as stables.

We were given directions to Suayp Sehir, our first Assyrian city. *Sehir* was one of those clever words that, with only the slightest variation, did for 'city' from Turkey to Nepal, as 'nan' for bread and 'pis' for what it sounds like. Suayp was partially an underground city again, though without the depth of the ones up in Cappadocia and with evidence of magnificent above-ground building. After we'd rooted around for half the afternoon we turned North to the sun temple. We reckoned, rightly, that we'd reach it by nightfall; we reckoned, wrongly, that we'd reach the tarmac by lunch-time the next day.

The landscape even before we reached the sun temple was creepy. Out of the sandy ground loomed oddly smooth, totally bare, and clearly stratified rock forms, the size of small hills. We thought we must be almost upon it. Then, turning a corner, there it was – the 'solar system': a central, dominant hill standing for the sun, encircled by six subservient 'planet' hills: believed to be the layout of the universe by these early medieval pagans even before Galileo proved it. It was even weirder when we'd scrambled on hands and knees up to the graveyard on top of the 'sun': like the women's eyes, indefinable, but the same kind of creepiness as when, in Dorset once, we'd put our tent up against the sealing stone of a Neolithic burial mound miles from nowhere. Back down in Sogmatar village which clusters irrever-ently round the base of the temple hill, the people's wild appearance and behaviour didn't make us feel any easier.

As we passed a police post at the exit to the village we were charged to explain ourselves. To the best of our abilities we did and asked if we could possibly sleep in their enclosure. They were genuinely sorry but the

'Komdat' was out on business and they didn't have the liberty to let us in. We tried to relieve their mortification by saying that we had an idea of where we could camp, which was true. One soldier came running after us as we left, rifle chinking against metal buttons, and tipped army food rations into our baskets before we could stop him.

'What d'you need a military post out here for anyway?' we tried to formulate. He gestured vaguely southwards and we thought we caught the words 'Surya', 'Kurd', and '*yeni yil*' in among the otherwise incomprehensible torrent. 'Oh well' . . . We pushed off to the rocky overhang we'd passed as we'd come in. It had looked as if it could protect a tent from people and weather, though all we were unsuspectingly thinking of then was the frost which had lain on the ground that morning. As we were fixing the guy ropes one part of what the soldier had been saying suddenly slotted into place: '*yeni yil*' – new year. Here it was, New Year's Eve and here we were about to go to bed before six. We ate in the tent, spreading a towel out in hopes of catching the crumbs in the pitch black, then settled down, Anna with tubigrips pulled up over her knees under all her other layers and a shawl, quartered, down the seat of her trousers. In the sleeping bag she'd begun to feel the cold most in her bottom and knees, probably because one or the other lay nearest to the zip, which, though bevelled, was still the most pregnable part. She was just glad there was no one but Howard to see her with her bulky, sagging nappy and straitened knees.

We fell asleep easily that evening after the excitement and exertions of the day but at some indeterminable hour the tent was bathed in headlights, there was a crunching of heavy boots round our heads and a sharply issued order which had something to do with 'now' and 'the Komdat'. We groped our way, groaning, out of dreams about colour TVs in sun temples and Howard tried, in the first few seconds before we realised we were under arrest, to negotiate through the zip with these darned hospitable Turks: 'Look we're fine, really – got everything we need. My wife's so comfy she's fast asleep still.' There was a rapidly reiterated order and, as the clouds scudding across the sky parted for a minute, Howard saw the bayonets glinting. 'Darling' he whispered urgently, 'it's no use pretending. It's the police. Get your nappy off quick. We've got to go with them.' And that, with a soldier ahead and two at our rear, we blearily did.

We might have been excused for thinking we'd come to the wrong place when, at an inner sanctum in the police post, we were confronted by a fresh-faced twenty-one-year-old behind a desk. When our guards closed the door behind us though, respectfully clicking their boots together, it was obvious that, smooth cheeked or no, this was the Komdat and the Komdat meant business. We sat and waited as he and another of those noble Arab types, this time sporting a silk suit below his *kuffiyah* and wielding a fat cigar, dealt with a man with a fresh and bloody wound on his head. The examinee appeared utterly cowed by both the Arab and the Komdat who was obviously keen we should note his interrogation techniques. It took us a bit longer to fathom the relationship between this duo.

We sat mute, furiously trying to work out what on earth we were doing there and what we were going to say when we came under fire. Finally the defendant was dismissed and we were called to order. 'Do you want some tea?' the first question barked out. We dared not catch one another's eye but we managed to remain respectful as it became abundantly clear we were in custody mainly for the offence of arousing the commandant's curiosity. We'd also committed a heinous crime against the laws of hospitality by not seeking accommodation from the

village chief – the noble Arab. Now his presence was
explained.

Of course, in the eyes of the state a village chief has no
legal power, but here his actual power was as strong as
the day Atatürk had formally abolished it. Old habits die
hard, particularly out in this no man's land where the
concept of the Turkish nation carries little or no weight.
We were so close to the Syrian border that the people
didn't count themselves as Turks, even when they
weren't among the substantial number of Kurds co-
existing there. They regarded themselves as Arabs: all
part of *Ummah*, the Islamic brotherhood, but beyond
that they proudly refuse to be labelled. The existence of
a police post here was, in part, to enforce exactly the
national cohesion our commandant was now shrewdly
overlooking. He knew he could never hope to break the
chief's rule, so instead he'd won the chief over by
flattering him with the notion that they were keeping
order in tandem. If ever the commandant wanted to
implement something he knew wouldn't go down too
well with the villager-serfs, he simply delegated it to the
chief, proposing it to him as another opportunity of
proving who really ruled the roost. The villagers,
because they think they're still subject to the tribal
authority they instituted, seldom dream of disobeying.

It was a canny system we couldn't but help admiring
the Komdat for. When in the course of the conversation
about our accommodation it seemed (were we hearing
aright?) that it was a question of which of the chief's
wives we should stay with, we realised that the commandant was actually having to turn a blind eye to more than
simply an illicit power structure. We couldn't blame him.
Everything about the Arab spelt command. We wouldn't
have liked to get on the wrong side of him. However, the
last thing we wanted to do was to have to pack up
everything and shift camp, so we suggested, cautiously,
that it would be most undiplomatic for the chief's

marital relations if we were to prevail upon one spouse and not another and we'd do much better to go back to our tent where we were most comfortable. 'Really fine,' we insisted, trying not to yawn too obviously but just enough that they got the message. At length we were acquitted and escorted back to the tent and fell asleep again.

Eleven o'clock, however, and 'crunch, crunch, crunch' came the sound of heavy boots round our heads and the Komdat wanted to see us again. This time we stalled for longer but it was no good. A gentle rain had begun to fall since we'd been asleep. 'Bet you he just can't bear the thought of us camping in the wet,' Howard grumbled wearily, and we were courteous but short when that, exactly, turned out to be it. We couldn't sulk for long however, when it transpired that we were now in the clutches of an entirely different commandant: one who, realising that he'd had no real grounds for the first arrest, or certainly not explained them, was concerned to rectify his manner in a second. From a self-important blusterer he became a charming young father whose eyes watered with smiling pride as he produced a photograph of his month-old son and shared with us his wife's impatience to get out of this backward hole and return to Ankara. Only two things carried over from the first meeting – the teas and the insistence that we couldn't sleep out. Besides the rain there was now a fuller explanation.

Our 'offence', this time, seemed to centre round the fact that we'd encamped too near to Syria, but the arrest, he assured us, was out of the kindness of his heart. On *yeni yil* terrorists (whether Kurdish or Syrian never seemed to be quite clear in their minds) were wont to make their most decisive sallies, assuming that the Turkish military would be off guard, partying in the New Year. 'Therefore,' he beamed at us, 'since I have to stay up all night, I thought I'd invite you to join me.' We

drew the line at that, but we'd warmed to the fellow by
now and compromised by waiting just long enough to
wish him a Happy New Year. At a minute after midnight we stepped gingerly round the boxes of grenades
to shake hands. It was the first of not a few occasions on
this particular stretch when we wished that the 'terrorists' would go hang for the havoc they caused in our
sleeping arrangements.

Anna ushered in the New Year with a real bang when,
stumbling with tiredness by now, she managed to pull a
barricade down not only on herself but on our three
soldier escorts and the commandant himself who'd
come to wave us off. They extricated themselves from
where they were all sprawling and we shook hands again
all round. Catching the eyes of the soldiers on duty
Howard could have sworn he caught a crinkle at the
corners but they were entirely po-faced by the time the
Komdat had brushed himself down. Settling down to
sleep again at one o'clock we agreed it wasn't the way we
might have chosen to celebrate New Year but it was
certainly worth writing home about.

As it turned out, 'we hadn't seen nothing yet.' When we
finally awoke, on 1st January the day did not dawn bright
and clear. We hoped that if we stayed put till lunch-time
the rain might abate. We cuddled down in our sleeping
bag and had the problem of what to do with the last hour
solved by — yes — the crunching of heavy boots and an
'invitation' from the Komdat. Guessing what it would be
we sprang to attention more promptly this time and were
rewarded by lunch and more photographs of baby.
Then, rain or no rain, we really had to go.

We set off confidently enough, furnished with a
sketch map by the commandant of the Tek-Tek mountains which had replaced the desert, but it was useless.
To a resident there might have been a subtle difference
between the size of the bewildering superabundance of
crisscrossing, stone groined tracks, but to city-slickers

like us, without a signpost in sight, they all looked exactly the same. Who needs a signpost when mobility is only relevant insofar as it affects grazing, and where everyone except the commandant's men had lived all their lives? We might not have laboured under quite such a long misconception that we were still headed the right way had it not been for the sudden language barrier that had sprung up between us and the lone shepherd we asked directions from every couple of hours. We knew enough Turkish ourselves by now to be certain these people weren't speaking that, and nor were they understanding ours. We were forced to proceed on only the most doubtful of 'Yes that's the way' signs and grunts. As night approached we had to admit that we were well and truly lost, soaked to the skin, and splattered with mud. The rocky landscape precluded any ideas of putting up the tent. What the herds find to eat on the barren slopes is a mystery.

From time to time we'd passed a sorry mud settlement clinging desperately to the hillside and showing, in this filthy weather, not a sign of life. From the outside it wasn't even clear whether they were human habitations at all but that, at present, was the least of our problems. First and foremost a roof was what we needed, and if we had to share it with the goats, it was still better than nothing at all. At the next one we pushed the bike up the incline and fell into the back yard of what emerged to be the domicile of another village chief.

The old man was a dear, raising his fist to Allah (or was it the evil one?) and the storm clouds, with bitter imprecations; hustling us into the parlour and giving double quick orders for tea. As our limbs began to thaw and our numbed wits to register, we took stock of the scene. If the simplicity at Hasan's, digital watches and Persian carpet notwithstanding, had given us pause, this was something else again with its dirt floor and barely translucent plastic sack for a window embedded in the

mud wall. There was one oil lamp on the wall illuminat-
ing a Koranic text, and the stove. Instead of a TV this
time (not much use without electricity) the only other
piece of furniture was . . . a cuckoo clock.

After that things proceeded pretty much as at Hasan's
except that no one appeared to have any more Turkish
than we, and the women were allowed to be with us in
between tasks. Before supper the chief and a limited
handful of the more senior men made their devotions.
They knew exactly where Mecca lay: in the direction of
the cuckoo clock. Before they prayed they washed, one
pouring from a jug over the other's forearms into a
large bowl, and stopping automatically as the hands
were removed. Before supper we were bidden to wash
likewise, but with a new, fragrant soap in our honour.
The old man ate first – *yufka* and spiced millet. When
he'd finished there was a sophisticated pecking order.
Guests came top of the list, with men and boys carefully
graduated thereafter. The women ate the leftovers in
the kitchen. Now we finally understood the comments
Howard's beard had attracted since we'd crossed the
border. To allow a beard to grow denoted that one was a
hajji, and had made the pilgrimage to Mecca exhorted of
the faithful. The bearded ones ate before the shaved.
Drinking water was passed round in a bowl with a
dipper. There was consternation and some nervous
laughter when Howard offered it to Anna first.

After the meal we got down to the real nitty gritty: our
marital status, and, because of the incident with the
drinking water, the status of Western (to them inter-
changeable with Christian) women. We went through the
usual explanations and distinctions but this lot were more
persistent than most, not satisfied with our 'no room on
the bike for children' which usually did the trick. There
was nothing obscene about the sign language but it didn't
take long to figure out that we were being asked whether
we slept together, and when we affirmed that one, 'Do

you, well ... you know, do you know how to make babies?' ('Wa-wa' with rocking motions was how they got round the word for baby.) When the general hilarity had subsided, Anna put a stop to the conversation with a '*Masallah*', eyes raised heavenwards.

Whether it was to give us a helping hand or whether this was the treatment all guests received, we were given that night what an estate agent would call the master bedroom, belonging to the most recently married son and his pregnant wife. After the scantness of the front room, the clutter in this one was another surprise: hammered brassware and beautiful textiles vying for pride of place with Pifco glass tumblers and plastic flowers. This time we didn't even try to demean ourselves with our sleeping bags, despite the wonder a demonstration of our Gore-Tex rain jackets had occasioned, with every member of the packed room testing out the Velcro and adjustable hoods for himself.

Too early the goats in the pen adjoining the bedroom woke us and we were even less enamoured of them when we discovered that it was their unpasteurised, still tepid milk, complete with floating hairs, which constituted our breakfast, along with more *yufka* for dipping. Anna made the mistake of drinking the pungent stuff in two long draughts to get it over with. The headsman was delighted and immediately presented her with another redolent tin-cupful. We had to leave then, though the rain had only marginally lessened. Which way to go only became more of a vexed question when, asking them to draw us a map, they produced a straight biro line with crosses on it at random points for landmarks. We learnt one thing for definite: yesterday we must have been within seven miles of the Syrian frontier as we circled round under the classic illusion that we were cycling in a straight line. The next rather crushing thing was that we'd have to retrace a good ten miles of yesterday's meander to rejoin the right path. The only way to

orientate ourselves was to try and transliterate the
names of the villages they said were along our way and
check as we went.

Dragging ourselves away wasn't so easy. First there
was the old man who touched his tearducts and his heart
repeatedly, rocking on his heels and vowing that we did
him a disservice to grace his threshold for so short a
time. Then there was the really disturbing exchange
with the father of a very sick baby they'd been trying to
feed the previous night. As was repeatedly to become
the case in the rural areas from now on, the assumption,
even before we complicated things by saying that our
journey was to raise money for health care, was that
because we had white faces we were doctors. They said
they'd been to some kind of doctor in the bazaar, but
that could mean anything out here, from a quack to a
professional. Looking at the charms round the child's
neck, more tattoos, and more eyes, we wondered
whether they'd invoked more than the doctor. We had
to disappoint them that we didn't have the cure-all
drugs in our panniers, but in the same breath impressed
the need for a real doctor or a hospital for the emaciated, sickly mite.

We left, and the ensuing day was perhaps the most
arduous of the whole trip as we followed our own tyre
marks in the mud back to a fork and struggled the
fifteen miles or so to the road from there. The rain came
and went. Within an hour we were as sodden as if we
had never hung our clothes out overnight, and the mud
. . . It was too depressing to calculate then, but we
probably spent as much time off the bike as on, clearing
it of the clods which locked the wheels every ten minutes
or so. Again and again we were driven to stop. It was
probably quicker to cycle than walk, but only very
marginally. As if yesterday's daubing hadn't been
enough we were smeared from head to toe by the time
we'd unclogged the bike enough to move, with sticks

that were desperately hard to find on this barren range. Half the time we ended up clawing it off with our fingers. Inevitably, too, the bike would squelch its last in the very middle of the unavoidable ponds that had formed in dips in the road, depositing us in them up to our ankles.

The last straw came when Howard admitted faintly to being on the verge of a hypoglycemic reaction. Just when he thought he could go no further, a village and, then a man appeared. He called us in beside the stove for generous helpings of *yufka* and granular butter. This time we had an English-speaking interpreter – who else but the village schoolteacher? – to assure us that we'd heard correctly when our Kurdish host introduced his five wives and thirty-five children.

So this was a Kurd, and a polygamous one at that. We might have been excused for having expected someone a little more fearsome, but Fasli Karadeniz, though he ruled with a rod of iron, was a perfect gent. He even gave us a taste of his tongue-shrivelling black coffee. We thought the half centimetre of liquid in the bottom of the white pottery cups was just that – a taste – but when we handed our cups back expectantly there was no response. After fifteen minutes' preparation, a centimetre between us! It was instant palpitation stuff. He prepared it himself (far too good for the women to spoil) and the others made do with tea. The only chink in his gallantry was on by now familiar ground. 'Two and a half years wed and no children? If I were you my boy,' leaning forward and tapping Howard sympathetically on the knee, 'I'd get another one. She's no use to you.'

Twenty minutes up the track we heard a shout from behind. It was three of Fasli's sons and the schoolteacher on an errand of mercy. Putting six people and a tandem with all its baggage on a tractor with no trailer is about ten times as impracticable as imagining it. We wondered as we clung on to whatever and whoever we could, handlebars in our laps, whether we were really that much better off. We wondered no such thing when – a nastily familiar problem – nine vicious dogs leapt out at a village they'd forewarned us about. The teacher, being the lowest hanging target, lost a shred of trouser but the rest of us escaped unharmed. Not even a full minute after the last one had given up the chase and disappeared from view, the engine gave a splutter and died. With the tarmac truly within reach now, we were all right, but they had to walk back to the dogs' village for petrol to get home. They were adamant that we should continue, however. That was the Turks all over: *çok güzel.*

7

NO EAST, NO WEST

Saturday, January 3rd

The sound of vehicles, audible before we could see them, was like sweet music – the whiffs of petrol positively pleasant. If someone had told us that back in Italy, after the shock of emerging from Venice's unmotorised oasis, or reminded us of it on virtually any major road from Iran onwards, we might have been excused for being scornful. Here, however, if we'd had the energy, we would have cheered when we topped the last rise and caught our first glimpse of the black velvet. We got off to free our wheels of mud for the final time and it was then, in our exhausted relief, that we decided who the dedicatee of our 'book' (if we ever wrote one) would be. We rolled down to the tarmac and, as we stood astride the bike, our feet positively *feeling* the solidity beneath us, we looked down the road. It was modern Turkey again. But beyond the last rise we'd just come from was a land of polygamy and heresy, subsistence and feudalism. It made us think of the categories people use to describe world living standards – North, South; yes. First World, Third World; yes, possibly. A finer distinction than either of these, we were to come to feel, was Tarmac, No Tarmac. Development spreads rapidly along its black ribbons; but off it, when it rains, it gets held up by the mud – simply.

'Civilisation' wasn't as easily won as all that, however. Asking expectantly at the T-junction for a *locanta* or simply a shop for food, we were told definitely, if kindly, that there was nothing for some miles. The armed soldier who had broken off from his steady beat guarding the police post to answer our queries, looked at the sun which was beginning to sink and advised us to make all haste to the next large town – Viransehir – for a bed. Under no circumstances, he said, should we sleep out. Kurdish terrorism was the reason again. We weren't prepared to take him very seriously. But neither did we want to stay in the tent that night, being so sodden and muddy. We smiled agreement therefore, repeating 'Viransehir' wisely after him, and lifted ourselves weakly back on to the saddles.

Pretty soon even we had to temper our new found enthusiasm for the road. It became abundantly apparent, some hundreds of oil lorries later, that this was the hotline to Iraqi oil. (The Iranians were not amused by this Turkish sponsorship of Iraqi arms purchases, as they saw it.) When we did a head count, the average came out fairly consistently as forty oil lorries to every car. Like dancing whales the lorries swayed and swerved round the potholes despite the DIKKAT (danger) signs painted over and among the flowers and rural scenes that adorn any self-respecting Turkish truck. It was the strangest and most hair raising convoy to be part of. 'I'd rather be at the mercy of a rebel Kurd any day,' Howard commented sourly as we were squeezed off into the verge again and again by a combination of pushy driving and torn up road.

At length a building with parked lorries outside suggested a *locanta* and in we went. We were in 'Fasli's place'; there was no doubt about that. This was the Turkish equivalent of Lil's caff, only instead of egg and chips it was kebabs and pitta, and the clientèle, to our eyes at least, was more exotic. They willingly made room

for us around the ubiquitous stove – the most ingenious
yet. A canister of black, sticky, crude trickled in constantly, syphoned off 'by arrangement' from the flotilla
passing outside who frequented the place. If it was
tipped slightly forward to increase the flow, the heat was
overpowering. Tea was produced in a matter of
seconds, the place of honour was given to Anna's
sodden boots, and we were just given time to rest our
weary limbs before they suggested a good wash at the
cold tap outside, and produced more tea and food. Only
then did they deem it courteous to give rein to their
burning curiosity and ask us to explain ourselves.

Some of these Arab-featured men wore head-dresses
and robes; others were more Western. The place of a
departing lorry driver would be taken by a weather-
beaten shepherd who'd lay his crook down, take off the
skin wrapped round his shoulders, and ask one of his
restaurateur brothers to hurry up with the *çai*. The
Yurtsevers were a big hearted, various family. Fasli
seemed to be the oldest, and in charge, though the real
respect went, again, in good biblical fashion, to the
elderly: Fasli's father for whom we all rose when he
strode slowly in for his in-between-milking pepper soup.
Again there was no sign of any women.

They laughed when we said we were planning on
sleeping at Viransehir. That soldier back at the T-
junction couldn't have had much experience of tandems,
for it was a good forty miles down the road and dusk
had fallen. We ended up in one of the small houses
behind the hotel, which seemed to constitute a veritable
hamlet, but which Fasli said all belonged to him. To our
dismay, a bevy of girls were shooed out of the warmest
one with the most mattresses and quilts in it, and we all –
including the seven or so brothers – spent a warm night
together.

In the morning one of our coats seemed to have

disappeared and no one was willing to take any respon-
sibility. We were in a pickle once we'd looked in all the
obvious places, not only because of the aspersion the
disappearance cast on them, but because we simply
couldn't do without those coats. They were essential;
tailor made for the trip from one of the latest camping
fabrics we'd bought wholesale. To have had to buy a
substitute here, with such a limited range available,
would have been to have to make do with something
which either didn't have double zips (perfect for a
sudden hill when you didn't want the thing flapping
around completely open but you wanted more air up
from the bottom), or the excellent drying qualities, or
the wind resistance, or the ability to double as soft, fleecy
pillows . . .

We had to ask, apologetically, embarrassedly, for a
wider search to be made. Still no luck. They offered us
tea. We refused. They looked some more. Still no luck.
They offered us more tea. We were beginning to get
suspicious, but then a child, very comfortably bundled
up in blue Polarfleece, which he seemed to have slept in,
toddled up. Finally we were able to leave, after the
inevitable photograph had been requested and, of
course, one last ('just one more') glass of tea. The
camera was so misted up and slow to respond after its
ordeal in the rain that we doubted whether the panoply
of carefully re-draped *kuffiyahs* would come out to best
effect. They too warned us against terrorists and sent us
on our way.

We were rather blasé about these warnings despite the
heavy police presence along the road for the only Kurds
we came across were the kindest people, if also the ones
with the most wives. Maybe we should have been more
cautious, for in the last few years there have been
hundreds of deaths in attacks by Iraq-based Kurdish
terrorist organisations, murders of village chiefs who co-
operate with the Turkish authorities, and even full scale

retaliatory bombing raids against their camps over the border.

We had an hour-long clean up at the first garage we came to. We got off as much dry mud as possible, then turned a hose full on the bike, prising off the most persistent bits with a stick and brush, and giving certain parts a petrol douse. We finished up by re-oiling, readjusting and then scrubbing the panniers down. We would have felt as good as new, had it not been obvious that Anna was coming down with 'flu, and from the preliminary signs, quite a bad bout. She knew exactly where she'd caught it — back at Hasan Ozbay's home, given the place of honour next to his streaming mum.

None of the few hotels along this stretch seemed to provide anything more than the very basics. We decided to make as speedy headway as the beached whales and broken road allowed, to the monastery outside Mardin we'd been told about by the pastor in Izmir. We hoped we might get a more congenial bed there for Anna to be ill and recuperate in. It was too far to reach in a day, so we spent the intervening night behind barbed wire at the home of a chief of police, who also wouldn't hear of us exposing ourselves to the wily Kurd. His was another case of simply counting the months till wife and three bonny children could be relieved of the rigours of the obligatory spell out in the sticks, and return to sit down lavatories and hot water in Istanbul. He, however, with the assurance that comes from age, had none of the self-important over-scrupulousness of his colleague down at the sun temple. His subordinates were disciplined and alert, but off duty enjoyed a good romp with the Komdat's children and a natter with his wife.

The next morning it was evident Anna couldn't cycle with a raging temperature, sore throat and runny nose. We gladly succumbed to what would have seemed back home an abuse of power. Without so much as a please or thank you, his rifle slung specially over his shoulder, the

chief went out into the road. 'Take these two to Mardin.'
And that was that.

The lorry was marvellous. It had half its windscreen
missing, the hole stuffed with tarpaulin, the doors flying
open at every pothole, and needed a service halfway.
The driver wasn't one whit abashed. 'British van,' he
beamed, patting the Bedford logo on the dashboard as
proudly as if it had been the sleekest Rolls, and made us
feel personally responsible for such munificent technology by buying us at least two teas on the seventeen-mile
stretch.

We left the Syrian plain to the south, climbing a
veritable mountain to get to Mardin. The driver didn't
know the monastery and dropped us at the beginning of
the town. We extracted the bike from where it lay in the
back on a pile of loose chippings which gave our water
bottles a permanent matt finish and took many moons to
get entirely out of the handlebar gloves' lining. Then we
stood by the side of the road waiting for someone to ask
for directions. Three very naughty boys with palms
stained bright red – we knew not why – came and stuck
their tongues out at us. Then a Toyota truck came by,
stopped, and, entirely Turkish once more, insisted we
pile in rather than cycle the few miles they said it was to
the monastery of Deyl Ul Zafferan.

By mid morning Anna was tucked up in vast, thick
quilts on the bed nearest the central stove of an eminently
warmable, though entirely stone, monk's cell. Cell 13
easily housed four iron bedsteads. It was on the third
storey of a many-tiered complex of courtyards and
towers, vaulted passageways and staircases, so that from
our barred floor-to-ceiling window we had a splendid
view on to the barren mountainside on which it was built.
So bare and windswept were the environs, that we feared
the regular supplies of olive wood, brought up by neophytes with lowered eyes, must be a scarce commodity
indeed. When we questioned them as to its availability,

however, these young boys stoutly refused to stop stag-
gering in with great armfuls and insisted on tending the
stove themselves. In the morning they'd push back the
little grille in the side, lie on the freezing stone floor, and
blow on what to us looked like dead ashes from the night
before. They would use kerosene and tinder only as a
last resort. The wood was deposited in tidy piles in one
of the many-ledged niches the room afforded, as
seemed entirely proper to a monk's cell.

It was a pleasure to have to decide where most neatly
to store our few belongings in this appealingly sparse
chamber. Some of the niches were infilled with sturdy
shelves, others boxed in with true-fitting, latched doors,
to make snug little cupboards. Others were left simply as
the arched alcoves which, with foliated capitals and
arcades in mellow, honey-coloured stone, characterised
the entire monastery. There was a well at the very heart
of the building and a diverted stream from up the hill
cleverly fed all manner of bathroom and kitchen tanks
on all floors, by means of grooved stone channels.

We couldn't have found a more peaceful place for
recuperation, though not a day of the five we spent
there went past without one or other of the brothers
visiting the sick. Most questions, once in the sickroom,
were directed at Howard, and any addressed to Anna
were with the same downcast eyes as the neophytes. One
old fellow, not a brother but the gatekeeper, spent many
a long half hour sitting on the opposite bed to Anna.
With his cap placed reverently on his knees, a drop of
cold hanging perpetually from his beaky nose, he never
uttered a word. He would smile, and raise his hands to
heaven, touch his heart, shake his head at Anna's
condition, again seemingly offer it up to God, make the
sign of the cross at himself and us, and vaguely in the
direction of where the stovepipe disappeared into the
ceiling. This was all accompanied by meaningful sighs.
We always knew it was he who was coming, for everyone

else waited to be invited in after they had knocked, and
kept rather more sociable hours than his occasional 6.00
a.m. visits. If Anna was asleep he'd sit down all the same,
even if Howard too was elsewhere, and ruminate gustily.
Why he bothered to come, since no communication was
possible between us, was imponderable but he was
faithful to the last, and never other than benevolent in
intention.

Besides our daily visitors we still wished for some
letters. Mardin post office had been one of the six poste
restante addresses we'd given to the folks back home.
Howard went a couple of times but with no success. One
evening however, he was called to the monastery's
general office to help decipher a strange document –
they thought it might be in English. Howard approached
through a circle of onlookers and there it was: a bit dog-
eared but spread out reverentially in the middle of the
wooden desk. 'Dear Howard and Anna' were the first
words he read. The postmaster, familiar only with his
mother tongue, had decided to send it out to the learned
monks at Deyl Ul Zafferan when it had come in his
postbag, to see if they could explain it. The mysterious
missive was one of our poste restante letters delivered
right to our door!

It was from a girl with whom we'd been at Cambridge
University. On the trip, getting letters from friends was
a real high point. Often, however, ones from our
university peers, many now launched into highly successful careers and buying their first houses, tended to
arouse a fear in us, latent since we'd elected to live such a
life style. Was life – the income earning, settled, 'normal'
type of life – passing us by? Would our trek out into the
bush make it very hard to slip back into the mainstream;
render us misfits professionally and socially? Our hostess
at a dinner party just before we'd left had drawn us aside
and asked us in hushed tones whether we were 'vegetar-
ians' and, if people didn't classify us as off-beat, there was

always the label 'missionary' to live down. We had to learn that 'I have prepared a place for you' was as true of our futures back home, as for the more immediate journey's end.

Meals at Deyl Ul Zafferan were taken thrice daily in a long, high refectory-cum-kitchen. They were cooked by village women who came in from outside to prepare great cauldrons of cereals, usually enlivened with some sort of vegetable or – very occasionally – meat. The least felicitous of these was served up on our first night, when atop a plain bed of boiled wheat were variously shaped parcels of intestine sewn up with what we didn't quite know or care to enquire. We did our best to attack the rubbery, greyish objects, but when an internal examination revealed simply more boiled wheat, this time a little seasoned, we filled up on the white ring loaves that accompanied every repast. Anna only made it to two of these occasions. The rest of the time she was served in Cell 13 by the same troupe of willing boys who provided wood, and candles when the electricity gave out from time to time. The two occasions on which she did go to the canteen she was struck by the way it was the few full adult brothers who served everyone else, only partaking themselves when dismissal had been sung and the company had risen either from the ground or from the benches and tables.

Howard attended nearly all the devotions despite the monkish hours at which some of them took place. Held in a regular round starting at 5.00 a.m. and finishing at midnight, they were almost entirely sung. The earliest surviving liturgies in Christendom, handwritten in Aramaic and leather bound, were placed on square tables at each side of the church. The monks stood round them to sing in the language Jesus Himself spoke. There was a curtain before the altar just like the Tabernacle from Exodus behind which some of the service took place before it was rent in twain for the Communion. Straight

after receiving it one walked out of the door. The
service was over. Strangest to us though, was the monks'
indifference to Western musical norms. All sang the
same tune; that was clear. But they all started on a
different note. To Howard it sounded like playing a line
of music on the piano with the palm of one's hand. By
chance, on one occasion, they even attained a unison
but, not a jot impressed with the result, were back to
their cacophony shortly afterwards. Howard had a look
at one of their books and, faced with a load of squiggles,
had to confess to not being able to distinguish between
the written words and the musical notes. They found
this ignorance very hard to understand until one of the
elder ones delved into a cupboard and produced
another book that had Western notation. They looked
over his shoulder at the incomprehensible squiggles and
were dumbfounded when he began to sing something
from it that they recognised! They joined in with great
glee – they knew them all off by heart – but all on
different notes of course . . .

The spiritual integrity of Deyl Ul Zafferan, as a
Christian foundation in a Moslem country, is maintained by its accepting that the Turkish Tourist Board
and visitors alike see it primarily as a building of historic
and cultural interest. We left refreshed in body and
soul, heading north-west despite the tempting observation that due south of Mardin, the next towns of any
note were Mecca and Medina. At Diyarbakir, with its
distinctive black and white striped basalt buildings, the
extreme cold caused us to heed repeated warnings that
we couldn't possibly cycle any further east. On closer
questioning it appeared that the snow we'd heard of
back in Urfa was still blocking roads, and fresh falls
made all but bus traffic unthinkable. No craft were
coming across Lake Van, which we'd hoped to cross by
boat for the adventure everyone said its black waters
afforded.

It was a disappointment to have to take to someone else's wheels again, but our Iranian visas meant we couldn't wait around for snow that might take who knew how long to clear. We had no doubt that deadlines would be observed by the Ayatollah. When we discovered that the bus we eventually boarded was actually the previous day's, nearly twenty-four hours late, we gave in with better grace, and "a cold coming we had of it". As we were waiting for the bus we were eagerly seized upon by reporters from one of Turkey's largest newspapers and flattered by the promise that they intended to send the story to Reuters. Whether they ever did, or what sort of report they produced, we never ascertained. That was to be the fate of the majority of reports we were stopped for, from Turkey onwards, though in each case we asked them to send any printed article on to us in Nepal.

Bus stations were a triumphant testimony to Atatürk's stress on the importance of communication. They teemed with business – human and animal. Our cycle was finally stowed away underneath the body of the bus, handlebars skewed, basket painstakingly removed with our wire cutters, among dripping hessian sacks of raw meat that they insisted on packing first, though we pointed out that our cycle was bigger and more awkward to manoeuvre. The meat had to come out again, but they knew best, and were quite self-righteously indignant by this time at the folly of putting a bike on a bus anyway. When you're a foreigner in someone else's country, people often slip into the role of preceptor, even when the issue in hand has nothing to do with their culture.

To pass the time and chase away the last of Anna's 'flu with some vitamin C, we bought tangerines from a man who made his own bags out of old magazines and newspapers. We shared them with a most serious theology graduate from Istanbul University who asked us how we could possibly worship three gods: the Father,

Jesus and Mary? Our hearts ached for more language to
try and explain when, having put him right on that one,
he still unsmilingly insisted that the concept of the
trinity meant we must be polytheists. There was a little
mihrab near the ticket office and a station copy of the
Koran, in a black leather outer case and seed pearl inner
bag, both in constant use. Atatürk might not have placed
them so high on his list of bus station priorities as they
evidently had become. It wasn't that Atatürk was unre-
ligious but his faith had allowed him in 1923 to create
out of Turkey the first Muslim state in the world to
separate the secular powers from the sacred.

Finally we were off, understanding enough Turkish
by now to be aware, had not the stares been proof
enough, that we were by far the most interesting thing
on the bus. When it got to the time for Anna's antibiotics, she heard the old man behind her fascinatedly
count them out as she shook them into her palm. He
then informed those around, 'That's two she swallowed.'
It wasn't maliciously meant, and by the time we halted at
midnight in a small mountain town, snowbound buses
and lorries literally nose to tail and triple parked, there
were any number of kindly offers to get us *çai*. The *çai*
shop profited from the pile-up by staying open all night
and doing a roaring trade. The police, with their fur-
collared uniform jackets, were highly efficient at man-
aging us and the three-metre drifts, but it was no good.
We were stuck for the night and, with the engine turned
off, we nearly froze.

At five-thirty the next morning it was our bus, for some
reason, that led the convoy over the pass, behind the
plough and the police towards Lake Van. In the town of
Van, our long cherished plan for entering Iran 'respect-
ably' in the eyes of the authorities, on the train that was
marked on our map and timetabled for that year by
Cook's, was dashed. 'Train discontinued,' the guard
repeated again and again, 'Never once more no train.

Gurbulak-Bazargan, there you go.' We'd never heard of either of these places, but he turned out to be right. Thither we had to go and the closer we got to Iran the more uptight we became. What if they simply said 'no bikes'? What if they wouldn't let us in at all? And, if they did, what awaited us once inside? Exactly what we feared we didn't know, but it had to do with hearsay, news reports, and people's reactions at home when we'd said we had a visa for Iran.

When we got to the last town before the border we decided we could just afford to spend a day there to collect our wits and prepare ourselves. That day we spent mending and patching, checking and oiling, priming and praying, was like a long, psychological, deep breath, which calmed us at least until the early morning of the next departure day. Instead of waiting as previously until we had got into the country itself to jot down our basic vocabulary, we asked the townspeople for our Farsi phrases. We wanted to be as on the ball as possible.

It was time for travellers' cheques again. In Turkish banks you get treated like a guest; in Iranian banks you get an abominable exchange rate and are obliged to change vast sums of money. We say this from hearsay, because we never had to do it, probably because people were so taken with the tandem that they forgot to make us go. Of all the travellers we met, we were the only ones exempt from changing between one and two hundred dollars' worth of money at the border, at an exchange rate nine hundred per cent less favourable than we got in Turkey.

We woke at six on the morning of our departure, too keyed up to sleep any longer. Our bags mostly packed the night before, we were too nervous even for breakfast. By ten past six we were on the saddle and making for the outskirts. In our agitated state the superb road, the snowy mountains, the brilliant sunshine which early dissipated a sharp frost, were out of tune with our mood. One mountain in particular stood out – a perfect, crystalline Mount Fuji shape to our left. We were so preoccupied with what lay ahead, that though we kept turning to look at its irradiated facets, we didn't put two and two together until the next day. It was the majesty of Mount Ararat, where the Ark had come to rest as the Flood receded, and Turkey's highest mountain.

Despite the fact that we wanted to get to the crossing early for time to deal with all eventualities, despite our frequent trips to the loo, the pace at which we covered the miles was disconcertingly quick. Before we knew it, Gurbulak-Bazargan was marked as one kilometre away and we jumped off, stomachs churning, to don Anna's purdah which we'd carefully tried out the day before. (Would they allow a woman to cycle?) We pinned her Turkish shawl over her head, round her neck, and up over the tip of her nose so that all that was visible were her eyes. We tried to take truly to heart God's constant assurances in Deuteronomy: 'Do not be afraid . . . for the LORD your God goes with you; he will never leave you nor forsake you'. (Deut 31:6). Then we made our way to the Turkish offices and wished that the staff weren't quite so efficient or quite so cheery.

It took exactly an hour to get through Gurbulak, the Turkish side. It took exactly the same again to get through Bazargan. 'Welcome to Iran', the officials greeted us and they were thoroughly taken by our *dunafer hastem* (the tandem); so taken that we were repeatedly instructed to by-pass the unending line of coaches and lorries between the passport office and the Customs shed, where one Japanese traveller we met up with again the next day said he'd spent fifty-two hours. He added that he'd heard that if you slipped the officials a pound, you could whizz through as speedily as we did . . . He also told us that as of November (we left in October) we needed visas to enter Pakistan: a retaliatory policy against Mrs Thatcher's demanding the same of

Pakistanis visiting Britain. If he was right, he'd done us a mighty big service. We could envisage arriving at the Pakistani border hundreds of miles after Teheran, on our last permitted day in Iran, without a visa to get out. We'd be illegal if we stayed or moved.

We might have ended up feeling somewhat over-prepared and a little foolish for our timidity, but there were enough indicators, despite all the 'enjoy your trips' and smiles, for us to feel that our circumspection hadn't been entirely misplaced. There was the way we were segregated at Immigration. (It was early enough in the whole process for us to feel it necessary to make spur-of-the-moment arrangements for what to do if we failed to meet up again.) Howard was told in no uncertain terms, when he presented our visas, that one day later and we would have been forbidden entry. There was the young guard, machine gun in hand, who barked at Howard to take the scarf off his head – that was only for women. His high, strained voice had something of the same manic quality that the endless military music blaring out of loudspeakers had – a bit of Pomp and Circumstance here, a bit of something else vaguely familiar there, all mixed in with something quite unfamiliar and presumably 'Persian'. 'Whisky? Sexy?' he questioned as he rifled through our panniers. Howard looked over at Anna, swathed from head to toe, and thought there was a good chance of getting away with a white lie. 'No,' he replied.

The slogans neatly painted on the walls at the border post and along the road when we'd got through – 'No East, no West, Islamic Republic' and the modest 'We want nothing but Islamic rules and regulations all over the world' – seemed to convey the same surreality, and the same warning: 'By all means come to our country. Admire our zeal and our purity, but just make sure you toe the line'. The bare facts were these: the Iranian Kerbala 5 offensive was launched just as we entered the country. In the two-and-a-half-week period covering the entire time we were in Iran, 1,800 civilians were killed by Iraqi bombs on non-economic targets. Proportionate to the half million dead since the war began in 1980, we had unwittingly chosen one of the most potentially dangerous times we could to have our little Persian jaunt. Looking at the situation in such a light, the congeniality and safety we enjoyed in Iran seem quite miraculous, though much more explicable – again with hindsight – when we discovered that at least three particular groups were specifically praying for us at this time, as well as a host of individuals.

Mount Ararat was finally eclipsed by the nearer ranges that flanked the road to the place at which we now planned to take the bus (*mashi*) to Teheran. There we would go straight to the British Interest Section of the Swedish Embassy, apparently the only official British presence left in the capital, to find out exactly how to travel in this land. We didn't know what stage hostilities had reached – perhaps thankfully in view of the facts. At a grey town pushed right up against the rock face, buildings strung out along the main road in the uninspired straight line that so often seemed to constitute urban planning in Iran, we stayed in a swish hotel (was it legal to camp? was another, as yet, unanswered question). We sat in the lounge with typically beautiful young women, their designer jeans and patent leather shoes not very carefully concealed by the black head-dress and overgarment. As we sipped our black tea in large clumsy glasses, we viewed bareheaded women on Russian television that leaked over the border. It felt as if we were in the lap of luxury, and we were particularly looking forward to a thorough clean up in the hotel bathroom.

As soon as one gets over the Channel, as every British person is proud to relate, the quality of public toilets deteriorates sharply. Things can sink even lower than those awful experiences we've all had in France, however. Electric lights became scarcer and scarcer and the

ceramic elephant's feet in the ground give way to
footpads of concrete moulded roughly into shape while
it was still wet. It's not the raw materials as much as how
you treat them that counts, though. The chief of police
who commandeered our lorry to Mardin proved that
even these makeshift affairs can be tolerable. At his
house all the soapy water from the basin was directed
down the lavatory hole, and a container of disinfectant
in the corner kept the room positively fragrant. In this
hotel, why on earth were all the bathroom windows
closed?

In the corridor outside the staff carefully overlapped
and pinned beautifully laundered sheets onto the duvets
that were spread out on the immaculate fitted carpets.
Inside the loo the air was so fetid you could taste it. The
basin fittings were swish and modern, so why was the
tape they'd been delivered in years before still stuck
around them? And – forgive the detail but the point is
important – why was the hole in the lavatory attempting
to defy all the laws of gravity by running *parallel* to the
floor? It was nice having it match the gentle curves and
colour of the basin, but no amount of will power was
going to get your deposit along (you can't say down) the
hole. Many of the more expensive 'conveniences' in
Turkey were almost as inexplicable. The water wasn't
directly beneath where you sat, it was – behind – and
there was always a little tassel brush to clean up with.
How can such design failures be perpetuated? Why is
there such a mental block about toilet cleanliness in
certain parts of the world?

We quickly realised that the unhurried privacy and
fresh air of the great outdoors was by far the most
preferable, until Pakistan that is, when the only privacy
to be had was well after dark. As time wore on, the
incidence of loo paper decreased, replaced by a tap in
the wall or a bucket and dipper. Not everyone appreci-
ates our standards though: 'Those Britishers. You've

looked in the bathroom? No water near the pot. I *never* believed it, but it's true, my God. They wipe their bottoms with paper only,' says the upper class Indian wife in Salman Rushdie's *Midnight's Children*.

We went off to the post office the next day and sent reassuring 'We're in' letters to our parents for, we thought, five pence each, and we peeked in the small, understocked shops: biros next to tinned peas next to toothpaste. Then we made for the bus, stopped along the way by the same questions that had been posed the day before, 'Have you anything to sell? Is your bicycle for sale?' in furtive whispers but gently and politely asked. 'Do you want to sell your sleeping bags? I give you good price.'

That overnight bus journey was probably one of our least happy adventures in Iran. Police checks were so frequent as to make sleep impossible. We were prime targets for suspicion, because of our nationality; we and a wealthy couple who'd obviously just been over the border for a spending spree on all the things they couldn't get with war and revolution restrictions. For their profligacy – in the eyes of the military guards who waved the buses down – they were subjected to the most detailed, humiliating searches. Madam's underwear came out on the verge alongside the new pressure cooker and Thermos flasks. We were treated with much less scorn, but a similar thoroughness. We were so put on edge by all this activity that we became scrupulously over-eager to show them everything as soon as they leapt aboard. We had our passports open at the right place, top items already out of the panniers, to show as willing and as unobstructive as we could. One guard seemed to perceive our nervousness. Howard was scrabbling in the dark to get from our passport photographs to the page that had our visa on it, when the man's face broke into a gentle, reassuring smile as he touched Howard on the shoulder as if to say 'Don't worry, I don't need to see everything. Calm down.'

Anna just kept quiet, no longer with her scarf right up over her nose, having seen what the Iranian women did, but making sure her wrists, neck, ears and hair were covered. Howard was obviously the one who was expected to do all the liaising. We weren't sure that our decision that she should speak only if spoken to and stand a little behind him was not a jot over the top, but neither did we want to test it out.

It was 3.00 a.m. and the bus had emptied enough for us to take a seat apiece to stretch out and try and get some sleep. Howard put his scarf over his eyes. Anna began to do the same, then a guard seated behind her caught her eye. She found it so impossible to believe that one of the purest, the most disciplined, the most zealous, should be giving her the come on, and that three feet away from her husband, that she decided she must be imagining it. The next thing she knew, her bottom was being poked from between the seats. She snatched the shawl from her eyes unbelievingly and he was leering at her over the top of the seat, beginning to gesture obscenely. When she woke Howard to swop seats with him and explained why, he found himself in exactly the same double bind as she: furious that someone should have taken liberties with his wife, but too intimidated by the milieu to make the kind of stand he would have done anywhere else.

We ground into Teheran bus station at 5.45 a.m. It was so dark we thought we were in a blackout. We weren't. The depot was simply eight kilometres from the centre of the city, where most of the electricity wasn't functioning. We extracted the bike from the luggage space under the bus, righted the handlebars, and prepared to nose our way to Avenue Ferdowsi where the British Interest Section of the Swedish Embassy was situated. Then Howard realised he'd lost our Swiss Army penknife. Looking back, our exaggerated reaction to this misfortune must have been a measure of our insecurity. Yes, it was jolly useful for everything from sawing away small thistle bushes from under the tent to slicing choice pieces of cheese, but the despair with which we eyed the rows of more than a hundred identical buses was not really proportionate to the inconvenience of losing it. When our persistent search under back seats miraculously produced the precious item, we suddenly felt able to face the worst Teheran could offer.

8

PERSIANS AND BABYLONIANS

Tuesday, January 13th

We didn't know it, but actually the worst the capital could offer just then was its appalling traffic which has wonderfully defied the attempts of a German team of systems analysts to make sense of it. The total anarchy, absence of working traffic lights, and explosive mixture of vehicles and pedestrians in the road, wasn't the worst we encountered, but relative to our previous experience was definitely the most striking.

We stopped off for breakfast after some six kilometres at a roadside café. This promised to be a new experience. Cross legged above a huge vat of seething gruel presided a glistening, grimy Buddha. From time to time he stirred the heaving depths with a great wooden stave like the ones Pakistani policemen use for crowd control, muscles rippling as the grey mass lumpily resisted. We filed past in line. The place was packed out with early morning commuters, and we watched as he dolloped our steaming ladleful into a bowl. He topped each portion with a teaspoon of white sugar, a teaspoon of brown, a sprinkling of cinnamon, and a tablespoon of hot, old cooking oil. With flat, factory-made squares of unleavened bread it made an extremely filling and surprisingly nice breakfast.

What the capital of a country at war is supposed to

look like we didn't know. Whatever we'd expected, somehow it wasn't this odd jumble. There'd be a stretch of grey, sad shops, half of them closed, the others pitifully depleted, or with queues of people outside waiting for the rations. The residential blocks seemed correspondingly shabby. Then we'd turn a corner and the area would appear to be smartening up, until we found ourselves either in the veritable Belgravia of Teheran, or its Oxford Street, where stores were spilling over with luxury goods from Japan – jewellery, electronic appliances, classy watches. There were even supermarkets with imported or indigenous specialities.

It was in one of these, later in the day, before we overcame a sense of impropriety at joining the ration queues, that we met a man who proved, in his cynicism, to be thoroughly representative of one sector at least of the population. He insisted on buying our bread for us (French stick lookalikes in cellophane wrap) and said that nothing had really changed since 1979. The war in the south meant food shortages up here in the north, and one occasionally saw a bus of conscripts making for the Front. Of course there were the constant radio, TV and *mullah* exhortations, and the incessant military music, but these were surface changes, no more. It was business as usual. The Great American Satan, he said wryly, gesturing at next door's video shop which sported Superman and Space Invaders cassettes, refused to be exorcised despite all efforts by the government. Had we met him only days later when Teheran was bombed for the first time after three years, he might have been less blasé. He advised Anna to keep her jacket on for propriety's sake though her head gear was fine, and directed us to Ferdowsi Avenue.

The young man who insisted on giving us a second breakfast before we got to the British Interest Section that morning represented the other side of the coin. We were caught at one of the functioning traffic lights on

Revolution Avenue when he leaned out of his car window.

'Where are you going? Please come for breakfast with me.' He pointed at the breads in his car that he'd just queued for. He was most insistent. Indeed, he said it was his duty; anyway, no self-respecting embassy was going to be open yet. For all we knew, this might be the only opportunity we had to see inside an Iranian home before we were advised to make haste to the Pakistani border, so we said that we'd already eaten, but wouldn't refuse a cup of tea. He was most relieved. The gleam in his eye, the military jacket, and the nature of the invitation itself should have warned us.

He led us into a three-roomed flat full of brothers and sisters, and brothers' wives, and sisters' children. We went into the living-room which, judging by the smell, had only just been vacated by sleepers. There was a rusty old filing cabinet, a table, a bookshelf, and a threadbare carpet. A large plastic cloth was laid on the floor, on which the bread and two pots of jam were laid. We were repeatedly urged to eat, despite our proviso, and some strange, sweet delicacies were brought out to tempt us when we stuck to our guns and our tea. Our host, it turned out, was a student at the University, still the hotbed of the Revolution, though they say that Iran Mac on Azadi Square is now at least as lively a venue! He was more than delighted to talk politics with us.

'What will happen when the Ayatollah dies?' we questioned him. 'He's over eighty, isn't he?'

'I pray,' he answered fervently, eyes shining, 'that our *Imam* may never die.'

The biggest eye-opener was yet to come. A man crawled in through the door on hands and knees, or what would have been knees had the stumps extended that far. 'My uncle,' the student said proudly, 'he is our living *shahid* (martyr) – her husband, their father,' pointing at one of the women feeding two children. 'We

have many martyrs in our family, for which we are
profoundly, deeply . . . most happy. That we should
serve Khomeini and our god in this way is our glory.' He
began to tick the martyrs excitedly off on his fingers.
'Her brother was killed last year; her mother has only
one son left . . . we' – he groped for the right word –
'laugh, because the *Imam* says it is for the cause.' He
leant forward, emphasising the point with his bread and
jam. 'If the Ayatollah says so, we will fight for twenty
years. We will allow our whole family to be martyred if
need be,' and he clenched the other fist in an upraised
symbol of victory. The whole room did likewise, with
little grunts or shouts of agreement. Uncle seemed to be
the least vigorous about it, but maybe he hadn't quite
caught on. His sight and hearing had also been impaired
in the blast though he promised, fixing his milky eyes on
a point just behind our heads, that he would pray for us.
They all murmured assent, the women as eloquent in
these interchanges as the men, for all their strict covering and downcast looks.

Anna began to feel sick. When the student tried to
extract the promise that we'd have lunch with them and
sleep there if we hadn't left the city by evening, we
parried desperately, trying to keep within the bounds of
politeness and wishing he wouldn't keep pointing out, as
every new offer was made, how it was his Muslim duty to
show such kindness to strangers. Finally, after he'd
pleaded with us for the 'privilege' of filling our water
bottles, he let us go. It had been his privilege to witness to
us about the real meaning of Islam, he said, and to clarify
the distinction between it and the sham that the 'godless
Ba'athists over the border' passed off on their people.

At the British Interest Section in the Swedish Embassy
we were briskly dealt with by a British woman with no
head gear, in a Marks and Spencer sweater. She'd got
our letter and saw no reason not to 'proceed as normal'.
She advised us not to go to the holy city of Qom (directly

on our planned route) because they didn't like 'infidel visitors' and since visa extensions were extremely hard to come by we should forget that idea. With only a two week transit visa we would have to take public transport some of the way. We were sick to the teeth. The bus to Teheran had been a sheer endurance test, but there was nothing for it; Iran is almost three times the size of France, and was thus impossible to cover by bike in the eleven days we had left. We were told that our Japanese friend's information about Pakistani visas was quite correct, but it was 'a simple matter' of going to the Pakistani Embassy and obtaining them. She thought we should know Teheran had been on red alert for the last three nights and that Isfahan had been bombed for the last four. She added, slightly wearily, that it was our decision whether or not we stay the night there. Then she dropped the bombshell about the exchange rate, and we were too stunned to keep her with any more questions.

We went and sat outside in the sun and tried every which way to wriggle out of the situation. We checked the piece of paper we'd been given at the border. The full amount of money we had on us was scrawled right across it. We thought of 'losing' the paper before they demanded it at the next border to see if we'd changed any on the internal black market. Then we reflected that many people must have tried the same thing. We considered altering the amount on the paper. We decided that was plain dishonest. Whichever way we looked at it, it didn't seem right – neither the exchange rate itself, nor the ways we were trying to avoid it – but we were darned if we were going to hand over five pounds and get back a tenth of that amount. We remembered the passage from Romans 13. 'Everyone must submit himself to the governing authorities . . . Do you want to be free from fear of the one in authority? Then do what is right, and he will commend you.' It was plain as the noses on our faces. The question still remained, though, if we weren't

prepared to exchange at that rate, was our remaining
eight pounds going to be enough for eleven days in
Iran, including transport costs? Presumably not, unless
we lived on bread and water.

'Unless we live on bread and water' we repeated
together. And that was what we decided to do. We
wanted to obey God, but we weren't also going to be
beaten by this Muslim imposition on our pockets.

One and a half hours later, having got to know
Teheran's posh north end intimately because our
address for the Pakistani Embassy did not tally with the
changed street names of the Revolutionary Government,
we were banging at a very closed and barred official door.
There were plenty of Pakistanis going in and out of the
side door, though, to inform us that the Visa Section was
closed till tomorrow, and anyway, we needed a letter
from the British Interest Section before we could obtain
them. We looked at one another. The British Interest
Section was closed now and wouldn't be open for another
two days. With our money situation the way we'd chosen
we couldn't afford to stay in Teheran for that long.
Howard held the bike while Anna went to explain our
predicament. 'Oh, well, perhaps you don't need a letter
after all,' someone said. 'Just come back tomorrow.' She
explained again. 'Get a letter to us by three o'clock this
afternoon and we'll see what we can do,' they beamed at
her. She re-explained. 'Sorry, you can only get visas
before twelve,' the answer came back.

Repeated negotiations proved fruitless. The midday
heat was sweltering. We began to peel our last Turkish
tangerines before setting off again, though to where we
weren't quite sure. Perhaps we could camp on the
outskirts of the enormously sprawling city for the night
and come back in. 'You want a visa mishter?' A man
dressed in a long cotton shirt over baggy matching
trousers, was beckoning to us.

He stood aside to let us enter the Visa Section. We sat

inside not daring to hope, expecting to be booted back out on the street still visa-less. We waited, and we waited, and we waited. After one and a half hours we decided to check with the pretty Pakistani receptionist. She made enquiries. We were ushered, with many apologies, into the bigwig's office.

'We did not realise you were still here. You sure you did not slip out for a drink?' 'Not likely,' thought Anna. The next thing we knew we were drinking milky coffee from fine china cups and saucers, and the three photographs essential for each visa ('oh no!') were being magnanimously waived as a lackey was sent to photocopy the ones we had in our passports.

We had a polite but friendly chat about what we were to encounter in his country. One thing he was most strong on was Pakistan's superiority in not obliging Anna to wear purdah. Finally we stepped out into the dusty, hot street, clutching our visas, pathetically grateful for the favour. The episode was an accurate foretaste of the unpredictability of Pakistani bureaucracy.

We decided it was now high time we got shot of Teheran and reached the place we really wanted to visit: Persepolis. We went to the railway station but were told that all the trains were closed to civilians. We made reluctantly for the Southern bus station instead. We didn't like buses at the best of times, and with the tandem they were a positive drag. Howard left Anna saying 'Just hold the bike while I get the tickets.' Three-quarters of an hour later she was still there, shivering in the approaching dusk, but far colder inside at the huddles of weeping mothers come to see their sons off to the Front, packing home-grown satsumas into protesting pockets and straightening new and unfamiliar uniforms on objecting young frames.

Teheran's Southern bus station is a vast, two storeyed, circular building in which a good twenty companies vie for custom for their buses parked all round the outside.

It looked like an ant hill just after it's been kicked over, and, blaring above the hubbub was a tape of soldiers at the Front, intoning their slogans till they were hoarse, and goaded on by a *mullah*. Howard went from one company to the next to be told the same story by each, 'Sorry, full up with troops'. Anna meanwhile became the butt of friendly curiosity from passers-by. There was an 'imponderable' curt handshake from a Revolutionary Guard, who said we must have supper with him that night, then disappeared. Then there was Sassan, a PhD student with excellent, soft-spoken English who, when he heard her story, plunged into the station to give Howard a helping hand.

Howard already had a helping hand – firmly grasping his thumb, and leading him through the press of troops so as not to lose him – but this man had been with him for three-quarters of an hour already, and was late for an appointment. Somehow Sassan found Howard and took over. After seventeen refusals because of services being requisitioned for the rush to the Front, he got us a bus scheduled for seven o'clock the following morning.

It was six o'clock. The hotel district was too far for Sassan to walk to, so he explained how to get there and said he'd take a bus and meet us. We begged him to just give us the hotel name and let us sort it out ourselves, but he wouldn't hear of it. Eastern hospitality. As he made his third flat refusal to leave us to our own devices, there was a thud, and all the luggage fell off the back of the bike. The rack had become detached, and there was no sign of the essential screw. The bike was uncyclable. We combed the ground with a torch borrowed from the growing crowd of onlookers. They were probably stepping on it. There was also a drain eighteen inches away. Hardly daring to hope, we delved into the tool kit and triumph-antly produced exactly the right screw which we had fitted within a matter of minutes. Every ounce of extra weight of spares had been worth it for a moment like that.

Sassan was faithful to the last, and, in fact, this was only the first of many hoped-for lasts. Meeting up with him at the hotel district wasn't as simple as he'd made it sound. We waited for thirty minutes at what we thought was the designated spot, and then we decided to check them out ourselves. The answers were the same at each hotel as with the bus companies. 'Sorry, we're full. Iranians fleeing from the south.' 'Sorry, we've got a place but this is strictly Iranians only, by government law. If the inspector caught us . . . Try next door.' 'Try the luxury hotels.' 'Sorry, really sorry, but we can't risk it.' We didn't blame them for sticking to the rules. The place was absolutely swarming with soldiers of all ranks, most probably just marking time before their conveyance to the Front left, but others perhaps more watchful. This was south Teheran, not only markedly poorer than the northern city, but where revolutionary fervour was supposed to be at its highest.

We were beginning to get that giddy feeling which comes when you've not slept, when the pavement makes contact with your foot before your foot is ready to make contact with it. Then Sassan turned up. He insisted on catching the bus once more, further up the boulevard – to the beginnings of the rich northern quarter, and meeting us where the luxury hotels were. We were in a dilemma. Money or no money, we had to sleep, and even had we wanted to capitulate, the banks were now closed. We clutched at the hope that if regular hotels were so cheap, luxury ones might not be wildly above our means. They were. Luxury means luxury in that city of contrasts. As soon as you get into the Westernised sector, prices also become all too Western.

We spent about two and a half hours looking for a hotel. Sassan never left us, as we boulevard-hopped, he on the bus, we on the bike, losing more and more time as we repeatedly lost and waited for each other. His kindly efforts became even more onerous to us than the search for a room and we finally persuaded him to leave by saying, 'Sassan, we shall go and try at the Embassy,' though secretly we didn't hold out any hope for it. He was very sorry he had 'failed', but insisted he would be there to see us off in the morning. We watched him jump on his fifth bus that evening, then we slumped. We were feeling nauseous with exhaustion and from not having eaten anything since a very scanty lunch.

After a long silence, we gathered ourselves together and climbed back on to the bike. We'd decided just to try the Swedish Embassy to ask them for somewhere – anywhere – to put the tent up. Somehow we got ourselves there, past giant cartoons of Thatcher, Reagan and Gorbachov on the walls along the side of the road. The aerosoled trio would have been a highly entertaining anomaly had we had the energy or the heart for laughter. We rang the bell. The Swedish guards, blond and blue-eyed the pair of them, listened carefully to our story through the gate, then swung it open and put us in the gatehouse and went to phone the 'Second Officer'. In next to no time we were being handed the receiver. A very British, very urbane voice told us to follow the guard to his quarters.

We passed through more gates, past the Embassy building proper, into a large, grassed expanse, bordered with carefully planted plane trees just like Hyde Park. Then we reached the residential quarters, and there was the Second Officer, a Cambridge contemporary of Anna's, with Drambuies at the ready. They'd probably sat in the same examination hall four summers ago. We were made entirely at home; pressed to sample a concoction from the newest shipment of Sainsbury's tuna and pasta. He'd got our letter and was sorry the receptionist hadn't contacted him as requested when we'd shown up that morning. We had a lot in common, it seemed, and we would have loved to have found out more about his job, but our eyes were closing and we had to be up at six-thirty for the bus. He promised to visit us in Nepal, and one thing we did get sorted out before bed, apart from under the stairs being the safest place to sit in the event of an air raid, was the exact status of the British Interest Section of the Swedish Embassy.

Aside from its name, the 'Swedish Embassy' was as British as it had always been in the days when, on exactly the same premises, and with exactly the same staff, it had been the British Embassy. The Revolution had decided to put a stop to all but a token British presence but – part of the strange double-handedness with which foreign affairs can be conducted by governments – it functioned in all but name exactly as it always had done. Those 'Swedish' guards were as British as they came. The fact that the Swedes had two embassies, their own up in the north end of town and this 'new' one down here, seemed to pose no problem. It was a joke we had many a chortle about, till we got to Nepal and discovered that in the intervening period every single Brit but one had been decisively ejected from the country.

To our relief, the painstaking Sassan failed to make it to the bus station the next morning. As on the previous bus people were courteously solicitous of our well being. It was never too much trouble to help us out at *dast shooey* (toilet) and food stops, where we'd suddenly find a large mixed salad of fresh coriander leaves, parsley and spring onions brought to enliven our bread, or some tea. Those who didn't buy food would suddenly produce saucepans out of bags and from under purdah and all the family and friends dipped in. This busload was almost entirely female, and their behaviour seemed to confirm what we'd perceived in the zealot's flat. Purdah was no curb on lively, intelligent participation in everything that was going on, though the women preferred to relate to Anna rather than Howard. We pulled into Isfahan in the late afternoon, past the manned anti-aircraft guns. Anna was quietly, immovably firm about one thing. The best mosques in Persia were to be seen here but they could keep them as far as she was concerned; she was not going to stay the night in a city that had been bombed now for five nights in a row. Howard, conversely, would have loved to have been in the thick of an air raid. It was at times such as these that we realised, for all our usual agreement once in a blue moon we could not be further apart.

We set about putting the various bits of the bike to rights which had been removed or loosened to get it on the bus. As Howard tightened the screw which kept his saddle and Anna's handlebars facing forwards instead of swivelling on their axes, his attention was caught by something on the other side of the road. There was a sharp crack, and the alloy screw designed for lightness more than strength, snapped in half. We didn't have a replica of that particular part, because we'd done exactly the same thing on a previous trip, used our spare, and sworn we'd not be so silly again.

We went from shop to shop searching for an identical screw. Many of the places we went into didn't even sell screws; but Eastern shops are confusing to Western eyes, lacking the same comprehensive display of goods but needing a simple question, for which we hadn't the language, for the required item to be produced from some dark corner. Anna was getting touchier by the minute as the prospect of having to stay in the city for the night became more and more likely. We couldn't cycle any distance with wobbly handlebars and saddle though, and Isfahan was the last big town for several days where we might be lucky enough to find the right screw. We asked a man hard at work outside his garage where we might obtain one. He looked at the broken one and at his blow torch and said something to the effect of 'You don't need to bother about getting a new one. I'll stick it together for you.' He meant exactly that. He was going to fuse the two pieces with his blow torch. It was useless trying gently to point out that this was a precision made item with a thread that had to fit exactly. We were up against another good hearted, but determined 'I know better'.

The two broken pieces were carefully clamped in place, then welded together. It could only have happened out East, where anything and everything is used and reused till it's exhausted. A well-meaning throng had gathered round us chattering and questioning, waiting for the moment of truth when Iranian savvy was to save the Brits' day. The moment came. The screw, of course, didn't fit. Even then he refused to accept defeat, taking it back, reclamping it, reheating it, and trying to file it down. Without appearing downright ungrateful, we couldn't simply reclaim it and press on with our search for a new one. We watched helplessly.

Finally, perhaps forty-five minutes after we had first been stopped, he admitted defeat. As he handed back the by now mangled and unrecognisable item, useless even for interim measures, someone in the crowd reached out and intercepted it.

'I think I can find one the same,' he said in broken English, disappeared into a nearby workshop, and was back two minutes later with an old iron bolt that fitted perfectly – for no charge of course.

We put it on, thanked all and sundry, and left the city as evening drew in, calculating that as we were exiting south-east, and the Iraqis entered and departed in the west, we didn't need to get too far out to be able to avoid possible bombing. To our right we passed acres of fenced off military zone with regular warning signs not to trespass and not to take photographs. To our left, at times reaching right down to the road, were the mountains. We were going to have to camp on the scree. We spied a likely outcrop and hauled the bike up over the loose stones to its shelter. Perhaps we spent too much time trying to get the tent pegs into the hard ground.

Perhaps it was because we were overlooking the military zone. Perhaps a country at war is all the more alert to foreigners. Whatever the reason, we'd barely got our first peg in when four armed soldiers scrunched over the ridge above us. Anna dived for her purdah and then imitated Howard in raising her hands high above her head.

They flashed their torch at the bike, our bags, our tent, and indicated that we should explain ourselves. With perhaps five words of Farsi on our side and five of English on theirs, we indicated that we meant to conceal nothing. One thing, however, was obvious to them, whether from a sense of hospitality or sheer opinionatedness: we couldn't sleep where we had chosen. We must go back to Isfahan they told us, where there were hotels. At that Anna, hitherto mute, muffled, and submissive, emitted a determined 'No'. The soldiers seemed quite taken aback. Howard was a little alarmed, but it may have been just the thing, for after a few more attempts at persuasion, they gave up. Once they'd gone we took to an early bed after a quick supper. Bread and water is not to be lingered over. We were asleep by eight o'clock.

In our innocence we'd thought that an air raid would be an ear-splitting blast. When, at 11.00 p.m., the ground rocked beneath us and our hearts leapt into our mouths, it was a sinister dead thud that heralded our first cluster bomb. We lay not daring to move for another couple of seconds as the explosions continued, than we unzipped the flap, hearts pounding, and peeked out. Full-faced above us was the moon. Every prickle of every thistle on the slope down to the road was visible. Isfahan however, which had twinkled prettily below us when we'd first retired, was quite black, all lights extinguished and in the shadow of the mountains. The sky above the city, though, was alive to the flares of anti-aircraft fire, zipping through the air like so many short-lived fireworks. It was utterly terrifying. We had a glimpse of what the worst of our parents' childhood must have been like. It made no difference that we were in no personal danger. The sheer proximity of *war* was enough to cause even Howard trouble in getting back to sleep when the cacophony and lights eventually receded, the Iraqi planes beat their retreat, and the city was left to pick up its pieces.

*   *   *

In many ways, Iran produced the best cycling environment of the journey. The Zagros mountains lie in a band down the west of the country with an enormously long, flat corridor between the crazily angled ranges on both sides. This gives the thrill of mountain scenery – rich browns receding to mauves and white caps – but you cycle on the flat. It explained how the ancient Persians had such a good mail system between their major centres. The terrain, coupled with the Shah's excellent tarmac, produced our fastest cycling averages and an exhilarating feeling of space and freedom. We passed splendid *hans* and entire square townships enclosed by thatched, mud walls, still inhabited.

There was the continued kindness too: a man who found us looking for bread in a town which apparently had none, for instance. A quarter of an hour later we were intercepted on the road, where he proceeded to pass us a great pile of it, still hot. Then he reached his hand into a humid plastic bag and held out a scoop of warm, dripping goat's cheese in his palm for us to pack away – somehow! There was the night we found ourselves in a cosy spot in the lee of one of the deserted buildings – often great estates gone to seed – which are a poignant legacy of pre-revolution days. At midnight we were woken by a police van all set to ferry us off to more comfortable quarters, we knew and cared not whither. In general though, Iranian attentions were more controlled than Turkish. Drivers would discreetly pull into the verge some fifty yards further on from where they'd seen us to get a closer look as we pedalled past. They smiled, but wouldn't usually prevail upon us. There was a graciousness and a dignity about these people.

There was also Homayun. In the pre-revolutionary days he had been champion of the national cycle team. When his friends spotted us in their village, they jumped into their car and shot ahead to warn him that we were coming. They knew that he would want to rise to the occasion. Homayun was waiting for us on the road opposite his father's farm as we freewheeled towards him, discussing when and where to kip down. He leapt into our path, imploring us to stop, begging us not to be frightened, beseeching us to believe him when he said there was nothing more he would like than to put us up for the night. It was getting late he said, and we couldn't possibly sleep up the road in the mountains. He himself hunted tigers on their heights, and continually had to protect his father's flock from foraging mountain wolves.

It wouldn't be quite accurate to say that we gave in. We didn't have much choice. Homayun would have died rather than let us go on. Stepping over the threshold of the Soleimany farmhouse was one of those real contrasts which characterised our experience of this land. Our feet sank into carpets that spelt 'Persian luxury'. We were served tea and more tangerines than we could eat from the farm as we reclined on plush velvet cushions and drank in the happy, family atmosphere that constituted prayer day at Papa Soleimany's. If your house was more than a certain distance from the mosque, one cousin told us with a twinkle in his eye, you were let off Friday attendance; so Friday was the day the children and grandchildren piled into their cars and spent the day at Papa's, legitimately out of reach of the nearest *mullah*'s harangue.

The women, some three-quarters of an hour after our arrival, having satisfied themselves as to our allegiances, calmly divested themselves of their head-covering. We nearly died. It turned out that Papa had been one of the Shah's secret police. He had been one of the lucky ones – or perhaps simply timed his exit well. Now he spent his days virtually in internal exile, rearing a fine breed of sheep, tending acres of fruit trees, and enjoying his family. Perhaps that was why he knew so well how 'to love those who are aliens' (Deut 10:19) because he himself 'lived as an alien in his country.' He had a token, obligatory picture of the Ayatollah in an obscure corner of the room. When we asked him why he tuned into Israeli radio for his news, he answered by switching on the television, with its endless stills of heroic battle scenes and the same gross advertisements that were on roadside hoardings: toddlers with pink cheeks and sparkling eyes, in army boots and cocking rifles.

'Only from those outside my country can I hope to get some measure of the truth of what is going on,' he said quietly. 'This,' as the latest statistics pertaining to Iranian victories and Iraqi defeats flashed up on the screen, 'is all lies.'

'This Government,' broke in Homayun with a characteristic, endearing use of English 'is wery extrawaygant. Wery. This *jang* (war) is wery wasteful.'

We took hot showers and ate mutton and aromatic rice, eggs, yoghourt, leavened bread, all farm produced and all quite delicious to lips cracked from our bread and water diet. Anna was quietly, closely questioned by the younger women about how she managed to remain childless since getting married. The Revolution, it appeared, had put an end to contraception like so much else.

That night we slept beside the huge oil stove that more than heated the whole of the open-planned lower storey of the farm house. No Karrimats for us that night. We lay on deep-pile, sumptuous rugs. We departed weighed down with home-produced honey. Iran's chief exports make a fine list: oil, caviar, rugs, fruits, nuts, opium, and tragacanth. At the Soleimany farm, this sumptuous catalogue seemed probable in a way that was so unlikely in the zealot's tenement flat. The best of Iran however, was still to come. We were going to Persepolis.

We climbed and climbed through the bare outcrops of rock, up to the highest point we'd reached since the Alps. The landscape reminded us of the American Mid-West in its breadth and starkness. Months before we had scrutinised the atlas and feared this part of the route. It was going to be bitterly cold at that height in the middle of January, it was probably going to be illegal to cycle off on our own in Iran, but it would all be worth it for the prize of visiting the palaces and tombs of the ancient kings of Persia. We had visions of tramping through the snow to get to the remains. But here we were, feeling the sun burn if we stood still in it, and the only snow was that visible on the mountain peaks far to the left and right.

Howard could hardly contain his excitement as he kept checking the map, willing the place to become visible on the horizon. At long last, there was a little sign announcing the direction in English – a remnant of the Shah – and we turned into a beautiful avenue and cycled up it in the flickering sunlight, past women in flouncy, bright dresses and no stockings or headcoverings. They were too far from Teheran to have taken to Western dressing under the Shah, and they hadn't yet taken to the black *chaddr* under the Ayatollah. It added to the sense of timelessness as the busy road petered out into a broad, flat space with the mighty monument in the middle of it.

In the year 587 BC, a man named Jeremiah bought a field from his cousin. It was a significant purchase because it was currently in the possession of the hostile army of the King of Babylon, and the town near whose walls it lay was about to capitulate after a long-standing siege. Jeremiah by this act endorsed his confidence that, after the certain destruction, the Lord, the God of Israel would somehow restore Jerusalem and the fields around it to the people of Judah. The city did fall, and the surrounding countryside was largely depopulated, with many prisoners taken to Babylon.

Decades later, one of those prisoners was so to distinguish himself that successive kings of Babylon would trust him as their intimate adviser. The prisoner's name was Daniel, and he was in the capital that memorable night when it was taken by the Persians. Just as Babylon had taken Jerusalem into its empire, so now Babylon was taken into Persia's. The man responsible for it was Cyrus the Great whose tomb we had come to see. Xenophon and Herodotus tell how Cyrus's satrap, 'Darius the Mede', diverted the river Euphrates upstream from Babylon thus enabling the Persians to enter the city along the dry river bed while Belshazzar and his nobles were feasting in the royal palace. The city was taken in a single night.

The Scriptures tell the same story, too, with chilling vividness in Daniel 5:1. 'King Belshazzar gave a great banquet for a thousand of his nobles and drank wine with them.' This was the night the sacred vessels that his grandfather had taken from Jerusalem a few weeks after Jeremiah bought his field were put to sacrilegious use. This was the night of the writing on the wall, and 'that very night Belshazzar, king of the Babylonians, was slain,' and his kingdom divided. (Dan 5:30)

The record continues 'It pleased Darius to appoint one hundred and twenty satraps to rule throughout the kingdom with three administrators over them, one of whom was Daniel.' That made Daniel one of the very most senior officials in a vast, rambling imperial structure that the Persians were creating for themselves. We know from outside Scripture that Cyrus himself arrived at Babylon shortly after its spectacular storming, on

October 16th 539 BC. In the circumstances it is highly
likely that he met Daniel, crucial link-man that he was in
the exercise of imperial control. And here we were at
the spot where Cyrus had lived, where he built his
palace, and where he was buried.

The tomb is on the site of Pasagardae, 'the camp of
the Persians' which as its name suggests was more of an
elaborate camping ground than a palace. The Empire
was so vast that it needed five Royal capitals and the
court was constantly on the move to see, and be seen in,
all the corners of the Kingdom (as is the King of Nepal's
today). Pasagardae was a complex of luxurious facilities
for the court to move into, dispense justice, and leave
behind again deserted until the next time they came.
Sadly, very little of it is visible now, except the great
tomb. We bought a ticket issued by the Islamic Republic's Ministry of Culture from an excited man who
followed us round, as interested in us as we were in the
tomb. Plutarch records the inscription:

> Oh man, whoever thou art, and whencesoever
> thou comest, for I know that thou will come, I am
> Cyrus, and I won for the Persians their Empire. Do
> not, therefore, begrudge me this little earth that
> covers my body.

It was an ironic touch for so vast an edifice. We were
given special dispensation to break all the rules and
climb up the smooth soapstone edifice to reach the
small, dark, cool chamber at the top where the remains
had lain. Once inside we stood silently.

Cyrus not only probably met Daniel, but he also
carried the notable distinction in Scripture of being
described as a specific instrument of God's will. 'He is
my shepherd' says Isaiah (44:28), who goes on to
describe him as 'the Lord's anointed'. Both these
descriptions are the same as are used to mark out

Above: The tent sagging as we begin to dismantle it one cold Alpine morning: our daily task for five months till the 'people factor' in India made camping impossible. (Page 24)

Below: Sindon: not snow white in a hygienically sealed plastic bag from the chemist's, but cotton buds in the raw. (Page 58)

Right: Lunch overlooking the great amphitheatre at Philippi. (Page 64)

Below: Breakfast at Ibrahim's. From bottom left: slices of *halumi*, granulated honey, eggs from the backyard, *chai* in the ubiquitous tulip glass, teapot with built-in top-up... Turkish hospitality! (Page 80)

Left: Thessalonica's churches are hardly photogenic but they are unique. (Page 61)

Below: Getting in line in Pakistan: Winter wear bundled away, headcoverings for the sun, and, for Anna, for modesty – as with her ample Afghani *cameez* and Turkish *sholvars*. (Page 210)

Above: A hitch in our sixty-mile Bolan descent: the metal grid was the underpinning for the tarmac, both washed away in flash flooding. We are cycling down the river bed. (Page 234)

Below: Intended as a picture of Sukkur Bazaar, by the time we'd clicked the shutter this became one of the 'people factor', not to mention a splendid display of sequined Pakistani hats! (Page 244)

Left: Which was more interesting – Anna taking the photo, or Howard having his hair cut? And they loved fingering our washing, safety-pinned to dry on the end of the tent bag. (Page 251)

Below: A close shave for a sacred calf in Delhi, but Mum and Dad are quite unperturbed. (Page 275)

Above: An obscure corner kiosk of the Taj, designed to catch the maximum breeze. Vultures on the roof wait for drooping tourists. (Page 278)

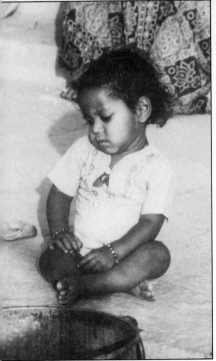

Above: A woman soaps clothes on a slab before lifting them above her head to thwack down as her neighbour is doing. Then she lays them out to dry on the sand. (Page 278)

Left: Toddler on the *ghats* at Benares: charm round her neck and *kohl* round her eyes, presumably to protect her from the fate of the smouldering bodies not twenty yards away. (Page 282)

Inset: All we wanted, in the heat of the Indian plain, were the Himalayan snows. 'That's going to be home, my love.' (Page 291)

Above: Looking across rice terraces tumbling down to the river, at the last stretch of road between Butwal and Pokhara. (Page 290)

bishops of the early church and it is startling to see such imagery used of a non-Jewish king at this stage in the Old Testament.

Cyrus had indeed 'won the Persians their empire'. His successor but one, Darius the Great (who is nothing to do with Darius the Mede) extended its boundaries right through Turkey, over the Bosphorus, and into Greece where he successfully fought the battle of Marathon. It was he who built the great Persepolis some miles down the road from Pasagardae. Persepolis, 'the city of Persia' was probably intentionally so named to point up the difference between the new capital and Cyrus's old one. The Persians were renowned in their Golden Age under Darius for the most fabulous opulence. Persian carpets were legendary in the time of Xenophon. Financed by a vast tax network throughout the Empire, there was a positive cult of luxury surrounding the King, and it is embodied to this day in Persepolis. We were back on Alexander's trail here. It so epitomised for him the ostentatiousness of the Persians who had overrun his Macedonia that, uncharacteristically, he razed it when he passed. His policy overall was characterised by a tolerant respect for all that he conquered. But with Persepolis it was different.

When we were there, a young man told us how it really happened – the local knowledge that didn't get into the history books. Alexander couldn't believe that he'd really defeated the Persians while the splendour of Persepolis still stood, but try as he might, it was too well built for his army to pull down. The chief obstacle was the Apadana, the great throne room, or the Hall of a Hundred Columns, whose roof was so secure that for days it withstood their attempts to destroy it. The locals showed great satisfaction at his inability, and he felt sure they knew something he didn't about why it wouldn't move. How to get at the secret, though? He bullied and threatened them, but they said not a word. There was

only one other hope. He would have to try gentle
persuasion where force had failed, and singling out a
young girl from the village where they were billeted, he
seduced her heartlessly and dropped his idle question at
the end of the night. Overwhelmed by being so
favoured by the conqueror of all the world, she melted
and in the silence before dawn she softly whispered the
fateful secret . . . By the time the sun was up, so was the
whole army, gathering together a huge fire to light in
the middle of the throne room. The great blocks of
stone had been fixed together with molten lead which
had hardened to form hitherto impregnable joints. Only
melt the lead and the building would slide down of its
own accord . . .

Enough of it remains, thankfully, to tell of the mag-
nificence once displayed there. Its situation, its groundplan, its architectural style, and its artistic decoration all
serve to glorify the King's person. It is situated against a
vast, barren, rocky outcrop and from any point a glance
to the north shows Persepolis to be almost a snub to
nature. Where she could not support any crops, or
grass, or even scrub, there the King would lay his
splendid surroundings of the finest imported stone his
empire could afford. Its groundplan is unusual in that it
is impossible to enter the city without climbing up stairs.
The north is sealed off by the unclimbable outcrop, but
the other three sides are all raised fifteen feet off the
ground. In practical terms no one could enter without
first dismounting from his horse. In addition to that, the
steps themselves are so shallow and so long that it's
impossible to rush up them. It's as if the architect 'builds
in' a reverent approach and forces you to arrive with
dignity. Howard had practically tripped over himself
trying to bound up.

Up on stage, the scale of the architecture is still
breathtaking, the elaborate capitals which are distinct to
this site, the towering doorways with massive carved

gryphons and eagles in attendance, and the natural path that leads without diversion to the Hall of a Hundred Columns. The decorative reliefs finish it off. There is no doorway without life-sized carved sentries on the inside to lead you through and remind you of the power of the 'King of Kings'. Inside, there is no window without attendants with fans and flyswats carved in to keep the King comfortable in the heat. Most impressive of all is the secondary stage, within the first, also with its shallow steps, and with literally hundreds of attendants milling there with you, chatting and stepping up or down beside you in the stone. At the top stands a wall of armed guards strictly to attention that wait, tireless, on the King's pleasure.

Standing in the centre of the palace one can look out far to the west and just make out the site of the cliff-face tombs of four of Cyrus's successors. All flesh is grass, after all. Great Darius lies there among them at Naqsh-i-Rustan. He too left a memorable epitaph: 'Saith Darius the King: by favour of Ahura Mazda, I am of such a sort that I am a friend to right. I am not a friend to wrong. It is not my desire that the weak man should have wrong done to him by the mighty; nor is it my desire that the mighty should have wrong done to him by the weak.'

All four of the kings buried there have appearances in the Jewish history of the period, and an unmistakable picture emerges of a small number of Jews exerting a disproportionate amount of influence in the Persian court during successive reigns. There is Darius who arbitrates in the local dispute between the Jews and their enemies who opposed their attempts to rebuild the Temple. Then there's Xerxes I, or Ahasuerus as the Jews called him, who wound up taking a Jewish wife whose story is told in the book of Esther. (He also received local complaints about the Jews' return to prosperity.) Next was Artaxerxes I who was first persuaded by the dire warnings of yet another official complaint by anti-Jewish elements in Judah, but changed his mind dramatically and sent there both Ezra with powers to 'appoint magistrates and judges to administer justice' and then Nehemiah, his cup bearer, to 'rebuild the walls of Jerusalem'. Finally comes Darius II who gets just a brief mention in Nehemiah.

The fascinating thing about the tombs is that the style of the reliefs cut into the rock face around the small black entrances is very cosmopolitan. There is nothing distinctively Persian about it. It betrays in its style the same inclusive imperial policy that allowed the tiny Jewish race to rise to such high positions of authority that we hear about in the biblical record. We squinted through the sunlight at the scenes forty or fifty feet above us. They would have had to hoist the bodies up on long ladders to get them up there. Each one depicts the funeral ceremony with the image of Ahura Mazda, the god of the prophet Zarathustra hovering about the proceedings. Shown too is the fire temple that stands in reality still at the base of the four tombs, remarkably untouched after 2,300 years. The fire is a sacramental expression of the presence of god and is eternally attended by the priesthood; an outward sign in which the boundaries of symbol and reality are deliberately blurred.

Imagine our surprise, two months later in a bank in Lahore, when we met a current-day adherent of the Zoroastrian faith! They are known as Parsis now (the word for Persia again) and can rightly claim to be members of the faith that first advocated a one and only invisible God. Only a few remain now in any numbers; in Shiraz in Iran, Karachi in Pakistan, and Bombay. But our friend did assure us that there is a flourishing little fire temple in California.

Leaving these ancient spots that afternoon was something of a culture shock. The immaculate vandalism of nineteenth century British diplomatic staff and officers who carved their rank and regimental crests when they came to visit, reminded us that we were not the first tourists to find Persepolis. The Persepolis Hotel, where we had a bite to eat, was an example of the vacuum left by the abrupt end to the Shah's open-door policy. The paint was flaking, the pool empty, the faded glamour almost a caricature of itself, the room empty, the waiters sullen, and the salad dry. The only life came from the radio, still blurting out the military music, trying to enthuse nobody in particular. As we set off on the road to Shiraz, we noticed that the grounds to the side of the archaeological site had been taken over by the Revolutionary Guards as a training camp for officers.

In the place where the Shah had invited the rulers of the world to celebrate 3,000 years of the Persian monarchy with an ostentation worthy of his predecessors, the forces of the Glorious Islamic Revolution were plotting the next moves in the war with Iraq. We should be grateful for their presence though, because our guide told us that there had been a nasty moment during the course of the Revolution when the symbolic weight of Persepolis had almost been too much to tolerate. Bitter memories of the Shah's display there looked like being unleashed into another destruction of the precious site. It was only with hesitation that the Ministry of Culture took it under its protective wing and released money for the continuation of the restoration programme. The Revolutionary Guards have appropriated it for themselves, and perhaps it is not so ironic after all. For are not Iranian and Iraqi, Persian and Babylonian, still fighting one another in a macabre replay of ancient animosities?

9

'HELLO MISHTER!'

Monday, January 19th

After the heights of Persepolis, things could only go downhill – with the architectural splendours of the ancient Persian kings fresh in our mind's eye, Shiraz, that same afternoon, made a poor and dusty showing. The bus station, where we went to buy our tickets for the next day's journey, to as near the Pakistan border as we could get was tucked away in a stinking back yard. Travellers, their luggage pecked at by roosters and waiting for eternally delayed buses, were driven by desperation only to drink tea in a sleazy cellar. They were easy prey too for the beggars who surreptitiously pulled aside scanty sackcloth to reveal their war wounds – irritated to a fresh soreness, we were told, by skilful rubbing with turmeric and grime. The command 'to be open-handed towards ... the poor and needy' (Deut 15:11) was one of the less attractive aspects of the Exodus story to take on a new and graphic meaning.

Any travellers going East, particularly the ones who set out in the belief that they've saved up their last penny for their journey of a lifetime, would do well to make a decision about their giving fairly soon after the begging starts; deciding to give so much to so many so many times a day, or somesuch. We dithered for a long time, disorientated by the extent of the problem. Tithing is all very well, but even a tenth of our comparatively vast

income falls hopelessly short of the demands of the
'starving millions'. We felt a lot better when we'd made
our own guidelines, able to look beggars in the eye
throughout any interchange. But the problem was never
completely solved. The reason is simple: 'There will
always be poor people in the land' (Deut 15:11).

To be fair, Shiraz had its high points too: four miles of
bazaar – stone passageways, vaulted and spacious, quite
unlike the warrenlike ones of Turkey. We visited the
sights, the tombs of the great Sufi poets Hafez and Saadi
who had become, like the Mevlâna, objects of worship in
their own right. This hagiolatry, so reminiscent of
medieval Catholicism, didn't surprise us in Turkey,
where the emphasis on unadulterated doctrine isn't so
strong, but it was strange to see that both Iran and
Pakistan, who pride themselves on the purity of their
faith, allow – or perhaps can't stamp out – such unortho-
doxies. Some use Saadi's poems as a way of planning
their lives, opening the book at random for immediate
guidance. In the mosque of the Fourth Imam, Rezad, a
spot of such significance for the Muslim that we were
surprised to be allowed in, we puzzled over little padlocks
attached to the grille surrounding his tomb. We were told
that this was how the faithful ensured their prayers didn't
get lost. Once over the border, and in Pakistan we were in
the 'Third World': limp, grubby strings and ribbons were
reverently knotted on instead of padlocks. They'd be
snipped off at the end of the day by the guards who'd
also sell flower offerings to scatter on the monuments.

We tried to conceal our lack of appreciation at the
tarnished pieces of mirror which crudely mosaiced the
entire building from chest height upwards, for
Homayun was as proud of Rezad's memorial as of
Persepolis. Its glitzy vulgarity reminded us of that first
provincial mosque in Turkey with its multicoloured
bathroom tiles. Outside a martyrium had rolled up, one
of a number of mobile booths we saw in which the
photographs of people killed in the war were festooned

with fairy lights and bunting, and lauded by an indistinct tape recorder concealed inside. More amazed at the phenomenon than sad at the dead, we nodded awkwardly at the 'driver' and scuttled away.

We had left Homayun only with great difficulty that evening. He'd come all the way to Shiraz and pressed upon us every conceivable delicacy the war-depleted city had to offer, in an effort to put off the evil moment of parting. No wonder he'd urged us to visit Hafez's tomb, for the poet's language was only marginally more elaborate than his own when it came to 'the pain transcending' when 'soul-friends depart asunder . . . ' (*Rapture's Vision*). If we hadn't experienced the old Arab's eye wiping, hand wringing, farewell down by the Syrian border, Homayun's tears and hyperbolic professions – 'Wery keen fooehling. I weep all night' – might have seemed quite false. The apparently excessive language of Eastern hospitality cannot, however be written off as insincere. It's rather like Elizabethan Court poetry: the most tender, anguished tropes addressed to an entirely fictitious lover. The excellence of the verse isn't one whit compromised by the absence of actual personal experience, because writer and reader are complicit in the idea that 'the truest poetry is the most feigning'. We now receive letters from Homayun like this one:

> My brother Howard, my sister Anna, couple never to be forgotten. Helo to you Resistance and manifestation power . . . I want to sure you that you are always in my heart. I shall never forget you . . . my father, brother, stepmother, and all my ralatives, and bees and queen bees and flower bees say 1000 to you,

with pictures of weeping eyes and puddles of 'weep water' and 'hearts-ease pansya' in the margins.

How to respond to Homayun that night in Shiraz,

without appearing strangely cold? Our inability to squeeze out a tear must have been as foreign to him as his effusions were to us but, however heartfelt our appreciation of the Soleimanys' superabundant kindness, Homayun was surely aware that we were hardly soul-mates. To put it even more bluntly, we were dog-tired and needed to find a tent site in the city, which wasn't going to be easy.

At first, Homayun couldn't even bear to help us look for one. It would bring the hour of parting too close. He took us to an ice-cream parlour in the richest area of town where women talked to one another over coffee in best porcelain cups and German biscuits bought on the black market. Homayun had a brainwave: we could come and sleep with him on the bee farm he was on his way to. We pointed out that it was sixty miles away and we had to catch the bus the following morning because our visa was running out. He tried to buy our ticket. Then he had another idea. Friends of his in the city could put us up. We protested, but it was the least he could do. They weren't in. The sun was setting. As we stood on the doorstep, we spied a piece of waste land behind us and were sure it was suitable for the tent. Homayun couldn't bring himself to leave till all the guy ropes were in place to his satisfaction. Finally, he sprinted off to his pick-up (he never walked when he could run) and returned two minutes later with the tears still standing in his eyes.

'Tomorrow, I will come back. I cannot leave you thus, my friends.'

We were sure he didn't mean it seriously. It was a hundred and twenty mile round trip to and from the bee farm.

But in the morning there he was — nowhere near the campsite, or the bus station — but sprinting down the teeming boulevard in a city big enough to be bombed by the Iraqis a couple of days after we left.

'My father taught me how to tracking. I am looking, looking, looking, asking, asking, asking. I have your scent. I know,' he explained proudly. He gave us hamburgers and Pepsi in a sad little bar where we met another wan shadow from the days of the Shah – an ex-tourist guide with immaculate English, delighted to talk to us. There was no work for him now, of course. Homayun only quitted us after waiting the two and a half hours our bus was delayed, and finally pressing a kilo of pistachios into our hands and weeping.

No town after fifteen hours on a bus looks its best, but at dawn, after we'd had to get the bike off the roof of the bus ourselves or pay once again for the privilege of putting it there, Zahedan had a desperate ends-of-the-earth aura about it: the sort only border towns can exude. We tried to get breakfast. There were no eggs to be had, ever, in this town, we were told. We couldn't decide which tasted the soapier: the bread, *halumi* or the tea we'd settled for, but were assured that the cheese, too, was the only lot to be had in town. We had a long search for oranges – up till now, juicy and delicious – to freshen our mouths. We finally found some truly desiccated specimens. The throng round the bike as we worked out what we could buy that would use up our last ryals got so oppressive that the redoubtable fruit-seller lost patience. She wasn't in the least impressed by the tandem, and even less so by those who were, and suddenly turned a hose on us all to give her more space. It was mainly directed at the onlookers, we thought, so didn't take it personally and stood by appreciating the cool shower.

Zahedan may have been the least prepossessing town of our time in Iran, but it did provide us with two escorts on the way out. The first was a delightful bevy of excited vehicles, many still wet from their dousing, who shouted and clapped after us, young teenagers racing ahead, men on motorbikes pretending not to be part of the throng really, old gents caught up in the moment, and a toddler astride his plastic tractor, making more noise than the rest of them put together and being pushed at breakneck speed down the middle of the road by his obliging, only slightly older brother. We couldn't get any sense out of them as to how to get out of town, so we stopped a couple of policemen quietly pocketing a fee extorted from a lorry driver, hidden, they thought, in the shade of his vehicle. They sprang to a blustering attention and personally accompanied us to the border road, slowly cruising ahead of us like a presidential bodyguard.

Some way down that road, we ran into less exalted travelling companions: the densest swarm of flies imaginable. There were so many that we couldn't even brush them off without squashing them into one another and on to our hands. We passed a couple of children sitting by the road, seemingly miles from anywhere, who'd obviously got used to them. As they got up to have a look at us, a black cloud rose from them, and by the time we passed, settled again. Fortunately, it was a good, flat road and at exactly seventeen miles per hour, we were going too fast for them to land again, once removed. We fled from them into a formidable landscape of desert and sharp mountains forming the natural boundary between Iran and Afghanistan. Entering the unknown is always worse than being there. We pressed on, with not a little trepidation.

The Ayatollah's message to the passing infidel is painted in large neat letters on an antiseptically scrubbed wall at the border post:

CLEANLINESS IS DIRECTLY RELATED TO THE MAN'S PERSONALITY

Our treatment was quick and business-like. Anna was frisked by a 'Sister of Mercy', those same who are reputed to have hidden razor blades in the cloths they use to wipe the lipstick off their erring sisters' mouths. Not a word was mentioned about that piece of paper we were supposed to produce as evidence that we'd not changed money illegally. Considering some horror stories we'd heard about people getting snarled up at this end, we concluded once again that it was the tandem which had got us preferential treatment.

Business done, we wheeled the bike towards the heavy, green gates. Anna peered through the bars as they were swung back by smartly uniformed, unsmiling guards.

'What do you suppose all those tents and shacks are, Howard? How far do you think it is to the border town?'

Tarmac immediately gave way to sand. The gates clanged shut on Iran's final graffitied word – DEATH TO THE AMERICANS. We were through. Immediately a physical sensation of relief overcame and surprised us – a kind of weightlessness as if we'd suddenly shed a load of anxiety and fear we'd been unaware of harbouring after those first tense days.

We were surrounded all at once by smiling, brown faces, hands pointing, gesturing, touching every part of the bike.

'Look, look! A Mr and Mrs Bicycle!' 'Hello Mishter,' (addressed to both of us).

'First class tip-top cycle.'

More and more men gathered.

'How var you?' 'Okay, okay?'

'How many children do you?'

It didn't matter that those on the fringes couldn't see what was drawing the crowd. The important thing was to be involved in the excitement somehow or other. We tried to wheel the bike forwards, but were blocked by a wall of grinning men.

'Excuse me,' we said.

Still they grinned, not unkindly. We looked behind

for a way to back out, but there was another human
barrier and still more men came to enjoy this new
spectacle. Information was relayed back to them by
those in the know:

'Iran . . . *Ingrejee* . . . *dugna* (double) cycle.'

'Excuse me,' we said.

They didn't budge. We were getting impatient.

'Please let us through. We have to get to Taftan
today.'

'*Vair* ar you gowing mishter?'

'Taftan,' we said.

'Taftan?'

'Yes. We have to go today – Immigration – passports . . . '

'This *is* Taftan.'

We looked at the cardboard box and corrugated iron
lean-tos, propping one another up, some lucky enough
to be screened on the fourth side by a piece of torn rush
matting. Howard extracted a piece of goat's dung from
the pedals. A chicken with a fluorescent pink head
darted past Anna's legs for the possibility of remaining
crumbs in a packet of 'real *zeera*' (cumin) biscuits, 'both
saltish and sweet'. It shouldn't have bothered. This was
Pakistan. There were no remaining biscuit crumbs.

'*This* is Taftan?'

A ripple of laughter.

'Yes Mishter.'

Then another host of questions:

'Change money?'

'Eat?'

'Hotl room?'

'Can I help you?'

'How much this cycle please?'

'Vair are you from?'

'Vot is your job?'

'Where's the bank, please?' we asked.

It was travellers' cheque time again. They nudged one another.

'It's closed.'

It was a sad reflection on what we thought of them, but we reckoned that was just as likely to be untrue as true.

'We'd rather find out for ourselves,' Anna said quietly. The surprise at hearing a woman taking the initiative must have been why the flanks opened a crack and we were able to move again. The problem was, we didn't know where we were going. We kept walking in order to avoid being trapped once more and asked again as we walked,

'Where's the bank?'

'That way.' (Circular arm movements which returned to the speaker's chest.)

'Sorry, *which* way?'

'That way.' (More circular arm movements, and a slightly injured tone of voice at our apparent incomprehension of their English.)

'Maybe the bank's closed,' someone suggested.

'Maybe,' we replied.

'I give you good rate. American dollars?' This last with unbelieving hopefulness.

We laughed, suddenly seeing the funny side of the contrast between these men and their militant brothers on the other side of the great iron gate.

'We're going to the bank – after Immigration.'

The only way to fob off their attentions was to promise that we'd consider their rate if the bank really was closed.

'We'll wait for you,' they promised, and we were sure they would.

So much for the precious visa we'd struggled to get in Teheran. We'd gone past Immigration before we realised what it was. In fact, we only identified it because it was one of the four concrete buildings in Taftan. There were six officials inside. Thigh-length shirts *(cameez)* hung down from underneath their British Army supply sweaters, girded about with massy buckled belts. The lower ranks wore baggy cotton trousers *(sholwars)* secured by a drawstring at the waist or *lungis* (oblongs of cloth tied round into a skirt), to our eyes comically out of keeping with the more important officials' army trousers ending in gaiters and heavy boots. Maybe Anna's ski boots didn't look so ridiculous in the blazing sun after all. If they weren't in turbans or variously swathed scarves, they wore embroidered, mirrorwork hats.

Their dress was typical of that strange mixture, of Pakistani and British, the legacy of the Raj. While served *cafee* (mouth-screwingly strong black tea) at eleven o'clock sharp, in Minton china lookalikes – with a mango cream biscuit manufactured by Peek Frean of Karachi, the expatriate would do well to remember that his little 'tiffin' was first so named by his hosts.

Anna showed our documents to an unimpressed officer in a small dusty room. She expected to have to take her turn at guarding the bike outside while Howard presented himself in person, but was summarily dismissed with no such request, only with a warning: not that we shouldn't change our money unofficially, but that we should expect a worse rate if we did.

This cursory treatment of our official documents was the first of many times in Pakistan when we were to wonder whether anything really mattered so much it could be termed 'essential'. There'd be a lot of bureaucratic humming and hawing and official buck passing, and waiting, and smiling if anything was a little out of the ordinary, but the problem would always be overridden with a noble speech about service to their brothers being their duty – and another cup of tea. We soon understood why the Pakistanis and the Iranians were so (tolerantly) disrespectful of each other, despite their spiritual fraternity. To the Pakistanis, their brothers' ideological fervour was simply too much effort. To the Iranians, such a laissez faire attitude was nothing short of heresy. Anyway, to our Western minds it was essential to change some money.

In Iran, you get a raw deal at the bank. In Pakistan you get a barefooted guard with a wooden rifle to announce your arrival – and a guess at the exchange rate. The guard escorted us inside and couldn't refrain from introducing us in terms of our strange mode of transport to his two superiors. They sat behind the couple of desks that, with a filing cabinet, constituted the sum of the furniture. He was despatched immediately and returned with a tray of guavas and tangerines, four cups, and a Thermos of syrupy sweet all-milk tea for us. The manager was so delighted to hear our story and practise his English that nothing much financial occurred for quite a while. When it did it was like a novel.

Howard was still a bit edgy about finance at borders and wanted to check the exchange rate. There was a lot of looking around on the shelves, but no, there was no indication of what the rate was today, or yesterday, or last week.

'A hundred rupees is about four pounds,' we were assured.

He was right we discovered when we got to our first newspaper nearly a fortnight later and Howard felt a bit churlish for having made a thing of it. The next problem was the Standard Chartered cheques. They weren't on the manager's list of accredited banks of the world. Things looked a bit desperate for a moment until we found their address written in our diary.

'They really are a bank. Look, they've got a branch in Karachi – Abdullah Haroon Road.'

'Oh yes.' The manager knew Abdullah Haroon Road so they must exist, because Abdullah Haroon Road definitely existed. Paperwork could begin now. The manager, the guard with the gun, and we all watched in silence as the clerk registered the details in splendid, leather bound ledgers with a black fountain pen and careful Roman lettering. The manager then authorised in red and blotted it. A dank mustiness tickled our nostrils as the huge books were opened and banged shut. The smell must have been at least as old as Partition. Business was finally declared to be at an end and seeing as all this was going on after hours, the guard set to with a large bunch of keys.

That done, we were directed to The Taftan 'Hotl' – a step up from some of its neighbours on account of its personal tap and mud walls. We were offered a six rupee bed, but said we only wanted to put the bike somewhere safe and eat before we got going. They solved the bike problem by bringing it right into the middle of the restaurant and we concentrated instead on a new hurdle: how to eat rice and gravy with our fingers. Impossible as it sounds, it's actually not that difficult. As we'd been told back in Britain, the secret was to use one's thumb as a lever. Black tea was served in a blue enamel 'Habitat' teapot, with cheap, factory produced cups. We paid, then made our way down the alley, peering into each little three-sided shop to see what we could purchase to eat on the road.

There were biscuits galore, all made by Peek Freans, and plenty of fruit – satsumas, and guavas – but we were after bread and cheese.

'Cheese?' they queried, eyes sliding past to get a better view of our strange two saddled appurtenance.

'*Peynir?*' We tried the word which had passed in Turkey and Iran.

'Oh, *peynir*. No, no. Not in Taftan. Maybe in Lahore.'

We weren't going to be there for another month. They shrugged, smiling.

'Vich country you are from?' . . . and at each stop an all male crowd would gather to comment and smile, and hang on one another's shoulders, and try to persuade us to go by bus to Quetta, the capital of the province four hundred miles away. We thought they must be agents for the bus company, so dismissive were they of the prospect of us cycling out of Taftan. Besides, by now we'd seen these famous buses parked in the sand, affording useful shade for the goats.

To a Western mind there was nothing buslike about these phantasms by the time 'Fancy Bodywork Co, Bundag Road, Lahore' had sheathed the original body in a beaten and chased tin casing. If anything could clink or tinkle it was dangled, in curtains, from this new frame. If anything could sparkle or dazzle, it was applied to the psychedelia already painted and inlaid round the windows. And what windows – Fancy Bodywork wouldn't have stooped to anything quite so unimaginative as a simple square of glass. If there was glass (it was self-preservation as well as cycling pride which had made us recoil from abandoning ourselves to their jangling embrace) the gleaming tin of the body was cut around it to produce ovals and heart shapes – a curlicued prong waltzing across the passenger's vision here, a shaft of shimmering falling stars there. There were little fantasy scenes on the low roof-rack: maidens plucking glassy dates from zanily curving palm trees, reflected in wildly undulating oceans which lapped at impossibly gold shores. Who wanted to travel in one of these when on the outside and looking on it was like watching a carnival?

On the outskirts of town, we passed tents stamped 'Afghan Relief Organisation'. Then the town disappeared and we began to negotiate the ruts. Had there never been a road there, it might have been better, because the remains of this one were a positive obstacle course. One thing we'd determined upon in the Iranian buses was that once in Pakistan, every mile would again be personally pedalled. We hadn't bargained for this, though. We remembered that day on the Gallipoli

peninsula, when a cloud of dust ahead warned us that
the tarmac was about to give out. There at least the
surface had been loose and gave a bit under the tyres. It
seemed like a carpet compared with this 'washboarding':
one or two inch ridges, less than a foot apart, and totally
unyielding.

Every hour or so, a silver monster would roar past.
We'd know it was coming minutes before it swayed
round the last rocky outcrop, by the clanking. As soon as
it knew what was coming, it made sure we knew it knew.
'Screech' went the brake, squealing with pain at the
effort, gasping wheezily to draw breath before the next
exhalation. The chinking chains hanging from the back
gave little shudders of sympathy. Every loose piece of
fancy bodywork clattered its protest against the groaning real body. Out of windows – real or imagined – and
from the roof rack would hang the nationals, fascinated
by our double act:

'*Dubbal* cycle!'
'*Dubbal* chain!'
'*Dubbal* saddle!'
'*Dubbal* pedal cycle!'
'Mishter, cam on, cam on!'

Then would come a lorry, close first cousin to the
buses, vying in PVC appliquéd splendour and plastic
scrollwork, equally insistent that we pitch the bike on top
of their load and lurch off fraternally into the wide,
dusty yonder. We'd refuse, smiling and waving. Finally
our bottoms grew too sore and our bodies too weary to
look up and make contact. By now, we were really
scared something major might snap, and occasionally
we'd abandon the road for the deceptively flatter packed
stone and sand beside it. It was a gorgeous relief. We'd
skim along until we'd suddenly sink to a halt, and have
to pull-push the bike back to the ruts.

Our bones were aching and bruised from our jolting
progress. We'd done fifteen miles in four hours. That

meant sixty-five to go before tarmac. A Suzuki pick-up
ground to a halt beside us. A turbanned man stepped
out and spoke quietly, a courteous smile on his lips.

'You need help, my brother and sister? My *British*
brother and sister?'

Howard saw the look on Anna's face and answered
yes to both questions. He and the bike were squeezed
into the back with two other fellows. Anna was sandwiched between the speaker and another man. They
took it in turns to drive, shooting over the bumps at sixty
miles per hour, reasonably supposing that speed would
iron them out somewhat – or at least get them over and
done with quicker. Anna sat wondering how to address
this austere figure.

'Where are you going?' she tried.

'To Nukundi, where the black road begins and you
can eat and sleep.' Encouraged, she tried again:

'Where are you from?'

'Rabat,' (just inside the Afghan border. He must have
slipped over that afternoon). Anna went hot, and then
cold. She swallowed so loudly that she was sure he would
have heard her had it not been for the hundreds of
stones spurting up from the wheels and pelting the
vehicle. The Afghani turned towards her. She noticed
the eyelid which hooded the left eye. Tensing herself,
she blurted out the first social nicety which came to
mind:

'Er . . . what's your job?'

'I am a mujayad.'

That was *it*. She tried furiously to think how she could
attract Howard's attention. The mujayad was still looking at her, smiling. He smelt faintly of Pond's cold
cream. She tried to smile too, as if it was the most normal
thing in the world to be riding in a pick-up with an
Afghan freedom fighter.

From time to time, we'd pass a vehicle to which the
road had done its worst: more than once a whole

busload squatting in the dust would ask us to bear the news to the first service station in Nukundi, or take some passengers. Anna had used the first of these stops to tell Howard of the predicament. His eyes had lit up, and then he'd noticed her expression, squeezed her hand, and climbed again into the back. We'd occasionally pass buildings, some with electricity ('own generator' we were informed), some not. Otherwise there was virtually nothing. Other vehicles, including the Japanese pickups that had passed most frequently, were getting scarcer and scarcer as evening drew on. We were alone. The mujayad rattled an order and we jerked to a halt.

'Please get out.'

This was it, then. Anna's fear had been justified, while, in the back, Howard had been mentally writing the story of how we'd been given a lift by an Afghan rebel in the middle of the Baluchi desert. She began to open the door, slowly, playing for time. Four men versus one man and a woman. What could we do?

'Excuse me,' the mujayad said politely, 'We must go and pray.'

Spluttering with relieved laughter, Anna watched the four figures racing off the road, water bottles in hand. The evening breeze skimmed over the sand as they completed cursory hand to elbow, foot to knee, and facial ablutions, prostrated themselves towards the sunset on the desert floor, incanted, adjusted their robes, and hurried back to the truck. We'd now seen almost 180° of the Islamic world. In Istanbul, Mecca had lain to the south-east; here they simply used the setting sun.

'Okay?' The hood came down over the left eye as the smile flashed. A waft of Pond's and we were off again.

At long last the black road kissed our wheels with silence. We were dropped on the outskirts of Nukundi and directed to a 'hotl' for food and a bed if we couldn't find a tent spot suitably protected from marauding

Afghan rebels . . . Our mujayad had brushed aside our thank-yous with a matter of fact: 'Your country helps my country (trigger pulling motions with forefinger). It is natural that I should wish to help you,' which, on reflection, made us think that paying our taxes had its benefits after all. We were offered tin plates of curried vegetables, dal, or goat meat, swimming in ghee (clarified butter). They bubbled away in *daichies* – straight sided, handleless, silver pots – over holes scooped out of a mud wall with fires inside.

In the kerosene lamplight we watched the chapatti wallah kneading a tin bathtub full of dough with his forearm. He broke off a ball, stretched it deftly from hand to hand to form a thin disc, draped the *rotee* (the generic name for bread) over a wetted rag pad and . . . asked us to move. We were rather reluctant. Our bottoms were pleasantly if inexplicably warm on the mud verandah floor. When he lifted up the metal cover in front of us we saw why. We'd been sitting right on top of a huge fiery pit – the *tandour* for bread. He slapped the chapatti on to the inside wall and hooked it out three minutes later, crisply delicious with a soft inside (tough as old boots though when we'd carried it all day through the desert). We wondered whether it was something like the 'unleavened bread' the writer of Exodus seems to suggest is something of a privation after bread made with yeast (cf Ex 23:15). Except in the desert where hotels were too infrequent to be counted on, we all but stopped carrying our food. It was much easier and as cheap to eat under a hotel's bamboo matting roof.

That night we slept in the two-roomed house belonging to a schoolmaster. He'd brushed aside our attempt to pay for our meal, with a laughing 'Why not?', a phrase to become almost as familiar as 'Hello Mishter'. Why not, indeed? We capitulated, when it dawned on us that the hotel likewise had only two rooms whence issued all-male snores from at least twenty sleepers. At dawn we were woken by the schoolmaster, Syed Sultan Ibrahim Shah, rummaging quietly through our baggage. We feigned sleep as we tried to work out how best to tackle this one. He furtively withdrew his prayer mat from underneath our panniers and rolled it out as Mecca-wards as our recumbent bodies, taking up most of the small room, would allow.

The regularity of Moslem devotions, regardless of circumstances, took us some while to get used to. Moslems are supposed to pray five times a day – at daybreak, noon, mid-afternoon, after sunset, and in the early part of the night. Miles from anywhere, we'd hap upon a circle or square marked out in stones beside the road. The *mihrab* would be especially beautifully swept. There'd be a lone traveller praying in it, face down on the ground. There was something beautifully uncluttered and symbolic about this cameo of man's need to acknowledge God's omnipotence – not perhaps in spite of, but rather because of these starkest of surroundings – and wonderfully disciplined too. 'Remember how the LORD your God led you all the way in the desert . . . to humble you and test you in order to know what was in your heart.' (Deut 8:2)

Frequent repetition of set prayers wasn't new to us of course. Christians have done it here and there all through their history, but if the primary or only ingredient of a spiritual diet, it seemed to us rather unbalanced. It would have been good to be able to ask these men what other sorts of spiritual expression they had a taste for. It would have been good to know more about their sense of obligation to it all. Each time Moslems pray they're supposed to make a profession of sincerity beforehand. How much did they do it because they had to, or how much were they freed from that into something more personally felt?

In Pakistan, as in Turkey and Iran, most hotels and trucking stops had, at the very least, an area for worship marked out by a mat, or a niche in the wall facing Saudi. At wayside restaurants, flocks of fed travellers would wash the crumbs and gravy from their fingers, defecate in the nearest convenient place (turning one's back seemed to constitute invisibility and the long *cameezes* helped), and dive into the nearest mosque before continuing their journey. Moslems are taught, like Christians, that forgiveness is only to be obtained because God gives it to us freely. It is not obtainable by merit. Paradoxically, to be worthy of attaining it, they are taught unremitting prayer and performance of good works – one of which is hospitality. We were, of course often the target of this 'good work'. Once in a while, duty carried out, we'd find ourselves despatched with disconcerting haste.

One afternoon we were getting badly short of energy – having had sweet tea – but no food – pressed upon us in each village we passed through. We had the temerity to refuse an offer of a coke from an insistent man who surprised us by suddenly pulling the bike towards his hotl while Howard was holding it and looking in the other direction. It was food we needed, not liquid; and we were short of time. Our would-be benefactor, evidently a person not a little pleased to be the only English speaker in a crowd of otherwise unremarkable villagers, placed his shawl proprietorially in our front basket.

'You need to drink,' he said. 'Food is not important. Stop please and talk.'

He snapped his fingers for a minion to fetch the coke we'd just declined as politely as we could. We repeated ourselves to no avail.

'It is my duty. You must wait. You must drink. Vot is your country?'

Howard replied with equal decisiveness, 'I am sorry it is your duty, but I have already said that I have drunk and I'm looking for some food. Thank you again for your offer, but I must refuse. Please take your *chaddr* from my basket.'

He took not a blind bit of notice – just placed his hand fraternally on one handlebar and asked whether we were married or not. Howard offered him back his shawl. He refused to take it. Howard indicated that he'd put it on the ground if he didn't take it back. He still refused so Howard did so. Before we could move, however, a coke bottle was pushed, literally, to Howard's teeth with an unsmiling:

'My brother – drink. I have bought you coke. It is my duty.'

Anna's bottle was being pressed upon her only a little less forcefully. Howard thrust both open bottles into the front basket without meeting our donor's eye and cycled off extremely determinedly, obliging him to move smartly out of our way.

When something like that happens, you spend all day wondering whether your behaviour was excusable, and chide yourself for your cultural heavy-handedness. This was probably one of the most extreme of many situations in which we had the uncomfortable feeling that there was a curiously heartless aspect to what we were experiencing. We couldn't help thinking of Jesus's words: 'when you give ... do not let your left hand know what your right hand is doing'. None the less, a truly hospitable Moslem is unmatchable. Surely it's when giving becomes, in the words of the Prayer Book, 'not only our duty but our joy', that we know we're at the heart and not simply the letter of the law. Our experiences on the trip gave us a new perspective on Paul's otherwise rather bald 'Practise hospitality'. They also pointed out to us that when we learn how to give in the right spirit, it's usually only then that we really know how to receive. That was presumably why, for a large part of our journey, we were rather uptight beneficiaries.

Syed Sultan Ibrahim Shah was a 'heart' giver. We

were pressed to visit him miles up the road, where he was going to visit his family in a few days' time. Eyes shining, he produced a crumpled, official letter from his pocket granting 'Syed S I Shah, schoolteacher, leave to change his teaching post to Dalbandin on compassionate grounds'. It was like the schoolteachers in rural Turkey, though we had the feeling that the Turks would never have consigned a father of four to the sticks for three years without the means to take his family too. He shared out aerated white bread called 'double *rotee*' for breakfast, which tasted like sweetened Nimble. After we'd left, despite repeated invitations to stay just one more night – why not? – we discovered satsumas, biscuits, and nuts sneaked into our basket.

10

PADDLING PALMS AND PINCHING FINGERS

Tuesday, January 27th

That week of desert cycling might have been tedious; in fact it stands out in our memories as one of the happiest periods of the whole trip. For six days we negotiated a road whose surface, though infinitely superior to the one we'd started on, was variable. It often narrowed to the point where a vehicle could not pass with all four wheels on the surface. For the first three days it was almost consistently dead level. Like a genie flickering from a bottle, an oncoming vehicle, distorted by the shimmering air, might be visible on the horizon as far as four miles away. (We measured landmarks with our milometer.) As it drew closer, it became recognisable and then sped past in a cloud of dust that made us close our eyes and hold our breath. Apart from these intrusions we were very much alone. For the first time in our lives we found ourselves absolutely the only trace of life for as far as the eye could see: not a weed or a bug or a bird or a beetle in evidence. Nothing at all could be detected buzzing or rustling when one stopped to listen.

We didn't identify it precisely then but later we discovered that each of us had suffered waves of melancholy at that time and had been struggling with fears of the other's death. Our first guess was that we had been fearful for our safety. But no, that wasn't it. Afghan rebels were really the least of our problems and once in a while a bus or a lorry or a pick-up did overtake us (though we didn't see a private car till three days in). Our final diagnosis was that our journey was so satisfying, so simple, and stimulating an experience, so precious and such fun, our twosome working so well in our common endeavour, the answers to life's deepest questions so uncluttered and sure, that – like Cinderella just before midnight – we couldn't bear it to end, and couldn't believe it would last. Just as the idyll of the trip had to come to an end, so also, for some reason, would our time in this currently so pleasurable world.

'Desert' is an umbrella term for a multitude of terrains – not only flat, golden sands and an occasional palm tree. In time we had plenty of the latter, though our first tree was so many days in coming that we just stood and gazed with pure pleasure at its torn, drooping leaves and balding bole. There'd be hours of pancake flatness, then wrinkles and lappings in the sand lifted by the wind, that would build up into hummocks. Sometimes a mirage would play games with the land either side of the road, giving the impression that we were approaching some great wall or gully instead of the gently undulating dunes. For a while after there had been no vegetation at all, there might be a few shrivelled thistles, and then some shrubs which one could call green, if not verdant. The sand ranged from white to creamy, to yellow, to buff. When it verged on black, that usually meant mountains were encroaching. Thereafter, it would become shingly, then stony, then positively rocky. When the mountains came very close to the road, big outcrops of rock meant good tent cover. During those first Baluchi days, picking a tent spot undisturbed was not the fine art it later had to become.

It was almost incredible to contemplate, but we were

virtually on Alexander the Great's route again. Once more the road gave out. It looked as if it had been waterlogged last season and the resulting hard-packed surface was excellent for cycling. The trouble was, when the road disappeared, the lorries just peeled off across the sand in a variety of directions. They knew where they were going, but we didn't, and we weren't fast enough to keep up with them. After much trial and error, we began to use the sun and a particular mountain peak as our guide, and congratulated ourselves for photocopying a large scale map of the area at the Pakistan tourist office in Holborn, to supplement our Bartholomew one of the Indian Subcontinent. Being as scientific as we could we managed all right, if somewhat loop the loop.

A product of the spirit level conditions was the railway line running alongside. One afternoon, the words 'Darlington Steel 1909' stamped in it caught our eye. What a strange thing Empire was. It made us suddenly think of Elgar and Britain before the Great War, of an almost unbelievable time when it was economically viable to produce steel in the north of England, transport it to the ends of the earth, and lay a railway line to nowhere in particular. Perhaps it had been part of the as yet unfulfilled dream to have a railway service from Paris to the Punjab. It made us think of our honeymoon as well, when we'd wheeled our brand new tandem across the old cobbles in Darlington station. Perhaps these lengths of steel had passed that way, too?

Villages had grown up round the railway stations, at seven mile intervals. Between them – understandably, since even the soapy water which tainted our tea had to be brought in by rail or truck – there was precious little. A rattling and clattering behind us *without* a horn meant a lonely cyclist loaded up with pots and pans, tin plates and cups, all tied together with string, peddling and pedalling his wares from one station to the next. Cycling bow legged to accommodate a cluster of kettles hanging down from the crossbar and to avoid catching his pyjama-striped *sholwars* in the chain, a sturdy Indian bicycle at least thirty years old would draw abreast of us with a delighted,

'Cycle-wycle!' (To add a rhyming, nonsense word is commonplace in Subcontinental parlance and hasn't our connotations of baby talk.)

We'd have a companion, and predictable conversation, till we came to the next station when he'd veer off into the sand to the side of us. First he'd pass the mud mosque, forecourt and facing wall topped with thickly sculpted cross and circle shapes. He'd haul his bike across the line, then push it through the deepening sand to the mud houses nestling in the shade of the fifteen-foot concrete walls of the vast station building proper.

It didn't seem to matter how bad the road was, how hot it was, or how far it was out of their way, fellow cyclists usually found it irresistible to prove that these two on their fancy bike with fifteen gears and water bottles weren't going to daunt a Pakistani on a gearless boneshaker. Off they'd go, trousers ballooning, shirt tails flapping wildly, glitzy sandals going nineteen to the dozen. If grandpa was sitting on the back (Subcontinentals aren't ones to waste vital transport space: we'd often see a family of four variously distributed on a single bicycle), he'd join in the breathless laughter, cackling and wheezing. Stick thin legs bouncing up and down in time to the various tinsel pennants and plastic folderols attached to every spare inch of the old frame, he'd hang on for dear life. Usually it was a near thing for, on the flat, our fifteen gears didn't give us much of an advantage. Nor could we muster up the motivation to race all out; we had several more hours to do in the day, as likely as not.

The race would come to an end as suddenly as it had begun, with the other bike making a sharp, unannounced

dive across our front wheel to join some track in the
sand, visible to their eyes only, leading to a similarly
invisible village. As unaccountably as they'd arrived, so
would they go, with a few cock-a-snook wheelies, and
the last we'd see of them would be a shimmer on the
horizon before we were quite alone again. In Baluchistan these occasional contests were not so frequent as to
be tedious, and the country was still new enough for
them not to be the energy-sapping endurance tests they
were unfortunately to turn into.

Of all our chance acquaintances, we enjoyed our times
with the Afghanis the most. It was not only because they
drank their black tea with a sweet or a lump of
unrefined, ungranulated sugar wedged between upper
and lower front teeth instead of putting it in with the
water. This meant that we who dislike sweet tea could
save our sweetener till afterwards (they found this
hilarious). It was also because they were unfailingly
gracious and dignified towards us and one another.
They had the same ability as the Kurds and Arabs down
near the Syrian border to entertain us with the least
amount of fuss, while ensuring we had the best they
could give. Unlike the Baluchis – though even they had
a relative restraint we only appreciated when we began
to be mobbed daily in the more populated provinces of
Sind and Punjab – their fascination with the bike and us
was always courteous.

They'd often squat in a row of three or four, deliber-
ating together on how the bike worked. The hub brake
gave the most trouble. They knowingly informed one
another, that it was the 'engine' and that the water
bottles had petrol in them. (The wire to the hub brake
was obviously the petrol feed.) There was none of the
poking and pinching that the people on the plains were
to do as a matter of course. We never felt worried for
our luggage. On one occasion, one of the men couldn't
tear himself away, even after his friends had come back

to the fire. We watched him shake his head in disbelief. About five minutes later he was still there. He shook his head again, and without taking his eyes off the bike lay down on his side in the sand, head resting on his hand, to get comfortable for a good long look. He would have gone to sleep there and dreamt of double cycles for sure if we hadn't had to move on.

Anna's expectation that Pakistan, in respect of her status as a woman, was going to be a relief after Iran had been fuelled by the assurances of the official who'd issued our Pakistani visas in Teheran. Accordingly, with no reliable information to put her right until meeting Pakistani Christians in Quetta, she'd whipped off her headscarf and heavy jacket at the first opportunity and was cycling in T-shirt and her Turkish *sholvars*. She was planning on sending her sweltering boots ahead as soon as she could find a cool pair of shoes suitable for the bicycle, and a large post office. She was just about able to wear them still by taking out the laces, which hardly flattered her appearance, but did let in a little more air.

The fact that for the first three days we saw perhaps one woman to every two hundred men, and then from afar, covered from head to foot and never alone, didn't worry us unduly. We began to get more of a feel for things one day in a station settlement. We were wheeling the bike along, looking for the hotel we'd been 'directed' to, when a tall septuagenarian dressed in a flowing white robe and elegant turban, halted us with what we took to be a smile of pure, old man's delight. He held out his hand beaming. Anna, being the one whose hands were free, naturally took it. His smile widened, pushing a curled and greased moustachio further up toward equally groomed and imposing eyebrows. He spoke to us in his language. We replied in ours. He was still holding Anna's hand. He spoke some more and Howard, making eating motions, suggested 'hotl?' Anna suddenly felt the old man's little finger curl inwards from the hand still holding hers, and begin to tickle her palm suggestively. Howard, quite unaware, was still trying to establish where he could get his dinner.

'Er, darling, this man's tickling my palm. Do you think I should take my hand away, or is it a cultural thing?' she faltered.

Howard paused, torn between the anger that naturally came up when someone insulted his wife, and the possibility that this was quite different from Shakespearean England, where 'paddling palms and pinching fingers' were definitely out, replied 'Keep smiling and withdraw your hand gently.'

Little by little, from observation and what people told us, we pieced together a code of conduct for Anna as a white woman in that culture. Given the fact that she was doing the unheard of anyway, by riding a bicycle, we hoped we proved our willingness not to offend. As far as the bicycle allowed, Anna tried to get her clothes into line with native women's dress which offered a range of options.

Most extreme was the *burkha*, a cone of material resembling a shuttlecock, that concealed the body literally from head to toe. The top was shaped like a little cap from which hung a tent of material, often in exquisite narrow pleats. To see, a little oblong lattice was crocheted at eye level, sometimes repeating the fine embroidery stitches in the cap or round the hem. There might be slits for the arms – covered to the wrist. They were worn more in small towns which were, as in the West, frequently more conservative than villages or large towns. Indeed, in small towns, it was a status symbol to wear one, for it showed you were firmly in the middle classes. The really low class workers in the fields couldn't possibly have managed with one of these.

The strange thing about *burkhas*, like the saris and other all-over coverings, was that though their aim was to conceal, they were often the most eye-catching of

magentas, brilliant blues, or deep oranges. We came to
the conclusion that this had to do with the same impulse
that transformed the buses, frilled and furbelowed
bicycles and tractors, decorated radios and livestock.
Hindus rather condescendingly single out this pretti-
fying tendency as a hallmark of Moslems. Perhaps it's
partly an over-reaction to the original Islamic prohibition
against representing the natural world in art because it
comes too close to idolatry: if you can't depict 'real'
things, go to town on embellishment. On a more mun-
dane level, it's also a way of distinguishing your stock
from your neighbour's. If saris or *sholwar-cameez* (these
were for women as well) were worn, the *dupatta*, a long
wide scarf covering both head and breast, or even
completely veiling the face, was essential.

Like *burkhas* and saris, a *dupatta* was impractical on the
bike. Anna resigned herself again to her rejected headscarf and, at the first opportunity, had a *cameez* made on
Quetta's Jinnah Road by a tailor in the employ of an
Afghani refugee. Women's *cameez* came in so many styles
– calf length, knee length, full, tight, dress type, shirt like,
embroidered – not that it was easy to design one wide
enough in the skirt so that she could get on the saddle, but
narrow and short enough not to get caught in the chain.
The Afghani's beautiful mirrorwork and embroidered
wares caught our eye, and his unobtrusive manner, in
contrast to his relentlessly persistent companions in the
trade, won our custom. Business was done over a cup of
green tea.

In respect of their appearance, the Koran says that
women should 'guard their unseen parts. They that
defame honourable women shall be given eighty lashes.'
This, as is so often the case with religious dicta of any
persuasion, has been so extremely interpreted by men
and by custom that, not only are women consigned to
trammelling, often stifling, dress (allowed to remove
their *dupatta* only in the presence of their immediate

family) but they are forced to use the communal tap, that's frequently the only place for washing, after dark and fully dressed. After this, it came as quite a shock to see bare-breasted Nepali women at the village pump, seemingly quite unconcerned. The discretion which most men in Nepal would seek not to look or pass too close seemed entirely right. In Pakistan however, it appeared that such common decency was out of the question. Here it was the women who bore the burden of both male and female sexuality, despite the Koranic injunction to 'tell the believing men to lower their gaze and be modest . . . Allah is aware of what they do.'

Women always seemed to keep their side of the bargain. If the *dupatta* had slipped from their heads during their exertions in the fields, they'd replace it as soon as they saw us coming. Sometimes they'd turn their backs, sometimes even run out of sight. In a rural economy, where female labour is indispensable, one way of partially solving the tension between the need to remain out of sight and the need to work, was to leave a screen of unharvested crop abutting the road, behind which they could scythe in relative privacy. It was women who suffered the medical consequences, in the most conservative areas, of not being able to go out into the fields to relieve themselves during the daylight hours, for fear of being seen. It was women who suffered the results of houses designed with two passage-ways and a suite of rooms at the back to avoid the meeting of the sexes. In the Koran, wives of the prophet are told 'stay in your homes' and many women since have had to follow suit. This immuring in turn became an excuse to leave them all the household tasks, and not even the release of enjoying the company which came in and out of the front door, and for whom they cooked and cleaned.

Men, though, seemed unable to keep their side of the bargain, certainly where Anna was concerned. There was probably a combination of reasons for that of which uppermost was irrepressible curiosity and the fact that they recognised that the rules needed somehow to be modified for a white woman. The worst analysis was that her whiteness denoted promiscuity, for the attitude in this part of the world towards women can encompass very little beyond one of two extremes. Either her sexuality is so precious she is to be covered from head to foot, not allowed out in the bazaar except on the rarest occasions, and then always accompanied; or she is the harlot of harlots, every man's property, and the butt of the lewdest vulgarity. The one attitude, of course, breeds the other. White women for a number of reasons, almost invariably fall into the latter category. This has something to do with the hippy trail out East in the 1960s, the infiltration of Western sex videos and films, and incipient tourism which renders the Westerner the subject of the liveliest discussion and the closest questioning.

From these the Pakistanis draw true inferences about latter day, Western sexual mores but extend them into false generalisations. Via this generalising process, an all too common train of thought on seeing a Westerner can run something like this: white, therefore Christian, therefore pig-eating, therefore contemptible; Christian, therefore polytheistic; white, therefore having much more money than is good for them; white, therefore having a taste for women who have passed themselves round the community, therefore despicable; white, therefore alcohol drinkers, therefore drunkards; and so on.

The complicating factor is that white also symbolises all things progressive in technology and materialism, both of which are highly desirable. White also spells 'aid' which, along with certain bequests from the Raj, such as pukka roads, the railway system, and the irrigation system, is gratefully – even effusively – acknowledged. Another major factor in the whole uneasy equation is the strict Islamic enjoinder to treat travellers well. The equation does not, cannot, balance. Its various terms go some way, however, to explaining the veritable panoply of responses we engendered.

In time, assured that hand-shaking between men and women was not in order she refused to comply, giving the faintest smile for politeness' sake and lowering her eyes immediately. If forced she would give the merest touch of her fingertips before withdrawing. If they were really persistent, and had enough English she'd ask them why they treated her in a way they wouldn't their own women.

What we called her 'demure and downcast look' came to seem the best remedy in all encounters of any type with the men, both for her peace of mind, and as an attempt not to 'cause anyone to stumble.' (1 Cor 10:32). What an imperfect remedy, though, for a situation that needs major surgery rather than an interim plaster.

Job rightly took the problem on his own shoulders: 'I made a covenant with my eyes not to look lustfully at a girl' (Job 31:1) It's not simply a case of male chauvinism and female repression, though. Society as a whole was missing out, and we couldn't help feeling that the seven-year-old boys who'd hound the girl from the crowd round the bike were as much victims of their situations as perpetuators of it: 'the sin of the fathers' being passed from generation to generation. (Ex 20:4)

One of the most present images we have of God is the combination of man and woman. 'So God created man in his own image, in the image of God he created him; male and female he created them.' (Gen 1:27). God is not best described as being so great and distant that He's sexless. Early Hebrews were bold enough to believe that He was able to be described as the fusion and fruit of men *and* women. When Paul thought of how close Jesus comes to mankind, he thought of how a husband loves his wife (Eph 5:25). In Pakistan we didn't like to make hasty judgments because we were just passing through, were biased, and had no language, but we couldn't help noticing the major imbalance. When we read the Koran it seemed to buttress our evaluation:

> You may marry other women who seem good to you; two, three, or four of them . . . A male shall inherit twice as much as the female . . . Men have authority over women because Allah has made the one superior to the other and they spend their wealth to maintain them . . . As for those from whom you fear disobedience, admonish them and send them to beds apart, and beat them . . . Women are your fields: go then into your fields and do as you please . . . We have made lawful to you the wives whom you have granted dowries and the slave girls whom Allah has given you as booty . . . You may put off any of your wives whom you please and take to your bed any of them you please . . . If any of your women commit fornication, confine them to their houses till death overtakes them.

The tone of this contrasts strikingly with our own much older Song of Songs where God has laid out a startlingly candid picture of what heights he intends for men and women together and as individuals.

Christian teaching wasn't all plain sailing for us in the early days of our marriage though. The Bible can be a difficult book to read, and even more difficult to trust in. Anna found it hard, fresh from a feminist, secular background to accept that chestnut in Ephesians 5:22 'Wives, submit to your husbands'. Howard wasn't temperamentally too keen on her doing so, either. Gradually though, we're realising that God really does desire every good thing for us, and find an outworking bound up in the previous verse, the one that critics of 'Christian

repressiveness of women' seem always to miss out:
'Submit to *one another*' (Eph 5:21). At our wedding Anna
vowed to 'honour and obey' and Howard consented to
her doing so. Howard obviously doesn't like telling her
what to do, and she doesn't like putting him in a position
where he has to. In practice then, no one orders anyone
around.

We asked our gentle, perceptive, Afghani tailor to
explain how you could possibly love with all your heart
('as Christ loved the church') more than one wife at the
same time. We feared that the idea of love within
marriage, being omitted from Islamic teaching, might
actually render the question irrelevant, but he considered it seriously, then avoided the answer with the
observation that financial considerations made polygamy
a rarity in practice. We pushed him to explain why men
could be polygamous but not women and he admitted
defeat, but – one in the eye for us – he said he deeply
loved his wife.

The irony of sexual segregation is that both sides miss
out on any relationship which would serve both to
reduce the depersonalising of women and provide some
realistic preparation for marriage. We were told by the
nurses who had to tend them and the missionary women
who'd got close to them, that the wedding night, far
from being the highest experience of mutual love, was
all too often the worst shock of a young girl's life.
Sometimes physically unready because of her extreme
youth, she might be totally ruined, both for childbearing
and for sexual relations with her husband by his literal-
istic interpretation of the Koran's 'women are your
fields'.

To add to the pressure, the wedding day is the first
protracted meeting of any kind that either bride or
groom will have had with a member of the opposite sex
outside the immediate family. In some houses we visited,
it was only patrilinear males who were allowed access to

the women of the family. Uncles, cousins, and nephews were all too remote, and they were segregated as Howard was. In contrast to the teaching in Genesis first to 'leave' your parents and then 'cleave' to your spouse, it was usual for the girl to go home to her mother the day after the wedding. She'd stay for a month or so – some say to recover.

We had an instructive afternoon with a Pakistani Christian couple. We generally found it difficult getting at these issues because the women were never around to give their view and, of course, language was mutually minimal. This time though, the husband spoke English. As the wife was backing out of the room after bringing tea, we strongly urged her to stay and, after demurring, she did sit with us. This in itself was an unprecedented departure from the rest of our experience in Pakistan. When Anna opened the questions, however, thinking them safer coming from a woman, the answers revealed the extent of the problem. The conversation foundered from the outset. Anna simply asked whether she'd like to go to the bazaar alone sometimes.

'It would depend whom I went with,' came the reply.

Fearing a misunderstanding, Anna came at it from another, and then yet another angle. The limitation of the woman's experience and her ignorance of the alternatives rendered her unable to grasp the question. Each reply came from a presupposition of the status quo and there was no breaking out of it. Even the converts from Islam, the very ones who might change things were still bound by the prevailing culture. What did this woman make of 'There is neither Jew nor Greek, slave nor free, male nor female, for you are all one in Christ Jesus'? (Gal 3:28).

Back in the desert, one meeting, once more with an old man, has remained in our minds. 'Captain William', as we came to call him, was again our lunch companion at a hotel, ushered thence, as the only English speaker of the village, by respectful younger men, that he might winkle our story out of us.

He told us his story, too.

'I spent seven years in your country, Mishter. Ledbury Road, it was, and it was very cold' (drawing the frayed Harris tweed jacket tighter over his *cameez* and shaking his head kindly at the folly of our bare arms – it was January and, by lunch-time, in the mid 70°s). 'We all wore shoes' (momentary ruminative surprise at his own bare brown toes in the dust). 'Even the women wore shoes . . . I have never seen such a bicycle as yours – never seen such a big bicycle . . . Not even in Britain have I seen such a big bicycle . . . And it was very cold in your country when I worked on the railways, Mishter' (a faint smile of remembrance). 'And when I came back from Ledbury Road . . . Do you know Ledbury Road, Mishter? After seven years in your country, I took a boat to Karachi with Captain William. Captain William was his name, and we took many days . . . Perhaps three, perhaps thirteen. I can't remember how long it took to get back. Ledbury Road, do you not know it? Captain William was very good to us' (old man's gratitude misting his once button-black eyes). 'But I never went back.'

He became aware again of the uncomprehending listeners, squatting around us.

'They have never seen such a big – such a very big bicycle. We do not have such cycles in Pakistan. But in your country you have many things. I came back in nineteen . . . nineteen thirty eight – on a big, big boat – to Karachi. It was very cold. This . . . double cycle . . . I never have seen.'

We wondered about the gaps and omissions. What memories had filled them? We urged him to recall the name of a town or a county, but there was nothing. What kind of treatment had this gentle, old man received as a 'Paki' in Ledbury Road, the experience which rendered him, despite his dotage, the wise one among the squatting young bucks?

Finding a place to pitch the tent in the desert had introduced us to new problems. The sand would often be too dry and loosely packed to hold the pegs, or too hard-packed to get them in. This, despite the fact that in such a setting there was hardly a dearth of empty sites, kept the urgency factor in tent-erecting time. Sometimes, it had been cold which necessitated speed; sometimes dogs; sometimes the possibility of onlookers; sometimes the prospect of total, unstarlit darkness; sometimes, in the mountains, the problem of solid rock. The evening after our meeting with Captain William our eyes hadn't deceived us when, hauling the bike over the railway tracks to put some distance between us and the occasional night vehicle, we tested a likely, browner belt of sand with the penknife.

As we began to slot the pole together and unroll the tent, an unnatural wind began to blow up. We'd noticed it on previous evenings and couldn't account for it. It was blowing at ground level. Standing still, we usually couldn't feel it, but could see the sand wisping round our feet. It had never been quite so strong as that night, though, and it was getting stronger, causing us to waste precious minutes as the sun sank, rewrapping our bread and checking all our zips. Sand, whether in your sandwich or your underwear, was a pest. We tried to slot the pole into its sheath, but the tent tugged out of our hands. One held the pole, now gritty in the joints, while the other chased the body across the tamarisk. By the time we got it back, the guys were all tangled. We unpicked the knots, squinting through dust and sand, and getting mouthfuls of it as we spoke. We remembered the laughing young man at the camping shop in Knightsbridge answering our question as to the resilience of the pole:

'I knew someone who broke their pole when they

were drunk, but otherwise you'd have to have a pretty strong wind. Anyway, you've got the repair kit.'

We decided to take no chances. We knew we were pretty much equidistant from stations, and didn't fancy cycling in search of shelter on what was going to be a moonless night. We laid the canvas down and tried to slot the pole in horizontally. We almost made it. The pole was nearly through when a sudden gust whipped the whole thing upright. We didn't let go quickly enough. There was a snap, and through the twilight haze we saw our igloo tent take on a much more conventional triangular shape.

There was no chance of just kipping down in that sand storm. Anna looked helplessly over the landscape, as if to conjure out of the massing, filtered greyness in which now not even the road or tracks were visible, some friendly 'Hello Mishter, can I help you?' For once there was none. Howard suddenly, uncharacteristically, began issuing orders:

'Tent bag. Repair kit. Pliers.'

We should have tested that famous repair kit in the security of Southwark Park SE1, like the tent itself. We'd assumed that the two inch long tubes one was supposed to be able to slip over the break as an interim mend would fit smoothly over the pole. They didn't. An hour later, having resorted to Nivea cream as a lubricant, we were forced to admit defeat, with sand lodged in every joint.

Night had fallen blackly, and the wind had not abated. Just finding our way back to the road was a soberingly zig-zag performance which brought back bad memories of the awful Tek-Teks. Our sand-filled clothes and shoes rubbed and itched like mad. Not that we attended too much to creature comforts – even to food after our seventy-mile day's cycling. We had the bumps and pot holes of a very poor stretch of road to deal with, without even knowing where it was leading us.

At length, after slipping off the tarmac down the bank a couple of times, we spied a pinprick of light to our left, abandoned the road, and made for it. Two men were sitting beside a tiny brush fire in a mud room. We couldn't understand a word either spoke; no Captain William here. We showed them our tent and made snapping noises. Not a flicker of recognition – not surprisingly, because the only tents they'd ever seen were nomads' animal skin affairs. Here were we with our Gore-Tex and aluminium alloy. We changed tack, acted out yawns and rubbed weary thighs, pointing at the bike, then, hopefully, at the adjoining mud chamber. Our mimes were wasted for they'd caught sight of the bike. For the next five minutes it was no longer we who were the object of their amazed contemplation.

It was one of the very few occasions on the trip that we felt really uneasy with someone. Our disquiet sprang partly from the fact that we could barely see them in the dying light of the fire and after we'd proffered Homayun's barely started kilo of pistachios as something to share the bag never came back to us. Howard shone our torch at our faces and then again in the direction of the next room. There was an excited expostulation, at what we couldn't guess. Were they bartering? They took the batteries out of the torch, pointed to them, to themselves, to us, to the room. Finally we got it. If we gave them the torch (or the batteries – we weren't sure which) we could have the room. We agreed, reluctantly enough, and because we still couldn't see their eyes, took the bike in with us and propped it and two large stones against the door before we lay down.

We have to be honest; we were both thinking 'why should they have our torch?' There were miles to go before we might get a new one. We didn't even know if we could get a new one in Pakistan. By morning, however, we'd changed our minds. We remembered how they'd pounced upon it – as if it were the most desirable item imaginable. We hadn't even bought the darned thing ourselves anyway. We'd picked it up off the Turkish highway. We considered the price of a hotel room (not in Pakistan – that would have purchased half a battery at the most) at home. We were shamed by the memory of the hospitality we'd received for so many months. Suddenly we recalled Christ's words: 'If some-one takes your coat, let him have your shirt as well'. How could we be so slow? When we emerged the younger man had disappeared. We gave the old man the torch. He didn't wait to see us off. The last we saw of him was an immodestly unwinding *lungi* as he hot-footed it up to the main station complex we saw now for the first time, clasping his precious prize.

Some way down the road from far over the dunes where no houses were apparent, came floating snatches of song, to our untutored ears indistinguishable from an Irish ballad, hyphenated and hiccuped as the singer negotiated a bumpy bit of ground. Reaching the main road, and catching sight of us, he uttered a long drawn out '*Shabash*' (the accent firmly on the second syllable) – that all purpose term of appreciation that is to the Subcontinental what *Cok güzel* is to Turks. We pedalled amicably together into the rising sun. Gradually, we were joined by more singers, rattling out of nowhere. They jumped off abruptly at a railway crossing. A Pakistani might have bells on his bike but rarely did he have such a thing as a functioning brake. We had a cup of tea then they unstrapped their spades from their bikes.

A British navvy would look askance at you if you handed him a spade whose blade turned back up towards its handle at an angle of forty-five degrees. This ready-made scoop made it possible to carry loads about the place with less effort. Most things Westerners prefer to do sitting or standing, Subcontinentals perform squatting, so the design presumably has something to do with this as well. A warm-hearted British Civil Service wife in days gone by, during her annual sojourn in Quetta to escape the heat of the Indus valley, provided the town road sweepers with 'proper' long-handled brooms. To her, the thought of bending and squatting all day with their two foot long clusters of sticks or sturdy grasses was intolerable. To this day, they say, long handled brooms adorn the walls of sweeper houses, immortalised as curios of the Raj, while the sweepers themselves go on as they always have done, in packs of four or five with hankies over their faces, bending and squatting. As for us expatriates, we're hardly any more adaptable. But just try squatting with the soles of your feet flat on the ground for any length of time, and you'll soon appreciate that it's actually a question of upbringing determining anatomy.

The Taftan to Quetta train goes down on Sundays and up on Mondays. The railwaymen kept their kit and took their siesta in little three-sided huts right beside the line, which they shared with the camel drovers. They were made of old sleepers, rushes and rags. One clear, starlit night we took it into our heads to sleep in one of these without stopping to think what day of the week it was. As we lay in our sleeping bags on top of our (by now mended) tent as groundcover, we tried to recall whether we'd ever slept outside in January before. Gazing up into the sky, our musings were interrupted by falling stars arcing across the heavens. Thoroughly contented with life, we fell asleep in the deep desert stillness.

One o'clock in the morning – something terrible was happening. Our peaceful slumbers were being ripped deafeningly apart. The Sunday train was bearing down upon us. Clasped together in an embrace of fear so tight it knocked the breath out of us, we knew our last hour had come. Our dream befuddled minds forgot in the clatter and roar that rails are to trains as husband is to wife. To anyone looking out of the train from Quetta as it passed us that night, we must have looked like two terrified rabbits caught in the headlights as we stared petrified, half in, half out, of our sleeping bag.

The terrain was changing and we were beginning to cycle long stretches right in the lee of the mountains we were going to have to climb to get to Quetta. We even had to change gear once or twice to accommodate inclines in the road, from which we looked down upon great white expanses of salt marsh, glistening like new fallen snow. One afternoon a new noise came to our ears – a steady 'put, put, put' echoing off the wall of a large black rock. We rounded the bend and there before us was a sight for sore eyes: intermittent plots of young, green wheat, shaded here and there by a clump (not just one – a clump!) of trees. It wasn't until we were splashing the bubbling water all over ourselves, fully dressed as Anna had to remain, throwing it at one another, replacing the stale water in our bottles, and doing our much needed washing at the pump, that we realised how constrained we'd felt by the scarcity: apologetic and guilty every time we'd had to request a refill of the precious stuff. It gushed clean and so cool out of a large pipe, drawn up from the water table by a beautiful old steam engine from a workshop in Lahore. It sat in its own little engine house and was immaculately maintained by an adoring engineer, who took Howard in to show it to him.

The fields were divided by neat little irrigation channels. It looked just like a charity calendar photograph and indeed, as pumps grew more frequent, but by no means the norm, we'd be pointed to the sign which gave the date and the cost of UNICEF's sinking a tube well. The desert floor, now that the water had come, was studded with dwellings, singly and in clusters, and punctuated always by mud mosques, crenellating sculptures picked out in white, the last thing to catch the final pink hues of those stupendous sunsets. Putting up the tent kept us out of doors at the going down of the sun throughout the journey: magical, last minutes in the canopy of the heavens which remain rosy in our memories when more exact reminiscences have slipped below the horizon. For the first time that night we had difficulty quitting the road without anyone seeing us and finding a tent spot out of sight. We slept with lights of human habitation on the horizon, hearing the odd bark of a dog, and with the distant put, put-ing of the water engine to lull us to sleep. We felt as if we were back at the hub of things!

Our road companions increased – human and animal. We'd pass a little donkey here, one or two sheep there, unfamiliar cattle we later identified as buffalo, and dogs, for the most part mangy specimens with ribs protruding, typical of the Subcontinent. Last but by no means least, there were the camels.

They would have seen us from miles away, but wouldn't let it spoil their lunch. They'd stand, top jaw wildly miscalculating width of bottom, chomping on some scrumptiously prickly desert foliage they'd hobblingly happed upon, front legs tied loosely together to prevent them from straying. As we approached, they'd go right on disdainfully mumbling, and slowly swivel their heads round 180° as we passed. If we chanced to look back, they'd still be staring after us, sneering and munching, but it wasn't that they were interested – oh no, nothing so demeaning as that. They'd seen it all before, and weren't in the least impressed. They were like an old hookah smoker we passed one morning as we cycled into a town in search of breakfast. He didn't bat an eyelid when we pedalled slowly past him over the cobbles. When we exited the same way, accompanied this time by the horde who'd come to marvel as we ate, he was still there on his doorstep and again, not a flicker of interest. He just went right on blowing bubbles.

Camels came in all shapes and sizes: big, small, tawny, chocolate brown, frisky babies, downy damsels, hairy youths, fraying middle-aged trendies, balding grand-parents. Somehow, when they had someone on their backs, the hip motion resulting from their advancing such long, thin legs made both animal and passenger appear complicit in the sauciest, most exaggerated, bottom-wiggle imaginable. We wondered what the RSPCA would say about the mirrors on their foreheads, the henna stars on their cheeks, or about the donkeys with bright orange hocks or pink spots, cows with coloured horns, and fluorescent chickens. Whatever the whys and wherefores, if you caught a camel's eye after laughing at it, the look you received in return unquestionably denoted a headmasterly injunction to 'wipe that foolish smirk off your face'.

Inevitably we had to hit something larger than a village sooner or later. We'd been getting quite excited about this place Nushki, written in larger letters on the map. It promised to be our first Pakistani town. Only a week later, we were by-passing them whenever possible. They made Taftan seem offish by comparison. The first cluster of shops in Nushki Bazaar were all bakeries of one sort or another. We bought a sponge cake which the baker turned out of its tin as we pointed to the shelf. We walked along the road peeling off the newspaper that served as greaseproof paper. It was oily, and smelt faintly of soda, but it was fresh, and we ate it with a gusto that resulted from our desert diet. We passed cobblers where they were making sandals out on the mud in front of their shop-dens cutting up huge pieces of leather with appropriately huge scissors, trimming with razor blades, and banging nails into the wooden heels. The selection was overwhelming. You could have embroidery, gold lamé, patent leather, beads, tassels, or mirrors. The world was your oyster but the straps had to be wide to take it all.

A fat, self-important eleven-year-old panted up to us on the shiniest, newest bike we'd seen since Iran, and shoved through the throng.

'You need hotl, Mishter?'

'We need tea and a rest.' (The journey out of town would be our first steep climb for weeks, and it was exceedingly hot.)

'You come to my hotl.'

'A rest': that was a joke. The child snapped his fingers and the tea wallah gave us a pot encrusted with flies. Flies were an unavoidable fact of life, markedly worse in towns. They were sated with sweet, milky tea. However we tried to spell it out, *'cheenee nehi'* ('no sugar') was never regarded as anything but our Western aberration. We'd think we had made ourselves clear and when it was brewed they'd hand it to us beaming 'no sugar, no sugar – just a *tiny* bit.' It wasn't worth making a fuss. They knew best and syrup was best. To be fair, too, there was a rationale behind it all: like the ubiquitous ghee, it was a merciful appetite cutter, and an energy booster, in a country where there wasn't always enough to eat. We sat down on a *charpoy* (string strung wooden bedframe) – with as many townspeople as could also push for a space. Our quiet, afternoon cup of tea to refresh us before the mountains had become an elbow-jogged interrogation, though with a couple of new permutations – 'Vair are you?' and 'Vair do you?' – which, if we were too frazzled to be amused by them, at least gave us pause for thought. We answered some questions, particularly 'She your wife?', which Howard had taken to responding to with a curt, surprised, 'Of course', in an effort to dispel the expectation that, because we were Westerners, we couldn't get married like any civilised people. The crowd grew, poking and commenting till, driven to distraction, we gave up and remounted.

We asked for a space ahead of us. They closed in even more. Anna got off and gestured so explicitly that a foot-wide tunnel was grudgingly allowed us. We'd just pushed down on the pedal when a newcomer arrived and stepped right into the newly cleared road to see what was in the space. That was the signal for everyone else to break ranks once more. We started all over again. Howard made road-clearing gestures, folding his arms with an 'I'm waiting' expression. Some of them saw the point and stepped back a little. Those behind couldn't see any of this, simply felt themselves being shoved backwards, and responded likewise, pushing people forwards into our path. We looked at one another helplessly. Then Anna caught sight of a policeman.

To give him his due, once we looked beseechingly he gallantly came forward, explaining to us phraseology that was to become familiar, that these were 'ignorant, uneducated' people, so we must excuse their 'rude country' curiosity, then smartly laid about them with his truncheon. The astonishing thing was not that they closed in again a moment later, but that they scattered without any indignation at their beating. Finally we got away.

This came to be entirely typical here of our crowd encounters – and most encounters in Pakistan were, by definition, crowd encounters. We devised a few strategies to lighten the strain. Whenever possible we'd eat in the first place we came to in a village so that we didn't attract quite such a large crowd as right in the centre. If there was a choice, we'd go to an establishment big enough to get the bike and us inside, and out of sight.

Once in a while there was what was called a 'family room' for the seclusion of travelling ladies. If only a curtained off area, it was hardly worth the bother. Half way through our first *paratha* – tasty layered and sautéd chapatti – we'd suddenly become aware of a row of eyes underneath and to the side which, as soon as they'd caught ours, took that as an invitation to pull the annoying piece of material aside and join us. If we could

bolt ourselves in, we'd do so and risk being closed in with
the rats and mice which were as much a part of tea-
houses as the curried vegetables.

If it was very hot, and we were very tired, we occasionally established a 'margin of desperation': an imaginary
boundary line between ourselves and them, such as the
edge of the verandah, or the threshold. The Pakistanis
love a game. We'd raise warning fingers at anyone who
infringed it, and they'd usually retreat behind it again to
a titter from the crowd, and shout their questions from
there.

It is impossible to convey the weariness that comes
from hours of cycling in subtropical temperatures, the
need it produces for entire relaxation, and the speed
with which predictable conversation becomes stale. We
wondered why anyone had ever longed to be famous.
We had to learn, though, that in the East, the gratifica-
tion of curiosity is viewed as a human right. At first, we
assumed that the amazed squeals and grunts that met
our ears as we cycled past, the 'wowees' and 'wa-haas'
must be coming from schoolboys. In fact it was as much
older and old men. Men of all ages would stand around,
hand in hand, or arms round one another's shoulders,
simply giggling at anything and everything. (Homo-
sexuality does exist in Pakistan, not surprisingly considering the strictures of male-female relationships, but
usually this kind of physical contact denoted no more
than friendship.)

We were a little daunted to be coming across signs to a
place called Lakpass, not marked on our maps, but
evidently some miles before Quetta. We couldn't be
certain of the exact distance because the kilometre signs
never quite agreed with the older, white milestones
(there could be as much as a three mile discrepancy) but
we guessed from our map contours and information
half understood over tea, that the road reached its
highest point at this Lakpass. Grinding up on to the

steppe after Nushki had been the very steepest cycling of the journey, and a shock after all that flat desert. We were determined to be more prepared for this. Accordingly, when we saw the wall of rock ahead of us and lorries crawling round its hairpin bends, we stopped for a second breakfast, listening to World Service news on someone's radio about exploits at a Dockland printing house just a mile from where we used to live. It sounded so bizarre in this setting. For extra sugar we bought cane from the squabbling vendors in the middle of the road who leapt out at every bus, passing up home-made sweets and biscuits and catching the rupees as they were thrown down.

We knew by now that the visible summit of a mountain road was never the actual summit, and rubbed Algipan into our calves to approving comments from onlookers who'd urged us to go up by lorry. We slipped into gear and began the climb, mute once more to conserve our energy. Eight or nine minutes later we looked at one another feeling very silly. We'd reached the top. Lakpass is just a hump in the road, albeit a huge one. It happens to be the tallest spot for miles around, but it's still only a hump. We hurtled down the other side, and careered into Quetta reeking of Algipan, with enough unused calories to see us through till evening.

Quetta: after our days in the desert, the bustling bazaar, the motorised rickshaws like the old bubble cars back home, the variety of food, the Christian hospital where we were kindly accommodated, the newspapers – all contributed to make it a veritable metropolis. This was where Field Marshal Montgomery had had a summer house. The spectacular formations and fissures in the cupping mountains are the result of one of the world's worst earthquakes in 1935. This also explains the seeming newness of Quetta though it is placed at a crucial junction on what has always been one of the major trading routes to Afghanistan.

Metropolis it might be, but that didn't daunt the
livestock that variously pecked and plodded, trotted and
darted its way, supervised or not, through the traffic. If
we ever suffered from culture shock — something the
slowness of our transition generally made us unaware of
— it was probably in having to come to terms with the fact
that any Subcontinental high street is like a day at
Smithfield.

We stuffed ourselves on *pakora* — spiced battered
vegetables — and toxically multicoloured sweets which
we selected, half-horrified, from oozing shiny pyramids.
Some were fudgelike and delicious, made of milk and
sugar and other unknown ingredients; others greasily
redolent of rosewater. Some had real silver laid on one
side, beaten so paper thin you could eat it — though it
didn't taste of anything much. We had an omelette and a
cup of tea — with no sugar, and no flies, in a restaurant
with glass windows and milk jugs, and blinked at the
seventy-five pence bill. We had Howard's clip-on sunglasses mended by a solderer in a street of tinkering,
tapping, metal workers. He refused to take any money
so we bought him a bright pink ice cream made by
'Kwality', and had one ourselves. We bought ridiculous
postcards of dark tubby beauties in hot pants, and
macho film stars in flares against studio backgrounds.
We were informed by the next expatriate we met that
they'd be unlikely to reach their destination since the
nationals considered them pornographic and would be
likely to remove them either to adorn their walls, or to
burn.

At this time we encountered that most wonderful of
Subcontinental figures, the Bureaucracy Broker. Post-
ing Anna's ski boots on to Nepal at the same time as the
cards, turned out to be over an hour's job, requiring a
tailor to make a muslin bag for them, filling in reams of
forms, standing at ten different counters, enclosing
Customs papers, and sewing up and sealing with wax

before we could begin buying the stamps. The man who effected all this for us, and without whom it would have taken a whole afternoon, was sitting in the dust outside the post office with a sturdy wooden box of glue, thread, candles, matches, sealing wax, declaration forms, a money box, ink, scissors, Customs stickers, an ink pad, rubber stamps and a fine Parker fountain pen from the good old days. He was an independent businessman, with a command of English, and inside knowledge of how to approach the inscrutable, illogical post office bureaucracy. He made his living by brokering between the ignorant and desperate customer and the all-knowing and unreasoning system. It was baffling enough to us. What it must have been like to the average Pakistani who wouldn't be likely to speak English, the language of officialdom, we could only guess.

It was astonishing. We were in Quetta for just three days, the bike was hidden away in the hospital from the moment we arrived, but everywhere we went, 'dubbal cycle . . . *Ingrejee* . . . ospotol' would buzz from shop to shop. News got around fast, even in big cities. We were subjected, inevitably, to constant questioning. We began to notice a serious strain in it. The earnestness with which we were asked 'Do you like my country?' was more than mere chit-chat and, unlike Turkey, it didn't confidently expect the answer 'Yes'. Except perhaps in Lahore, people could not comprehend why we were visiting their country, and were both relieved and puzzled when they discovered we were going to Nepal, a country poorer even than themselves. It tallied with their attitude to Iran: not being at war, they felt they had something at least over their neighbours. When we extolled the virtues of their country they looked pleased for a short while but then the question would creep back, 'This . . . Pakistan . . . you like?'

'This . . . Pakistan', in a half-wishful, half-despairing tone was how Pakistanis often described their country and it saddened us, until we were given the other side of the coin. We met a man who'd lived in Sweden for ten years before returning to Quetta. We asked him why he'd come back. Surely his prospects had been infinitely better in Scandinavia? With comic dismay he took in the beggars and the filthy gutters choked with the excreta of trade and humans, in an apologetic gesture:

'In spite of this,' he said, 'there's no place like home.'

11

INCHING UP THE INDUS

Thursday, January 29th

We pushed our way across the Quetta plain with a
column of sand to our right swerving and swaying
gracefully in a whirlwind so tall we couldn't see its top
up in the clouds. Baby whirlwinds skimmed across the
road once in a while, taking the sand from one side to
the other, but they never troubled us much. We were
steeling ourselves for getting over this Bolan Pass everyone had talked about, silently scanning the apparently
unbroken horseshoe of mountains for the breach we
would struggle up through. The railway was no help as a
guide. It had disappeared straight into a tunnel already.

In Quetta they'd been urging us to stay a 'little longer'
ever since we'd arrived. 'The hills are full of bandits' was
their most arresting excuse. 'Go by bus tomorrow. It'll
be safer.' We joked about these bandits as it got to five
o'clock. Should we sleep here on the plain before facing
the onslaught? The turrets of a pseudo-Norman castle
were coming into view – another bizarre legacy of
Victorian engineers – when nature played its second
and most stunning trick on us. Lakpass had been an
oddity that made us smile at our unwarranted trepidation. The Bolan was just so extraordinary that we halted
in disbelief and looked, and looked again to assure
ourselves it was really as it was. We sat peeling oranges

and drinking Long Life milk, to try and register just
what had happened.

Ever since Tarsus, back at Christmas, we'd been
gently climbing away from sea level. Brought up in
Britain, it had never really occurred to us that there was
anything other than mountains which were 'high up'
and everything else which wasn't. We hadn't absorbed
what the map had been telling us: the flat bits we'd been
on for weeks were themselves sometimes much taller
than any of the highest British peaks. The Bolan
marked the beginning of our stunning passage from
these now customary heights back to practically sea
level. At five-past five we had turned a sharp bend,
clicked down a gear or two, and had had to jam on the
brakes to stop ourselves running away down the precipi-
tous gorge that stretched before us as far as the eye
could see, as if opening up the very centre of the earth.
It didn't quite do that, but it did prove to be a sixty-mile
descent (the stuff of cyclists' dreams) plaiting with river
and railway into the 5,500 foot hollow.

That pass marked the greatest transformation of the
trip: cultural and environmental. We passed definitively
from spring to high summer in a single afternoon, from
sleeping bags and clothes to sultry hot nights. Flowers
and fresh greens seemed to burst forth at our passage.
The time of the singing of birds had suddenly come and
there didn't appear to be a familiar species among them.
We hurtled down, taking the longest way round the
tighter corners. At one bend dogs ate from the ribcage
of a camel; a pack of men flayed a horse at another; men
dangled out of passing lorries offering us hash. There
was a palpable wildness about these people which made
the warnings about bandits more credible. We had a bit
of a brush with the leader of a camel caravan picking its
way up to new pastures; real nomads with all their
chattels. He didn't like us taking photographs. Was it,

like the Hindus, because he feared taking the picture would also take away their soul?

When it came to bedtime we were uncharacteristically nervous, making a point of being quite invisible from the road, descending into the dry river bed, dragging the bike over boulders and getting behind an enormous rock. We unpacked in total silence to be sure of hearing the presence of any undesirable and Howard sat outside in the dusk for three or four minutes after all was ready, double checking that no one had seen us. We read in our guide book the following morning that an entire detachment of British soldiers from the Afghan wars in the 1840s had been drowned one night in their tents by flash flooding in that very same river bed.

The relative lushness of the Pass left us as suddenly as its jewel greens had delighted us. After Sibi – the town with the highest summer temperatures in the Subcontinent – where we were mobbed again, we were once more in desert. We wondered about claiming that we'd been in two deserts in a fortnight but the total absence of vegetation was real enough and the same seeming endlessness of the straight flat road. It was getting hotter by the day and though it went against the grain we decided we had to rest after an early lunch. Anna found it particularly frustrating though we filled this time with letter writing and Bible study. The Easterners' ability to just sit and 'be' doesn't only have to do with the heat and the under employment. If she could only take the time to learn, she felt sure they could help her with one of the commands she had most difficulty with: 'Be still and know that I am God' (Ps 46:10).

The day we first forced ourselves to take an afternoon break we holed up at a tiny teahouse in a railway station hamlet. There was nothing so sophisticated as a *charpoy* here. We sat on the mud but we couldn't start writing our postcards till they'd been passed round the group of men variously spinning the tandem pedals, fingering the luggage, pressing the milometer, adjusting the gears, and testing the brakes. The diary, the laminated map, and our 'Holy Book' were most closely inspected. Credentials established, this particular bunch of men were happy to leave us while they smoked and chewed *chars* – their name for best quality marijuana.

A shadow from outside the hole that served as a window fell across our letters. We looked up. A very hairy, very thin, very naked man was dancing up and down outside making imploring cigarette-puffing motions in our direction. He must have been the village madman cum beggar for the men were all matey with him. 'Malangar, Oh! Malangar', they'd call out when there was half a fag or a leftover chapatti going, and drop it into the filthy hand that shot through the aperture in response. He reminded us of the Elizabethan court jester. We wondered what the British Welfare State would have made of him. He'd have probably been as clean as a whistle and had a television to watch in a room full of easy chairs. His existence here was hardly the ideal but we wondered just how much an improvement our solution would have been for Malangar – neater for the community perhaps.

That night we were joined by our first eagle as we began to look for somewhere to sleep, its unmistakable shadow flashing across the tarmac in front of us. As we lifted the bike carefully over the thistly fields to an abandoned mud house beside the railway line, it circled overhead. When, with a distinctly human bending of knees, the camels grazing the tree tops gradually knelt down to rest, it was calmly roosting on a nearby branch. We allowed ourselves to become comfortably melancholy as we gazed into the flames of our furze fire and remembered our cosy chimney back in Rotherhithe.

The next day Howard woke with stomach cramps and diarrhoea. The nearest town was thirty miles away.

Because it was written in reasonably large print on our map we simply assumed that we could get not only a hotel there but the wherewithal to pay for it as our travellers' cheques had almost run out. The terrain changed again. Irrigation was so successful here that even the road was beautifully tree-lined. There was a good green smell from the rice paddies like rain on a British lawn. All manner of birds looped over the tarmac and skimmed in and out of the boughs: king-fishers with their legendary blue plumage, drongos (like very long-tailed swallows), all kinds of falcons, fish eagles with chests like bulldogs – and most canny of all, the cattle egrets like dainty white herons, perching on the backs of the water buffalo and de-leeching them with their long yellow beaks. That hot day, pushing to reach Jacobabad before the banks closed at eleven, we really envied those buffalo, wallowing in the pools between the paddies, huge grey flanks rolling lazily in the tepid water. Every now and again they'd give a huge sigh as if life was just too much for them.

We were stopped by a traffic policeman who wanted us to take tea with him. Howard's stomach wasn't up to it even if we'd had the time. The policeman however, wouldn't budge. 'The bank's closed' (shades of Taftan). 'It's a holiday,' he lied. 'Come and drink tea with me.' We could hardly contain our indignation. Policemen don't lie! In actual fact those two underhand officials in Zahedan quietly blackmailing the truck driver had been as much an indicator of things to come as the crowds of spectators, the lack of cheese and the flies. 'Do not pervert justice' we were reading; 'do not accept a bribe . . . Follow justice and justice alone . . . Do not spread false reports.' (Ex 23:1,8. Deut 16:20)

Sind, the province we were now in, was particularly notorious for its lawlessness and corruption. We were warned by so many people not to camp because of the dacoits that for once we judged the advice not to be the standard caution we'd received regularly since crossing the Alps, and slept in trucking stops, hotels and private houses. (Every missionary knew the next one and passed us on down the line.) In the West, and the government press, you hear about 'Pakistan'. When you get there you hear much more about Sind or Punjab and you only ever hear of Pakistan in editorials discussing whether it really exists or not.

There's a major identity crisis in the country and no news item you read will make proper sense unless you're aware that Pakistan is a loose federation of provinces with forces of decentralisation as strong as those of unity. The terrible intercommunal bloodbath that occurred in Karachi a month before we entered the country was actually the Sindis getting fed up with all the 'foreigners' (from other parts of Pakistan) crowding into the shanty suburbs. President Bhutto's execution was the Punjabis killing 'our' (Sind's) man. Areas in the North-West Territory Province were already officially autonomous from the national judiciary and state police force and subject instead to tribal law even before the Afghans began pouring over the border to flee (and propagate) the war with Russia. What the relationship is between Islamabad and these parts now is very questionable.

The Sindi dacoits weren't simply poor bandits finding that it paid to rob, but politically motivated adventurers trying to prove that the state has no control in Sind. We were chatting to a man staring out from the back of his donkey *howdah* one day, who said we were all right in Sind. If foreigners got molested here, he said, then the army would really have an excuse to move in and do goodness knows what.

The lack of unity hurts the Pakistanis all the more because of the centrality of the notion of brotherhood in their faith. Whether, or to what extent, to introduce *Sharia* (divine law) into the existing secular legislation as a remedy, inspired by the Iranian precedent, was discussed in the papers and over tea.

When we finally got past our somewhat more prosaic but no less insidious example of national corruption — that fibbing policeman — and into town, we ran into problems. There were only six cities in Pakistan, we were told, where you could change foreign currency and Jacobabad wasn't one of them. Telephoning one of these branches to get permission was out of the question in all except one bank where they said they'd got a flat refusal. We began to get a little desperate. Howard was a pale shade of grey and needing a toilet more and more often but we didn't even have the rupees for a hotel. The last bank we came to took pity on us.

'We'll lend you two hundred rupees,' said the manager, a rotund family man with a kindly smile, 'and take your passport numbers, then you can telex it back to us when you are able. No hurry.' There were plenty of good-hearted, honest Pakistanis as well.

We didn't mean to stay at the Christian hospital in Shikarpur, the town after Jacobabad. We just wanted a bit of expatriate company and perhaps a good British cup of tea. We didn't have much choice, though.

'My house is called the Taj Mahal,' said the nurse we first bumped into on the hospital compound, 'so it should be big enough for you two skinny cyclists to find a corner in and rest for a few days. Your husband doesn't look very well at all, you know,' she said to Anna. We weren't very well. The nurses knew exactly why: 'Didn't anyone tell you to purify your water?' they asked, dosing us up with a drug called Flagyl we were to become intimate with. We did have a stack of water purifying tablets but Howard never being one to follow the crowd without trying to work out why he should, had put the question in such a way that Anna could only agree. 'None of the natives purify the water, so why should we? Are we going to boil our water for three

years in Nepal? If we're going to get accustomed to it, we
might as well start now.' We were roundly scolded for
our foolishness. 'Just because Pakistanis don't boil their
water doesn't mean they're exempt from diarrhoea. You
can do permanent damage to your liver with unclean
water,' they remonstrated.

We rested up for five days, spending a great deal of
time in the British-built, marble bath tub, and washing
our sleeping bags, ingrained with three and a half
months' dirt. After weeks of chapattis and dal, beef stew
and sago seemed other worldly, as did 'real' tea. Ironically, what we usually got on the road was 'best quality
dust', the greater part of the leaf crop going to the West
for export.

One day Anna went round the wards with Sister. She
came back reeling with it all. She had seen one-day-old,
two-kilo mites who'd fitted between her wrist and elbow
and stared up with huge eyes heavy with mascara. On
the road we'd come across tiny girls and boys made up to
such a degree that we were unsure sometimes whether
we'd stumbled across child prostitutes. They didn't just
put it on for decoration. An important function of *kohl* is
to ward off the evil eye. (Here folk Islam comes close to
Hinduism, for the gold studs Hindu women wear in
their nostrils are to prevent the entrance of evil spirits as
well as for show.) The mothers use the same phial of *kohl*
as grandma has used on her infected eyes, believing the
nurses' warning only if the children get infections – or
worse, go blind. We'd never seen so many eye diseases as
when we were cycling in Pakistan.

A couple of babies had their heads in the depression
of a hollowed out wooden board.

'What's that for?' Anna asked.

'Oh,' Sister laughed, 'you wouldn't like to see this baby
grow up with a nasty round skull like those common
Baluchis would you? Flat-backed heads are the thing in
Sind. Besides you can keep your mirrorwork cap on

much better if you're kind of . . . square.' Sind is probably the only place in the world where babies' heads are shaped to fit their hats rather than vice versa.

Some of the babies wore little amulets round their necks with words from the Koran inside. When Anna asked what they were, Sister redirected the question to the mother.

'It's holy words,' the mother said 'to protect my baby,' though she didn't exactly know what they said. Sister smiled gently at her:

'What's the use of having the words round your neck?' she said. 'You need them in your heart.'

That was how they 'evangelised' at Shikarpur – quietly and intermittently. The patients obviously didn't find it offensive. Many of them joined the staff for their morning service in one of the wards, though most were Moslems. The Mission Hospital was far and away the most popular in the area, despite the funny persuasion of those who ran it.

When we saw how unscrupulous the bazaar doctors were in the Subcontinent we weren't surprised. If you go to one of these paramedics complaining of persistent headaches they're known to give one (not two) paracetamol and charge you the average daily wage for their – and your – pains. More frequently they will prescribe a 'tonic' or multi-vitamin syrup alongside the mainline drug. There's no harm in that, except the price. In a situation where there's money to spare these things might be a comfort even if not particularly effective. In a situation of total ignorance and real poverty on the part of the patients and the almost inevitable ownership of the drug shop by the practitioner, one can't help but question prescribing practice. We'd passed one sad, weeping huddle on her string strung bed. She'd been to a 'doctor' in the bazaar to induce her baby which was late and the medicine had brought on such violent contractions that the baby had been crushed. Sheer ignorance is so often the cause of disaster in Third World countries, with babies choking to death because mothers don't know to burp them. They parch to death because it's not realised that rehydration is essential for diarrhoea.

The Subcontinent teems with infants: a result of conflicting factors. The state advocates birth control because fewer babies mean less of a national economic burden. Islam, however, prohibits it, but it isn't only Islam that's responsible for the over-population. Children in the East are still on the whole perceived as an asset to the domestic economy as well as justifying a woman's existence. Barrenness constitutes grounds for divorce in Nepal. A man's virility is in question if no children are born. Ironically, though the high infant mortality rate has to do with poverty and ignorance, it's just that high mortality rate which actually results in more and more children being conceived as a safety measure. If one dies there must be another to take its place. Male supremacy is also a contributory factor. An Eastern woman hasn't really done her stuff if she hasn't produced a male heir, so she goes on trying. The youngest, especially if it's a boy, is grossly spoilt, until the next comes along and supersedes it at the breast. Often fairing hair is one of the signs that the neglected one is suffering from malnutrition.

Many of the patients wanted to know who Anna was. She was a bit fearful they might consider her a shameless hussy when they heard about the tandem, but they were full of admiration, patting her hand with wide smiles and telling her how brave she was and how they were sure God would bless her with children in time.

'Why don't they smile at me on the road then?' Anna asked.

'Oh, it's totally unacceptable for a woman to smile at someone she doesn't know,' was the answer. It was reassuring to find out that the stony faces of the few women we'd seen hadn't meant anything personal.

Our next port of call was Sukkur on the mighty Indus,

with its clog-shaped houseboats. We took our first tonga ride round the old streets with their exquisitely carved balconies and shutters, clinging on to the sides of the four seater trap as it lurched along at a cruel speed for the emaciated horse which was whipped when it flagged. We weren't sorry when we had to descend in the heart of the bazaar because the streets were too narrow for the horse to pass.

'Bazaar' in the Subcontinent doesn't just mean a particular type of commercial enclave distinct from shops with doors and windows. The bazaar is the shopping centre and the means of production are frequently brought right to the shop front. Where you buy your loaf tin is also where it's made, from sheets of thin metal by squatting men wielding rulers, scissor shears and little hammers. They cut and bend, overlap and tap, and fold in the raw edges like a hem on a garment. Then, hey presto! – there's your baking tin. Next door they'll be going in the oven in full view. Just past the Boadicea brassières – all seams and padding and points blowing gently in the wind – are weavers turning out receptacles of every shape and size from Ali Baba laundry baskets to chapatti trays. There were furniture makers inlaying exquisite ivory flowers into teak tables. It was funny how pliers of the same trade, including itinerant street vendors, would tend to congregate in the same place, and without the least animosity once the customer had chosen which one to patronise.

Coming in along the road to Sukkur we got an overview of a day in the life of the earthenware pots. We'd cycled past clay pits by the river or the village pond, which provide drinking water and washing places for clothes, humans, and animals. There we'd see children and adults often thigh deep in the slimy stuff, scooping it out with their fingers. They'd carry it along the road in flat baskets or on their heads (no wonder their deportment was so erect) or just in great handfuls, to the potter who'd slap balls of it on to the wheel, throw a pot, and line it up with hundreds of others to dry in the sun. A little further along the road we'd come across a barefoot man, as often as not accompanied by a child, who'd help him push his cartload of pots into town to distribute them to all the milk and tea shops. And there we were in Sukkur bazaar, not able to linger too long over our tea because the heat would gradually seep through the pot till it was impregnated and our tea had a slight – though not unpleasant – clayey taste. We couldn't even persuade the *chah* wallah to give us our second cup in the same one. He'd shake his head and point to the gutter where the shards of countless others lay in among the shreds of leaf plates laboriously sewn together with long grasses and, like the pots, the Eastern answer to paper plates. It struck us how often in the West so many of the steps of production are kept out of sight and untouched by human hand, the work done by factory machines. Sukkur bazaar was a delight with its bamboo matting overhead casting a mysterious shade over the hive of 'skill, ability, and knowledge in all kinds of crafts': (Ex 31:3). Finally we tore ourselves away – to Moenjodaro, the oldest urban archaeological site in the world.

As we'd travelled through Europe we'd been amazed each time we came across buildings still standing from before our 1066 consciousness. We'd ogle at an eighth century mosaic and wonder at a fifth century tomb and then in Greece we were as far back as Christ Himself. The thought at Persepolis that, if Christ had visited He too would have seen a ruin, was pretty amazing; but Moenjodaro was so old we just couldn't grasp it. As much time had elapsed between the building of these streets we were walking down and Jesus's birth, as between the beginning of our current calendar and today.

One of the most striking things about Moenjodaro, therefore, is the way its bricks could have been baked this

century. This illusory newness is surely partly why, for all
its fascination, Moenjodaro didn't have the same impact
on us as Persepolis. We made our way along its grid
pattern streets looking at the little shutes which served as
rubbish disposers in the walls of the houses. We thought
how strange it was that four thousand years ago they had
such an efficient system of waste disposal – squads of
dustmen would come round and pick up the deposits –
whereas today the streets of Pakistan are so often like
garbage tips. The same thing struck us about the excellent sewerage system and the sentry boxes for traffic
police at intervals along the ruler-straight pavements.

The Indus civilisation, of which Moenjodaro is the
most extensively preserved city, declined rapidly into
oblivion. Nobody can be sure why, but historians reckon
that the formidable brick production that took place to
build these models of orderliness deforested the valley
floor severely enough to upset the ecological balance
and ruin the climate. One thing these people's successors had learnt to do which they obviously hadn't was to
bake bricks using chaff. It gave off a terrible smell from
the tall chimneys along the road but it appealed to our
sense of economy, for it meant that not one bit of the
harvest was wasted. Going down the Moenjodaro road,
out of the corner of our eye we'd catch the flash of a
bright pink *chaddr* as men tossed spadefuls of grain up
into the sunshine to winnow them in the faint breeze;
grain which had been trampled by pairs of buffalo
yoked to a stave on the threshing floor and round which
they were forced to go, hour upon hour. No wonder
Deuteronomy stipulates, 'Do not muzzle an ox while it is
treading out the grain.' (Deut 25:4)

On a particularly deserted stretch, we saw three
massive forms in the distance. As we drew closer they
proved to be tombs with eagles' nests in the window
arches and cobwebs and birds' lime in the *mihrabs*. There
were just enough brilliant blue tiles left to help us later

to relate them to the fabulous Moghul edifices in Uch and Lahore, despite their crumbling bases, eroded by the saltpetre which lays whitely waste so much land in this area. There wasn't a dwelling in sight, but as we walked back to the bike, feet cracking the saline crust, a band of wellwishers suddenly appeared over the crystalline dunes to shower skirtfuls of tiny apples into our basket and cheer us off. It was that kind of totally gratuitous kindness which made up for so much in Pakistan. If only our stomachs could have taken the apples.

We inched our way up the Indus, once again utterly debilitated by diarrhoea and enforced physical exertion. We'd had no idea that gut rot could be so infinitely variable. Probably this was our worst bout but the ten days we spent with the next, providentially placed missionaries was one of the loveliest times of fellowship of the whole trip. Our hostess wasn't 'repressed' or soft; she'd simply learnt that 'godliness with contentment is great gain' (1 Tim 6:6) and therefore didn't need the escape routes Anna knew she'd have to have if she lived in that ultra conservative town. She told us gratefully, but with no longing, of infrequent picnics out in deserted woods where she'd lie on her back looking up into the leaves and meditating on the spacious place the Lord had brought her to.

Every missionary woman in Pakistan coped differently with the degree of restriction she was subject to, depending on her circumstances. Some took regular weekends away in hotels in the nearest, more permissive town. Others made their homes places where Muslim women could come and go without fearing the man of the house would encroach. Very occasionally we wondered whether some of these expatriate women weren't too self-sacrificial. One giggled a little as she described how women in her house would not only expect to be shown every room but would make an inventory of the cupboards as well. When it came to explaining why, in near nineties temperatures, she was wearing burning hot polyester she was less cheerful though no less resolute.

'I'd be looked down upon if I wore pure cottons,' she said. 'If I want to witness to these women I have to win their respect first.' It's a mark of wealth and elevated social standing in Pakistan to be able to buy synthetic imports instead of indigenous cotton. Pakistan didn't have an Indira who, for all her faults, was strong on denouncing this. One missionary broke many of the rules, cycling without a *dupatta* in the city where she was a doctor.

'We're different,' she said 'and it's no use pretending we're not.' But she qualified: 'It's all a question of individual situation and conviction.'

We went for a service at the adjoining house where to our amazement the Pastor proved to be a speaker of international repute. We wondered how he'd found Switzerland where he'd spoken at a conference, after this church where the majority of attendants were from the very poorest sweeper class and we all sat on the floor. They sat perfectly still for the two and a half hour service. We started shifting about on our numb bottoms after half an hour. Howard, physically unable to sit without his back up against something, found it one of the most humiliating of our inabilities to adapt. However, we felt much more comfortable here, with the clash of a *chimta* (two swords attached at the handle by a hinge and slapped together) accompanying local melodies and vernacular lyrics, than at almost any of the other churches in Pakistan and India that we went to. It was the Anglicanism of these which jarred, parts of Cranmer a seeming nonsense in this totally different culture.

This community was exemplary in its attempts to cross cultural barriers. One of the fellows was working, not with Muslims at all, but with a nearby Hindu community in whose Mahawari language he was fluent. The Christians from the tribe were having difficulty giving up their former baptisms of the dead. He was in the process of devising a Christian ceremony to replace these with something which satisfied, without heresy, their need for ritual. On our last night with these people, we noticed, over the bazaar, the full-faced moon. When it came to saying goodbye, the following morning, we were all rather tearful. It was good, however, to be back on the road. A man had given Howard some little brass halter bells for helping him out with his income tax forms – in English of course. Howard attached them to the basket with some multi-coloured tassels and we jingled along like Santa Claus.

With the onset of hot weather, and fewer layers of clothing, saddle-soreness had become a painful problem for Anna. Padding her saddle with a shawl helped. Those shawls were multi-purpose garments. You could carry your shopping in them; wrap them round the grass you'd scythed for the buffalo; shield yourself from the sun or the cold; make your turban out of them; and for the women, use them to carry the baby and veil yourself at the same time. When the night temperatures got really unbearable we put ours under the tap and used them as cooling bed covers. Pink was the colour in Sind, bright red in Punjab, but everywhere pure cotton – *sindon* – in glorious hues and subtle weaves, was the one commodity that wasn't scarce. It was the same in India: countless cotton ginning factories along the road and hanks of the stuff laid out in the sun to dry the dye. We remembered what a pleasure it had been to see those cotton plants in the Greek mountains.

We hadn't thought it possible, but when we crossed into Punjab the wildlife got even more varied, the land even lusher, and the people even more prevailing. This had something to do with the plenteous water supply (the word *punjab* means five waters and refers to the five rivers that flow through the province). There were more Western clothes, more English speakers and more schools. Despite this, Punjabi road services seemed worse than in Sind. Often we'd have to dismount and push the bike past armies of road-menders.

Though they usually did almost everything by hand, including the 'steamrolling', they made a beautiful job of widening the road (which had been fine in its day) with an almost imperceptibly added strip of macadam. They were always cheerfully interested in us, but we felt uncomfortable, sandwiched between those working on the road proper and the flange of stone breakers alongside. There was something grossly disproportionate about our pleasure trip and their labour. When we got to India and came across women working alongside the men with pickaxes and hammers we felt even worse, though there at least they sometimes wore goggles against the flying chips.

More stones meant stonethrowers – usually children – for the first time, though we were warned about them as far back as Turkey. Discipline among children seemed haphazard to us. Though there's plenty of belting in Pakistani upbringing, it's generally heartrendingly unsystematic and unpredictable. A believer told us that to expect consistency of his heavenly father was to limit his inscrutable greatness. Was there a link we wondered? It certainly contrasted strangely with our own: 'Know then in your heart that as a man disciplines his son, so the LORD your God disciplines you.' (Deut 8:5).

At their best the old British built roads in Punjab were dappled avenues alive with palm squirrels (like chipmunks) and more birds even than in Sind. There were the Indian rollers: unobtrusive brown birds till they lifted their wings. Flying they were totally transformed revealing only dazzling blues. There were hoopoes – fawn, with black and white zebra stripes on their wings and a brown crest which flicked up revealing black tips. They have the gentlest call by which they get their name. There were all kinds of woodpeckers and vivid hued parakeets, and many, many more that we couldn't identify. Perhaps most memorable of all were the weaver birds, not so much for themselves but for their extraordinary nests from which they too get their names. We thought these nests were coconuts at first till we got closer and saw how they hung from a skein of the same interwoven grasses from which the main body of the nest is formed. We saw the birds flying in from underneath and couldn't work out why the eggs didn't fall out till we chanced upon some abandoned nests (the male makes several but the female picks the one she likes best!). There appears to be no hole at all but if you pull at the bottom ever so gently an aperture appears which springs shut on itself. Elastic twigs. It was amazing.

By the waterways we saw our first mongooses which must have meant there were snakes, though we never saw any – except a small dried one with its tail inside its mouth. It was round a child's neck as a charm. As stealthy as the mongooses were the fishermen, wading waist high through the bullrushes with six-foot diameter nets shaped like cake covers held out before them. They'd see a fish and with a plunge of the net, trap it underneath and quickly scoop it up, bringing the net out upside down like a bowl.

Punjabi women had a freedom Sindis generally didn't, sometimes even waving and smiling shyly at Anna. The older Punjabi women seemed the freest and most contented of all, able to dispense with full purdah because of their age and treated with unquestioning respect. Sometimes they'd lay their hands over Anna's face in a tender gesture of blessing. One notable encounter with Punjabi women was in somewhat less touching circumstances.

Crowd dynamics are unpredictable. Choosing the

smallest of peripheral village hotels in which to eat lunch, we'd never have guessed that such a tenacious horde would gather. At breakfast we'd attracted fewer than fifteen observers though we'd been in the centre of town; now the head count produced 104 pressing, jostling, onlookers. When Anna took the veil, pulling her gauzy scarf right down over her face, the more daring just peeped up under it. The female chapatti wallah – in herself a Punjabi novelty – took up our case, brandishing her tandoor poker. But she couldn't possibly keep them all at bay as they scrambled across the wall and under and over *charpoys* to get a better look. Then into the breach came her formidable neighbour, hand on formidable hip. We didn't catch most of her twenty minute tirade but we understood enough to appreciate that Anna's veil should be honoured, that it was no use pretending it was only the bike they had come to look at – 'she knew' – and it was a disgusting way to treat guests in their country. One by one the multitude slunk shamefaced away. When we left, Anna shook her hand and held it a little while, trying to supplement the thank you she was trying to convey in English and pidgin Urdu, by smiling into her eyes woman to woman. Howard, of course, could only look grateful from a respectable distance.

That afternoon we got Howard a haircut. We'd been most intrigued by the outdoor barbers and just for the fun of it we chose one in the most isolated village we came across. He settled down under a palm tree with the road to one side and rice paddies to the other, to a dab of water on the head, a blunt pair of scissors with the screw loose, and an implement that looked like a dolls' house lawnmower. He got one of the smartest cuts he'd ever had. It cost about six pence.

The further East we got, the cheaper it became, but only if we kept our wits about us. Looking back through our diary the striking thing is not how persistently the

double dealing comes up but how soon we stopped
commenting on it because it simply became part of
everyday life. When we do note it, it's more usually a
new way of dealing with the problem. The basic rule in
hotls we discovered, was to ask the price before ordering
and if possible not from the vendor but from someone
sitting eating. He'd often blow our gaff by checking with
the shopkeeper first, but it was worth a try. That
though, wasn't enough in many places. You had not only
to ask but also to pay before eating, else you were liable
to find that the sum had magically changed once you'd
downed the last morsel, and of course there was no one
to verify the initial agreement except perhaps the lackeys who would inevitably stick to the proprietor's guns.

Being sensitive British flowers we didn't much like
paying in advance because it made the unspoken
assumption that we didn't trust the hotelier. For a while
we tried other ways. When he named some ridiculous
price, we might turn to some disinterested customer and
say:

'Do you hear what he's trying to charge me for a cup
of tea?' It was hopeless. Instead of replying, 'What a
rascal. That's not what I pay,' he'd turn to the offender
and ask in his own tongue, 'How much did you charge
these two for a cup of tea?' (a world of difference from
'What's the price of a cup of tea?'). Not for him to 'judge
fairly, whether the case is between brothers ... or
between one of them and an alien.' (Deut 1:16). He'd be
told the exorbitant price but wouldn't bat an eyelid;
simply relay it back to us *very slowly* so that we'd understand ... His unruffled compliance was however, often
as not totally unmalicious, for we were pretty slow to
grasp that 'Do not use dishonest standards' (Lev 19:35)
wasn't the issue at all. The question was whether one
charged according to the cost of the item or the size of
the customer's pocket. We'd turn away and go somewhere else. That might bring them both running after

us with a reasonable offer but not automatically, for the assumption seemed to be not that the shameful thing was to overcharge – in fact you were a mug not to if there was the chance of a picking – but that the really mortifying thing was to be caught at it. So we couldn't win. Even Howard's confident thesis that leaving the shop at least twice would get a fair deal, drew a blank with such a mind-set and we pretty soon stopped trying to be polite about it.

Perhaps we should have graciously acknowledged the fact that commerce was invented and developed in the East thousands of years before it hit the West. The money of course was usually negligible for our pockets but it was the dual assumption, first that the question of equity didn't enter into it, and second that the foreigner was a twit, which galled us. Natives are also subjected to the same treatment, though to a lesser extent. Moral considerations apart, it's quite difficult to smile when all you want is a cup of tea after sixty miles of cycling and you have to stand there arguing for quarter of an hour before they'll even put the kettle on. Often we were so exhausted and thirsty we'd just pay, but give them a piece of our minds when we'd wet our whistles. It didn't have the least impact except perhaps surprise and even admiration that we knew what they were up to, but it may have had some cathartic effect for us.

We went out of our way to go to Uch, not only as it's a centre of Sufism which we wanted to find out more about but also because it's likely to be one of the Alexandrias that the conquerer founded on his way down the Indus in 325 BC. The river marked the eastern boundary of his travels when he was persuaded by his weary army to turn back. The river has moved since his day, so exactly where he was isn't clear, but we wanted to round off our travels with him and Uch seemed like the most accurate cut-off point. When we discovered that Alexandrias weren't the only things he had founded on his travels and that the occasional fair-haired inhabitant was also reputedly traceable to his army, our sense of historicity was greatly strengthened.

We took one look at Uch's narrow streets and steep steps and decided to leave the bike at the police station. Quite apart from the mobbing it always occasioned, it was also obstinately awkward to manoeuvre throughout the journey, being so long and so laden with luggage. The police station was the usual Victorian garrison type, with cells either side of the entrance. Anyone entering the main courtyard could ogle at the felons through the floor to ceiling bars. We were kept waiting by the chief behind his desk out in the sun but were given tea and the best chairs to sit on. The upshot was that not only were we to leave the bike there but also he would provide us with a guide from his ranks and feed us when we got back.

Our guide took us round the medieval tombs, some badly crumbling and robbed of their glorious blue and buttercup tiling, others as pristine as the day they were built, and booming with business. The faithful flocked in to kiss and lay offerings on the main gravestone. Though they had to weave in and out of countless minor graves squashed up as near as possible to the principal one for extra sanctification, they never turned their backs to it. Outside the main courtyard with its pool for foot ablutions before you went in were scores of minor graves, also packed as close as possible and still being added to.

From Konya onwards we had noticed that these Sufic pilgrimage centres attracted the most rapturous, devout worshippers and the most perfunctory lip servers – both ready targets for the inevitable hawkers. When we made our way out of the dark interiors, lit only by candles and Christmas type lights which contrasted shabbily with the gorgeous carved and painted interiors, *pirs* (holy men) would try to bless us – for a fee – and someone would appear from the shadows of the porch to demand some money for taking care of our shoes which we thought we had just left there.

At the largest tomb, with its succession of exterior courtyards on different levels, the sound of children's voices reached us from the highest. The class sat outside, chalking on oblong slates bordered in wood and with a small handle at the bottom. When the space was filled up they'd wash the characters off at the pump. Sometimes these schools made a striking impression indeed, framed by the graceful colonnades and chanting quietly under the supervision of a *hajji*, his hair and beard dyed bright orange, and sporting a white crocheted cap as testimony of his Meccan pilgrimage.

Our policeman guide who spoke no English was insistent that we should visit a sight he obviously regarded as equal in importance to the tombs – the 'Well of Death'. It was a cylindrical tent whose exterior we ascended by a rickety ladder to a platform running all the way round the top. The cone shaped roof sheltered both us and events going on inside which we could look down upon. In the arena were thickly made up women in skimpy dress and high heels. When 1970s top-tens began to blare through a loudspeaker they started to dance suggestively, to the obvious appreciation of the male spectators on our platform. We looked back down at the policeman, bewildered. He motioned to us to stay, as if to indicate that the best was yet to come. The music changed and the girls each climbed on to a motorbike and cruised slowly around the tent. We never got to the bottom of the Well of Death – nor did we particularly want to.

We left Uch along a small back road which held two novelties for us: vultures – hook-necked and ugly as on the comic strips – and a bridge constructed from planks laid across four, moored puntlike boats. The police assured us we couldn't take it because it led straight to the 'jongol'. 'Jongol', we discovered, usually meant something perfectly able to be cycled, just rather out of the way. We'd come to have a nose for these *kachchee* (as opposed to *pukka*) roads, guessing at their existence when we saw a village marked on the map that appeared to have no road leading to it but which lay in a direct line between us and the next big place we were making for. Ninety-nine per cent of the time we were right, but we had a hard time persuading people that we preferred them to the busier, if smoother, route.

We chose the back roads because we just couldn't get into the swing of Subcontinental driving. People would come out of side roads right in front of us without indicating, easing round roundabouts backwards to get to the third exit, negotiating crossroads as if the lights weren't working, bearing down upon us as they over-took, as if we didn't exist, and crowning it with a hand on the horn as if to say: 'I'm warning you'. Howard even got to the stage of putting in earplugs.

For the lorry it's an easy life and there's always the black rag from the *pir* or an old shoe, painted or actual, on the mudguard for divine protection. For the spindly cycle it's like being bullied all day long. A feature of that culture and therefore to be 'understood and appreciated', it was nevertheless the similarity with the *backsheesh* system that struck us. Might is right; go for what you can get; the great 'I' is the supreme reference point; don't bother with things that are not for your immediate benefit.

12

GASPING DOWN THE GANGES

Thursday, March 5th

It was Anna's birthday. It had been lovely over the last
few days, cycling through an area rich in banana and
tangerine orchards, disturbed once or twice a day by
hissing steam trains, like us glistening and puffing their
way to Lahore. But what we really wanted to do was get
there in time to celebrate her birthday in style and
splash out on a good hotel for once. That morning we
were just thirty miles from the city. We made it by
elevenses. Cycling out of the early morning countryside
into the bustle and turmoil of the city, it was a change
indeed to find the road surfaces leading into the city so
well maintained and so wide that four lanes of traffic
could make their way, simultaneously and not get
snarled up. We were so dazzled by the white lines – the
first we had seen since Europe – and the occasional
bareheaded woman, that it took us some while to orientate ourselves before we eventually found a hotel and
flopped.

We took a dozen showers between us in twenty-four
hours, watched the test match on TV and had breakfast
the day after on room service. The bed, with blissfully
clean, cool sheets was easily twice as big and bouncy as
the tent. 'This is the monstruosity in love, lady, that the
will is infinite and the execution confined,' Troilus says

to Cressida. It had proven only too true during our rigorous trip.

We had a week to spend in Lahore till March 12th when the border to India would be open. Relations were so strained between the two countries that the border was opened only three times a month for those going to India and the same, though on the following day, for those going the other way. Just after we'd left Lahore a dozen people were killed in a bomb blast; just after we'd left Delhi it was put under curfew. Hindu-Moslem relations apart, the Sikhs were causing such unrest in the Punjab that we were going to have to go through there in a military convoy. It meant finding a vehicle willing to take both us and our tandem.

Despite the political situation, business in Lahore, as in Teheran, went on as usual, and business had a lot to do with food. It has to be said that hitherto we'd not enjoyed Pakistani cuisine. Too often, gasping for something cool and easy to eat, there'd been nothing but mouth-blasting, greasy curry and sickly tea, but Lahore is where Pakistani food comes into its own. There were the dairy shops with huge, earthenware bowls of yoghourt stacked on dividing slats of wood, just asking to have their creamy, wrinkle-free surfaces sliced with kidney-shaped metal scoops. You could buy puff pastry circles to crumble into your hot milk, bubbling away in vast woks. They'd sweeten it, then pass it back and forth with great panache and from great heights, from one metal beaker to another, till it was frothier than a *cappucino*. There was *kulfi*: pistachio ice cream on bamboo sticks, all the more tasty for being turned out of metal moulds on the spot by the barrow vendors. At one notable junction you could get *kulfi* and noodles — surely the strangest combination we'd yet come across, even counting the peppered fruit salad. And nearby was the lime juice, sweetened by sugar cane pulverised through a mangle.

There were the savouries too: every conceivable type of crisp, chip, samosa, puff pastry or battered delicacy for snacks, but there was also rice with seasoned and puréed spinach, or potato and egg salad, or chick peas and raisins. If you could face meat after passing the butcher's fly-infested slabs, shops hung about with intestines looking like macabre attempts at Christmas decorations, there was meat in plenty. Kebabs grilled on the spot with Turkish-type *pide*, and salad made from the bright red sweet carrots we'd become accustomed to, were our favourite.

One night we had our own tableside minstrel. He sang to a viol with a metal haired bow which had a bell on the tip. The viol itself – if that was the right family to ascribe it to – had three strings. Two produced a drone at the same time as the third was fingered, or perhaps more accurately fingernailed at the ivory inlaid neck.

We quite unashamedly gorged ourselves. We called it building up our cycling muscles. Even on our budget and counting the bad experiences, food was one of the unexpected pleasures of the trip. Not having to do the washing up afterwards was a welcome perk too, though we tried not to look too closely when, at the street stalls, our plate was consigned to a bucket of cold water with a hundred others, given a cursory finger rub with a bit of mud for abrasion if it was particularly greasy, then put out in the sun to dry – and for the flies. We thought we were avoiding the worst when we ate off the disposable leaf plates until we met someone who had caught worms from them. In fact, by Lahore, we'd finally beaten the runs. We'd been introduced to Diodoquin tablets which, until it had been proven they could cause blindness after protracted use, every missionary in Pakistan had taken daily. You could still get the drug, and for the short time we needed it, it was a life saver.

Central Lahore wears its history very much on its sleeve. If you know where to go, you can cycle back through the history of its four distinct cities along a very simple route. You start at the posh end of town. The names are all from the Victorians. 'Charing Cross' is where you find the brand new Hilton (where Anna bought Howard a copy of *The Independent* for his birthday) and the illuminated advertisements for Citibank, the department store and the shops with all the cameras and stereo systems. Carry on down 'The Mall' and you come to the second Victorian city proper where everything reminds you of St Pancras Station and the Law Courts in the Strand. Some, like the Government College, are straight Victorian Gothick, delightfully misplaced in the heat and flies and scrubby dry grass. Most of it though, like the central post office and the university, is that wonderful product of the Empire, 'Victorian (or Edwardian) Moghul': sober, stalwart British architects employing stylistic features from the very distinctive Moghul buildings of the area.

They take you right back to the days when young Oxbridge graduates in the Indian Civil Service were seeking to establish the infrastructure of a modern state with their own brand of broadmindedness to what was around them. In many cases they took much more care of the architectural and artistic heritage than the nationals had a mind to. For the great days of the Moghul Empire might have left monumental buildings, but they'd also left a bad taste in the mouths of the Hindu population who had not appreciated their Islamic rulers' construction of such mosques and tombs. How could they dishonour their dead so by refusing to cremate them? And then drawing attention to the omission by building a great tomb for everyone to come and visit!

It was Prince Albert who ensured that there was a museum here to house India's treasures, whoever's faith had inspired them. It was Rudyard Kipling's father who was the first curator there, and it was outside it that

Kipling's fictional character Kim 'sat, in defiance of municipal orders, astride the gun Zam-Zamah on her brick platform opposite the old Ajib-Gher – the Wonder House as the natives call the Lahore Museum.' It is there still and the 'natives', judging by the steady clientèle – villagers as well as city dwellers – haven't changed their opinion. We had only just left Alexander behind and this was the start of our time with Kim. It was nice not to be left alone. We followed him from 'Kim's Gun', through the book all the way to Benares, and we enjoyed his company.

When he is persuaded to leave his position astride the gun Kim disappears up into tiny alleys and closely packed rooftops. This is the third of Lahore's cities: the Old Town whose walls and gates still remain in parts, and whose streets are so packed and narrow that it really isn't very sociable to try and wheel a tandem through them. We couldn't think that things were so different there now from what they had been before the British got there. For us, this was Pakistan at its most dazzlingly entertaining and surprising, absolutely crammed with life and invention, decoration and handiwork, filth and idiosyncrasy. We squeezed our way up past the donkey carts bringing in sacks of corn and out at the top where there was at last a road wide enough to take two lanes of traffic.

It is here that the fourth city hits you. It is not a city really – just a mosque and a fort – but their impact is spectacular. It is claimed that the mosque is the largest in the world, but it wasn't so much the size that struck us, as the scale. The Badshahi appears immensely vast because of the claustrophobic conditions you have been struggling through for so long to get to it. We wandered silently along the outer walls of the courtyard which stretches almost interminably to the mosque chamber with its huge white onion domes that minimalise every-thing else in sight, thinking how horribly ignorant we were. So *these* were the Moghuls. An historian each of us, and till getting here we couldn't have told you the difference between a Moghul and a Mongol.

You get that when you travel sometimes. A crushing feeling of how small your life view is, of how careful you really ought to be before opening your mouth about anything. We came to learn that while Henry VIII was building Hampton Court the Moghuls were coming down from Afghanistan and beginning a mighty imperial rule in India, characterised by a genius for miniature painting and an exceptional gift for building. Some say that their decline was related to the fact that such a disproportionate amount of money went into the building programme. You can believe it when you see what impact they made, particularly in North India. We were able to enjoy the development of their architectural achievement across the national boundary from Lahore to the Taj Mahal.

The Moghuls had an amazing knack for keeping their buildings cool. Characteristically set in large monumental gardens, the grass and trees begin the process of considerably reducing the air temperature as their moisture evaporates, and to keep them from drying up to nothing as most vegetation there does, water flows round the site in carefully graded courses. The windows of the buildings themselves are usually filled with marble lattice work, whose circles and squares, to triangles and arabesques, are reflected, shiftingly, in the light and shadow on the paving stones.

Their hilltop placing probably had as much to do with the hope of wind as with the splendid views from afar. Some parts were designed solely as windtraps: boudoirs right out on an exposed corner of a site and up five flights of steps, or overlooking a river. The construction of buildings with long through passages running north, south, east and west had as much to do with creating wind tunnels as with a desire for symmetry. Finally, the

white marble stayed amazingly cool and refreshing to
the touch. As March drew on to April we were increasingly grateful to the Moghuls for being able to resort to
their beautiful and airy pavilions out of the stifling heat,
to write letters or read.

We'd spent far longer than planned in Pakistan – six
weeks – because of our illnesses. The morning we left
Lahore for the border we were very excited. We were
going to India. The very name brought back the anticipation we'd had back in London when we pored over
pictures of the Taj and elephants and expected this to be
the very summit of the journey.

*   *   *

Bam! Our tent, crumpling in on itself, had a boot
through the zip, Howard's glasses were bent from a
smack round the head, and Anna was scrabbling for
clothes. Howard grappled with the turbanned man as he
knocked over the tent, shrieking Hindi imprecations at
us. Another man in police uniform came running over
the field and forcibly restrained our assailant. In a
second he became docile as a lamb, putting his hand out
to rub Howard's temple appeasingly. In the events
leading up to the attack we'd suspected that we were
dealing with someone slightly unhinged. This last act
pretty much convinced us.

It was quarter-past-three in the morning. We'd been
dropped in the wilds of Haryana State an hour before.
Two German honeymooners had most obligingly stuffed
us, the tandem, and two Nigerian students into the back
of their Dormobile, to make it possible for us to pass
through the Punjab in the obligatory convoy. Possible
lifts had been very slow in coming at the border.
Though we'd got there around eight in the morning,
the first vehicle hadn't rolled up till ten thirty: a Turkish
tour coach too full to take us. At midday a British

overland bus with the space but not the will to convey us
had let out a bevy of miserable-looking passengers into
Immigration. We appreciated the driver's reasons. We
could, as he pointed out, be carrying anything (drugs
were his main fear) across the already hypersensitive
border. When the Germans arrived mid afternoon (the
border closed at six and wasn't open for another ten
days) they looked like our last hope. An unfortunate
Tamil, trying to get across without a passport, obviously
thought so too, but he was so desperate he by-passed the
niceties. When we climbed inside the van, he was
squashed up in the furthest corner, knees drawn up
under his chin, large frightened eyes in shrunken
cheeks pleading with them to give a person priority over
a bike. It wasn't the only time the size of our 'disco' (the
first, baffling, appellation the bike got from the Indians)
was a source of discomfort to us. Getting us all and the
tandem into the van was like one of those exercises in
spatial awareness you get if you go for vocational
guidance, though if anyone was good at packing things
into small spaces by then, it was us.

The sleepy, harvest-ripe Punjab we'd hurtled through
that evening, armed guards at our head and our tail,
hadn't felt at all like 'forbidden territory'. Nevertheless a
day later, when we heard that two more policemen had
just been murdered in Amritsar's Golden Temple which
we'd passed, the prohibition seemed more reasonable. It
hadn't been until we had tried to put up our tent that we
had begun to feel any sense of restriction. Two men, one
in police uniform, had come striding over the furrows to
prevent us. We had no Hindi as yet and they very little
English, but what they had stretched to a repeated
'prohibited area' which seemed, judging by their arm
movements, to encompass all the campable spots in the
vicinity. They were trying to get us to stay in a hotel in
Ambala, ten kilometres away. We had no pedals, no
basket, and no back wheel on the tandem, which had its

handlebars rotated flush with the line of the bike – all to get it into the Dormobile. We'd been up since before dawn the previous day and had no Indian money as yet for a hotel. Besides, as we understood, we'd just come out of the 'prohibited area' and we'd only moved fifty yards from where the soldiers had left us.

'Is this Punjab or Haryana?' we checked.

'Haryana.'

'Is this your land, then?'

'No.'

'Is it a military zone?'

'No.'

'Then why can't we sleep here?'

'No. Prohibited area.'

Imponderable. As we attempted to explain that we had very little option but to sleep here, the Sikh, for that was what the un-uniformed man was, began to raise his voice and push Howard by the shoulder. The policeman saw our point before the Sikh, who was shaking his head and rolling up the whites of his eyes pugnaciously. When the policeman explained our situation to him he quietened a little, but then offered us the money for the hotel in Ambala. We pointed silently at the dismantled tandem and half pitched tent, and then, with huge yawns, at our watches. He fumed and muttered some more, but finally the policeman prevailed, informing us that yes we might sleep there for just one night (as if we wanted to spend any longer) and led the Sikh away with soothing words.

It wasn't an entire surprise, then, when the boot appeared, but it made staying in the tent impossible.

'Tell your master to have the decency to turn his back while my wife dresses,' Howard said in his coldest voice. 'Then give us the money to stay at the trucking stop down the road.' The policeman translated, then simply wandered off. The Sikh produced the money but wouldn't turn his back. When we got to the trucking stop and caught the Sikh spying on our next bout of nocturnal preparations, we were sure he must be demented. He'd climbed up a ladder to the roof where we were stabled upon a bed of straw to play the silent voyeur.

The next morning it was drizzling; not what we'd expected of Indian weather. Things looked up when the proprietor of the trucking stop magnanimously gave us a free breakfast and, pedalling into Ambala mid morning, we passed a sign outside the police station saying, 'Requests, Complaints, Enquire Within'. It seemed like too pertinent an invitation to miss. They launched a full-scale inquiry: identity parades, long leafings through staff photographs, visits to the scene of the crime, and locals taken in for questioning. We never found the offender. The chief of police advised us not to camp in his country: 'I regret to have to include my own colleagues' – he twirled his beautifully waxed moustachios around his elegant, Victorian phraseology – 'but there have been incidences of inebriation . . . In short, desirable white damsels have fallen prey to unbridled lust, even within police compounds.'

When, two days later, we became unwitting victims of the 'Festival of Spring, Colour and the Brotherhood of Man' – *Holi* day – we decided we'd had a more than unfortunate introduction to the country we'd had such high expectations of. We'd had no idea what *Holi* was when we were pursued by an enlarged motorbike, cum three-wheeler, cum taxi they call a *tempo*, when Anna had sawdust and mud rubbed, hard, into her hair and water repeatedly flung at her. As we saw the young men draw up some distance down the four-laned highway to prepare for another assault, we crossed over the central reservation and cycled up the wrong side hoping this would deter them. As they came for us again, laughing, we lost our cool. Howard jumped off the bike, grabbing the padlock and chain.

'You come near my wife again, and you'll get it,' he bawled. Still they advanced, coloured dye in hand. As Howard lashed out, men from a nearby tea shop came running out to stop him.

'No, no. You do not understand. This is *Holi*. We are all brothers. This is fun.'

'This is not fun,' shouted Howard, letting his chain drop a little, but telling Anna to take the *tempo's* number down. 'The next police check I come to, I'm going to get the law on you. Then we'll see who'll have fun.' They tried to stay Anna's self-righteous pencil. The police didn't book anyone on *Holi*. The height of mutual cultural misunderstanding came when the chief offender leant forward to rub a smudge of dye on our foreheads as a sign of brotherhood, and we nearly started the fight again. We suddenly realised what we'd think of someone who couldn't take an April Fool's joke and submitted reluctantly. We were doused and buffeted till lunchtime when the jollity officially ceased.

In one respect that was perhaps a good thing, for until then, minor rubs and frazzles notwithstanding, we'd been so blissfully happy that we feared we'd never want to stop. But the most disquieting aspect of the disenchantment seemed to be spiritual, for Anna particularly. Since the moment we'd left the Pakistani border she had been aware of a sense of internal disturbance which had nothing to do, this time, with those 'new country nerves'. Its prominent manifestations were the inability to worship God with joy, and an indefinable fear. What was it? It may have been connected with the fact that we had entered the domain of foreign gods, blood sacrifice, 'detestable images' and sacred stones, carved stones to be bowed down to, cast idols and high places. 'The worship of their gods will certainly be a snare to you' we read in Exodus. Many travellers to India we've met have recounted a similar experience. We don't know much

about spiritual realms and forces, but we finally concluded they were something major here. The longer we
spend in a Hindu culture, the more we believe we were
right at that time to pray through the last chapter of
Ephesians, previously familiar to us mainly for the
ringing prose about the armour of God. Now the
phrases we'd hitherto glossed over suddenly seemed to
ring true as well:

> For our struggle is not against flesh and blood, but
> against the rulers, ... against the authorities,
> against the powers of this dark world and against
> the spiritual forces of evil in the heavenly realms.
> (Eph 6:12)

We were rather surprised to find ourselves largely
uninterested in things Hindu, preferring to stick to our
Moghul trail. Perhaps it was all part of the same thing.
At least in Islam we felt they were seeking the one true
God. If the truth be told, we were rather unscrupulously
commercial about Hinduism. *Daramsalas* are religious
guest houses, frequently open to non-believers, and can
cost as little as a few pence. Often you have to pull your
tooth-brushing water out of a well, and we have bad
memories of the toilets and things running across our
charpoys in some, but others were clean and spacious
with a fan and private bathroom. *Daramsalas* were a
boon to our pockets and our peace. We only tried
camping out three times in India. National curiosity and
the heat, both of which had been increasing steadily
since Baluchistan, finally put paid to our tent.

The 'people factor', for us, was worst in India, in
terms of sheer pushiness. We had to learn, though, that
it was not they who were different, but we. We did well
to remember that we were guests in their country when,
a test of tolerance won, we'd begin to feel just a tiny bit

superior. If we'd never seen a white face before, certainly never an *'ek doh* (one two) cycle' with clip-on luggage to match, our own response might have been similar. Ironically, it was also their eagerness to help foreigners and guests, that was one of the Indians' best qualities; this and an occasional unmatchable graciousness. If we could get behind the irritating action to the reason behind it, we'd often find it was as much our reaction that was the problem as the thing itself.

The persistent desire to bandy banal English phrases (quite often just out of conversational range) for instance, was not only for language practice but also had something to do with the wish to associate oneself with Western affluence, freedom, and style. We didn't mind the advances half as much if they came from educated, softly spoken adults, or via their children, as when they came from bunches of exuberant youths – again, more our problem. Persistent postcard- and fruit-sellers outside monuments drove us to distraction less speedily when we realised that their meagre livelihood depended on the likes of us, and that our developed sense of privacy and personal space is entirely foreign to them. If you share a tap with half the neighbourhood, and a bedroom with seven others, you soon lose any pretensions to that. We noticed, too, that if they saw us getting angry, they loved nothing more than to wind us up and occasionally the infuriating bargaining tactics were no more than a game. We knew, and they knew, that the price would come down in the end, but we had to go through the formula first.

One afternoon, on the plains of Uttar Pradesh, we were loath to take the chance that the next trucking stop would be remote enough to afford us the afternoon rest we'd been denied for many days by persistent onlookers. Seeing a shady tree a field away, we checked that there was no one in sight, plunged smartly to the left, and wheeled the bike quickly across to it. We kept our heads down and our voices low as we unrolled our Karrimats. For ten blissful minutes we thought we'd succeeded. And then they began to come – whence we knew not. We thought we'd been cycling along in the middle of nowhere for the last two hours, but from all sides they came, inciting one another forward. A few had a smattering of English.

'Just five minutes to look at your speed-wallah,' a middle-aged man pleaded. We knew how long Indian 'five minutes' were. Howard actually succeeded in driving the whole of one flank back thirty paces by taking hold, gently but firmly, of some shoulders. A physical gesture like this is much more tolerated than in Europe. We learnt that if a crowd simply wouldn't move aside for the bike, the only and perfectly acceptable thing to do was to nose the wheel right into the front line, though we hated doing it. They would tread on one another's toes and have a bit of a scuffle, but all totally without temper. To ask a sarcastic question like how long they wanted to stand there and stare before letting us go, would tend to upset and confuse. Having failed to get the children to go away, the men then told the women to '*chello*' (get away).

'Memsahib's not well. She can't stand the crowd,' they explained, looking understandingly at Anna, shoving the women away then resuming their places.

We wondered what Jesus would have done in such situations, remembering how He had to slip away from the multitudes for a breather. He'd probably have rebuked them for their selfishness, even raised His voice maybe, but He'd have done it out of love. Love: that was the crunch. Bottom line of course, it was for our own peace of mind and not for their sakes at all that we had to accept the 'people factor'. 'To be content whatever the circumstances' (Phil 4:11) was the goal, but sometimes it could be an uphill struggle in those temperatures. We certainly rarely dared exchange our hundred mile kisses on the mark in India: we usually had to wait until darkness fell and even then, it was dodgy.

The grand trunk road to Delhi was a strange combination. Lined with mango orchards and planted up the centre with bougainvillaea, it was a shock to count eleven head-on collisions in our first day, one of them a particularly vivid, recent smash between a donkey cart and a coach brought to mind what our fate would be if we didn't defer to oncoming overtakers. Warnings on road signs, and painted on to the back of vehicles seemed to make no difference. 'Accidents begins where safety ends', 'Speeding may be thrilling but it's killing' were self-explanatory, if ungrammatical, but the relevance of 'No pain, no gain' and 'Love is sweet poison', was uncertain. 'Horn, please' was unfortunately the only instruction scrupulously obeyed.

Indian roads were still like a day at Smithfield, but we reacted like any good Musulman at the addition of 'very hoggish, snuffly *pigs*' (our aghast diary entry for the day after we quitted Pakistan). They squealed uncleanly round the sacred cows, placidly munching on cardboard bang in the middle of the road. One thing the traffic was careful of was these deities, and it depended how concerned about the after life the particular vegetable-seller was if he allowed the cows to feed off his barrow.

Another thing that took some getting used to after Pakistan was the reappearance of women. Their dress ran the gamut, from saris and *sholwar cameez* to Western clothes (very dated or entirely up to the minute). When we passed a woman on a bicycle, and older women of particular sects wearing saris without the modest blouse underneath, that clinched it. Anna felt free to unveil; her troubles with Asian men must be over.

Our troubles with the heat were certainly not over. We were truly gasping down the Ganges. In all our preparations for the cold we'd never once thought we'd have to take the heat as seriously. The dehydration tablets we'd packed so reluctantly became life-savers, for it got to the point where our stomachs simply couldn't hold as much liquid as we wanted to swallow. When our appetites completely gave up on us in the mid and upper nineties temperatures, those despised, sweet, milky teas were indispensable for the energy they provided, and infinitely preferable to the chlorinated water in our bottles, redolent of swimming pools. The problem was convincing the tea-seller that we really wanted six glasses each.

'Six,' we'd say in Hindi, holding up six fingers, 'for her,' (pointing at Anna) 'and six,' holding up another six fingers 'for him.' Then, putting our fingers together to make twelve, '*Ek dojen chia*', we'd spell out. He'd nod, and his friends would translate; the first would come, and we'd down it in a gulp.

'That'll be one rupee,' he'd say, misinterpreting our looking round for the rest. We'd wheedle them out of him one by one, but by the time we'd got to the fifth our consumption had caused such an amazement among the audience that the effect of the first was lost in the exhaustion of, once again, being the centre of attention.

Our water bottles came in most handy for another beat-the-heat technique. It got to the stage when we had to drench ourselves totally every half hour: underwear, hair, and all, handpumps permitting. One would crouch under it, and the other would work the metal handle up and down. Then we'd quickly get back on the saddles, and push into the wind for momentary, gorgeous, cool relief. As, cycling along, we began to dry off, Anna would spray us with the bottle nozzle. It made a marginal difference, but there was nothing much you could do when it was sunbathable by 7.30 a.m. and by eleven o'clock like a hair dryer. Howard had long since abandoned his trousers for a *lungi*. When we'd read back home that an Indian winter is like a very good English summer, we'd been delighted. We hadn't realised that winter is over well before the March days we were cycling in.

It was an odd season to us: the green new growth of spring under a sun which in our eyes should mean midsummer, and golden grain harvests as if it were autumn. All we ungratefully wanted by then were the Himalayan snows. Getting up at dawn and taking a two hour siesta in Pakistan had seemed extreme, but there was nothing for it here except to get going well before sunrise, stop at half-past eleven in the morning, and wait till three or four o'clock in the afternoon when we could resume cycling till dusk. To have done anything else would have been a health hazard.

To be honest though, when it was good it was very good: lying on a *charpoy* after lunch (several glasses of tea) under the thatch of a hotel, goat kids dozing on one another under the table. There'd be no motor traffic for twenty minutes at a time – only the squeak of a bike, the measured chink of a camel wandering past, or the tidy clip-clop of a new horse and cart. The tone would be set by the snoozing proprietor and the remoteness of the place, our bike carefully chained somewhere out of sight. There'd be more tea at a word to the assistant, and tangerines in our basket to slake our thirst. We'd look across a shimmering lake to girls in splendid saris separating the wheat from the tares, and men would be harvesting with scythes, while children gathered nuts and berries in the shade, and exotic birds splashed at the pump.

13

'BYE BYE'

Sunday, March 15th

The endless avenues of the Ganges Plain wore on and on. We'd pass whole fields of coriander, the delicious scent matched. only by heady, night-flowering jasmine that reminded us as regular as clockwork that it was coming up for time to look for somewhere to sleep. The night before we hit Delhi, a young man serving us tea offered us a bed in his grandparents' rice mill. He had a gentle sadness about him as he said that it was unwise in these troubled times to sleep out. Later, sitting on the *charpoys* placed right in the middle of the biggest hangar for us, he told us that he was a Punjabi refugee whose parents had been killed by Sikh terrorists.

Then he left us to sleep, which Anna did immediately and deeply, while Howard established what was to become an increasingly frazzled relationship with the mosquitoes. Though they bit Anna, they really went for his pale skin. Pale skin produces a more severe systemic reaction to bites than dark skin with lots of melanin — which is providential for the nationals. Our Indian mosquito repellent was useless. In the heat it had separated into chalk and perfumed oil. It was far too hot to use the sleeping bags as protection. Even sleeping on them was sticky. Howard lay awake all night as bats and pigeons swooped and fluttered in the corrugated iron vaults, and rats tunnelled in and out of the mountains of rice about us. At one point the young man returned with four friends, standing and staring for five silent minutes at our recumbent forms in the light of the full-faced moon. We'd been on the road five months. By the next full moon it would all be over.

Despite the young man's story and our first encounter, we actually found the Sikhs restrained and gracious beside their fellow countrymen. Looking for someone to iron Anna's *cameez* in Delhi, we happed upon a Sikh tailor and dry-cleaner. He told us that until 1947 he'd been honoured to serve Europeans from his premises on Jinnah Road, Quetta – strangely, the very place where the *cameez* had been bought. The story of his displacement brought home the misery of Partition: he was regarded as a Hindu by the Muslims in Quetta and now as a subversive by the Hindus in Delhi. Forty years before, he'd fled his home for his life, left his business for an unknown enemy to appropriate, and sought refuge in what was for him a foreign land.

Delhi was larger than life. Popping out to buy a packet of biscuits, you'd bump into a whole cast of characters for your entertainment. There'd be a Tibetan lama with one tuft left on his shaved scalp to keep away the spirits, spinning a mantric prayer wheel, or Buddhist monks whose traditional saffron and crimson robes had been translated into yellow bobble hat, red rayon sweater and – in that heat – maroon wellington boots. There'd be Gandhi lookalikes with staves, and white and ochre lines and circles smeared on to their foreheads, signifying that they were followers of the destructor god, Shiva. These *tikkas* have the same function, basically, as the red circles you sometimes see on Asians in the West, setting them apart as Hindus. When they come in shiny plastic for women, at twelve for a rupee, they somehow lose the effect of those made of powdered dye. Rather disconcerting, too, are the dripping *tikkas* of rice and ghee, usually saved for particular festival days. Sharing with the pavement dwellers cooking up their *roti* on a pile of rubbish this distinguishing mark, but giving them a wide berth, business men would pass in silk suits reeking of Dior. Then we'd notice a Jain priest, or an enormously fat beldame with red in her parting to warn any possible suitors that she was already married.

We nearly bumped into an elephant carrying fire-wood down one of Delhi's busiest thoroughfares side by side with the 1950s British Morris Oxfords they call 'Ambassadors'. We were on our way to pick up tyres, this time from the Oxfam building. Once again, we had no luck. We could just make it to Nepal by putting on the solitary tyre we had left, if there were no major mishaps, but it didn't leave the leeway which had been our guiding principle in packing spares.

There were these and less entertaining street sights and sounds. The ground was covered in bright red/orange stains where people had spat their *pan*, a mixture of betel nut, spices, and condiments, which come rolled up in an edible leaf. They say *pan* chewing can become something for connoisseurs, with the classier concoctions including intoxicants, but we couldn't get past the Dracula mouth that was opened when we were addressed by a masticator, his words quite unintelligible thanks to the mouthful of crimson goo beginning to dribble down his chin.

There was the throat clearing: a long, drawn out gargle – hiss – eject that began way back in the oesophagus and joined the *pan* splatters on the sidewalk. There was the nose blowing: thumb and forefinger pressed just above the nostril, a slight stoop forwards, a vigorous ejection and yet more slime to pick your way round (though we were chastened to discover that Asians find our handkerchief up the sleeve just as disgusting). Compared with the blatant public toilet habits the national pastime of walking down the street brushing one's teeth

with a peeled twig purchased from an itinerant seller,
was barely noticeable after the first few days.

We couldn't leave Delhi till we'd got our panniers
restitched – eaten through by rats wanting to get at our
rehydration tablets. What with them, the puppy who'd
chewed his way through our towel, and the birds' nest in
the campsite showers, we hadn't done too well on the
domestic front, though the capital had again afforded
us a wonderful tour of Moghul architecture, including
the tomb of one of the emperors' barbers as resplendent
as any of the resting places of more exalted members of
the royal household. We particularly enjoyed the
buffalo-pulled lawnmower at Safdarjang's tomb, the
most ecologically sound piece of equipment we'd ever
seen. The gardener encouraged the buffalo up and
down the velvet lawns as we lay in the shade of a tree.
Suddenly we heard 'uh-oh' and it was all stations go.
The animal's tail had begun to rise, the buffalo wallah
snatched a handful of newly cut grass from the mower
and caught the steaming pile. In a moment it was on the
roses while the buffalo chomped from another heap of
fresh cuttings with a self-satisfied air.

Dung was something the Subcontinentals never
wasted. On the road from Delhi to Agra we passed little
houses made entirely of dung cakes, to serve as fuel or
building material and probably a hundred other things
we hadn't picked up on. As soon as they could understand, the little ones would know that if a buffalo
performed beside them, they were to pick up the
offering and take it to be patted and shaped into circular
cakes.

To get to Agra from Delhi, you can pass by Fatepur
Sikri, the tremendous ghost city of the Moghuls, perched
on an uncharacteristic rise, and visible as a commanding
silhouette for miles. We caught it in the evening as the
mists were coming up, a stupendous testimony to the
folly and vanity of man. Magnificently built as the capital

of the Empire, it was abandoned within a handful of years because the water supply was insufficient. The capital was transferred to Agra and we took the road there, warned about the bears that are trained to dance right out into your path to extort their fee. They were as disappointingly unresponsive for us as the snakes in the Red Fort had been, despite the charmer's attempts to rouse them.

It is in Agra, of course, that the greatest Moghul building stands, the Taj Mahal. Like Venice, its effect is even greater than all the hype would lead you to expect and equally indescribable; though who would share it with every tourist in India when if you go right at dawn you can have it to yourself and watch the bee wallah sweeping the dead workers from the plinth on which it stands? Thousands fall nightly from the huge nests hanging in the *muqarnas*.

In another Moghul 'kiosk', on the banks of the Yamuna River, we lazed away the hottest hours one day and sorted out our finances. We were near enough to journey's end to be able to predict how much we'd spend until then. That still left two thousand pounds from all our generous donors to give to the International Nepal Fellowship. We nearly lost the lot that very afternoon. Our attentions had been momentarily caught by the mesmeric motions of the *dhobis* (clothes washers) standing knee deep in the river and lifting the sheets in a wet twist above their heads to thwack out the dirt on large, flat stones in the water. A monkey came sneaking through a cusped arch, and went straight for the money pouch. In the nick of time we saw it, but we spent the rest of the afternoon spraying it off with our water bottles.

There were red-capped sarus cranes, picking their long legged way over the plains between Agra and Kanpur, and hundreds of the national birds – peacocks – strutting at the roadside. It was peacocks in the pipal tree overspreading our tent who gave away our idyllic camping spot — a field dense with dancing fireflies — when, for the third and final time in India, we tried sleeping in the great outdoors. They sounded a raucous alert and in no time at all, we were encircled by men with brands for torches. For all their fearsome aspect, they allowed us to stay in the end.

We'd met the unhappy British tour bus from the Pakistan border again, in Agra. The driver obligingly took a large bundle of our redundant winter wear to drop at a reputable Kathmandu hotel. Our load considerably lightened, there was space now for some additions. We stopped off at a village cobblers and bought Anna a pair of red leather shoes, with pointy upturned toes, for just over two pounds. They weren't quite as pretty as the inlaid and embroidered Pakistani ones we'd had no room for at the time, but they were the nearest thing.

The next night we were stopped by the mayor/ headmaster of a remote little town just before another boat bridge we had to cross. Seeing us reacting rather shortly to the mob round us he said that if we would explain ourselves to them they would leave us alone. He would provide sleeping facilities if we gave the school-children a talk, he said. He sent into the streets, and by word of mouth the entire two hundred and fifty strong school, plus interested parents and hangers on, were marshalled to the schoolyard to hear our story. Perhaps it had something to do with his being a Sikh; the dig-nified ease with which he organised the whole operation was quite remarkable. The other teachers resorted to the usual 'disciplinary' ear boxing and hair pulling, but in a quieter than speaking voice, he got them all into rows, still as mice. We were bidden to the place of honour on chairs at a table in front of the assembled company, and, to our discomfort, served tea and snacks in front of them all, the children round eyed and mentally digesting our every mouthful. We were asked then to 'please teach them a song'! We chose the hymn of St Francis, thinking it might appeal to the Hindu mind. Later that evening, the song went round and round Howard's head and he wondered whether St Francis's love of animals extended to mosquitoes as well.

Just outside Kanpur, aptly dubbed 'The Manchester of India' we were stopped and interviewed by a reporter who described himself in the report as 'this scribe'; promoted Howard, 'a British national who had undertaken an ambitious expedition on bi-cycle' to 'incharge' of the hospital he was simply going to administrate, and dismissed Anna as 'his colleague . . . Ms Anna, who was also working there . . . ' It was one of the few articles about ourselves that we ever got to see.

Perhaps once every three or four weeks, one or other of us would have a day when we just didn't feel very well. Our malaise was usually indefinable – perhaps just nature's way of telling us to rest for a while. In Kanpur, Anna spent the day in a *daramsala* bed, weak and without appetite, reading an Indian women's magazine. It was as much of a cultural eye opener as any day on the road. There was an inability to follow a logical line of argument that made the compilers of *Woman's Own* sound like Wittgenstein. The stories were like something out of 1950s magazines – not so much for the romantic slurp, but for their moral tags, the most consistent being the evils of pre-marital sex. The advertisements too, for cod liver oil and hilariously dated models of vacuum cleaners to 'replace your mother's broom' made wonderful reading. Best of all (if we didn't allow ourselves to think too seriously about the implications) were the matrimonial columns. This was a typical insert:

WANTED

Bride for handsome Punjabi doctor. No demands except: same caste, tall, slim, beautiful, convent-educated, adjustable, co-operative, submissive, homely. Preferably doing her house job or diploma in gynae. Must be able to bear children. Write with bio data to . . .

The next day Anna was up with the lark and we were packing in a vast breakfast to tackle the road to Lucknow. Lucknow featured prominently in the Indian Mutiny of 1857. The British Residency, its walls riddled with cannon shot, stands as a poignant reminder of the harrowing five months of siege the British withstood. It is a singular experience being a British tourist in India at some of the historical sights. Also fascinating was the way in which most of the principal monuments of Lucknow, built after the decline of the Moghuls show even more, via their bowdlerisation of the Imperial style, just how brilliant the originals were. Where water had been used as a creator of space in the gardens of Delhi and Lahore, here it was hidden in cramped enclosures bounded by Jerry built buildings with clumsily applied decoration. Vulgar gold domes completed the wedding cake effect.

From Lucknow, we could have made straight east to Gorakhpur and up to Nepal but we had time before the date we were expected to arrive to make a detour south to the 'eternal city' of Benares, or Varanasi. We caught a whiff of the place before we even got there, as we overtook a perfumed corpse being borne aloft on a bamboo stretcher. To be consigned, entire and weighted, or to have one's ashes scattered in the waters of the Holy Ganges in Benares, is to make more secure one's route out of the cycle of life and desire and into blissful oblivion. Better still is actually to die in the city.

The city reeks of death and worship. The air is nauseously heavy with the scent of the marigolds and white mogra blossoms which garland the temples and idols and are scattered on votive lintels with joss sticks. Even the tea in Benares tastes of patchouli. Entering the

maze of narrow streets in the old city, you pass *sadhus*
haggling over the price of a blessing with dazed country
pilgrims. Men with nose rings and bare feet tread in
holy cowpats. Too late you're rammed up against the
backside of a buffalo feeding off the rubbish in a street
so narrow you can only shunt it ahead of you before
wiping off the damage. It's collared by a tea-seller whose
shop has orange glass images in its shrine and he milks it
there and then.

You pass the silver door of the Golden Temple, walls
built into and around the massive branch-roots of age old
banyan trees. Monkeys – held to be reincarnations of the
god Humayan – dive bomb passers-by. You turn up
another dead end to the tinkling of ceremonial bells, and
a waft of incense, nearly fall down a sharp flight of steps,
and you're on the *ghats*. If the bazaar was suffocating, the
stench rising from the burning flesh is sickening. The
healthiest looking dogs in the whole of India prowl the
cremation pyres as you hasten to the bathing *ghats*
instead. Girls with dripping hair and wetly clinging silk
(Benares is famous all over India for its saris) push past
in excited, chattering groups. Police with spears keep
them in check. You round a temple leaning at an angle
of sixty degrees to the monsoon-eroded bank and in the
slimy green embrace of Mother Ganga are the hordes:
women with faces painted entirely yellow; yogis in
contortionist positions; PhDs who will swear to the
purity of the scummy depths; swamis waist deep in
rapturous prayer; all intent on washing away their sins.
Scowling down on all of them, from the highest point of
the city is the Emperor Aurangzeb's Great Mosque.

It's not hard to see why the city ranks as one of the top
'freak centres' in the Western guidebooks. 'When God is
dead, people do not believe in nothing, they believe in
anything,' said G K Chesterton. Where better than in
this holiest of cities where every second person is someone's guru or, better still, a *baghwan* (god)? Back down

near the Syrian border, we had little but instinct to guide us when we drew tentative links between the women's bewildered gaze and a possible bewilderment of faith. In Benares, the connection seemed unavoidable as we went from place to place for a room, finding them full of Western seekers with lustreless eyes. 'If your eyes are good, your whole body will be full of light, but if your eyes are bad, your whole body will be full of darkness.' (Matt 6:22-23). 'Gone' was the only way to describe them. Looking at some of these people, perhaps wearing only a filthy loincloth, matted hair way below their waists, so emaciated they looked as if they were about to disappear in a puff of marijuana, His final statement came to us with a terrible reality: 'If then the light within you is darkness, how great is that darkness!' (Matt 6:23).

Trying to find a lodge was a job and a half especially when the alleyways are all so narrow that you can barely get a tandem down them. We made our way out of these and on to the main road again, to try and get our bearings, but the trishaw riders who, despite the bike, always offered us their services, weren't prepared to give any directions to hotels they didn't get commission from. 'Burnt down' was the favourite phrase of the drivers of these our cousins, tricycles with a seat for two passengers behind. We got back on the bike to try and penetrate the labyrinth of the old city from further down the main road.

If male attention in Pakistan had occasionally been distressing, in India it was disgusting. Part of the problem was the Indians' greater ability to speak English. Many young men seemed to be fluent in obscenities, even if their more general vocabulary wasn't up to much. They didn't limit themselves to words, either. When two youths on a cycle drew alongside us and one grabbed Anna's breast, we could take no more.

The two men were no match for our double pedal power as we pelted round pigs and buses and rickshaws and sacred cows. We gained on them and rammed their back wheel. Both bikes went over in the middle of the main road, wheels spinning furiously as passing taxis honked at us. The lad on the back rack jumped off and fled down a back street but the other was pinioned, flailing, under his bike. Howard dragged him out. Anna had been insulted so many times by now that we knew exactly what we were going to do if we ever got the chance. Blind with rage, she walloped him round the face with her shoe, the most contemptuous weapon she could use because it came from the lowest and most debased part of the body to the Hindu – the foot. The effect was immediate. We released him and turned to go. The fascinated throng weren't going to let us leave without an explanation, however. When they heard what had happened, their indignation on Anna's behalf demanded an apology from the boy. He was forced to prostrate himself on the ground and kiss her feet.

It was utterly cathartic. Anna, drained from head to toe, quite unused to experiencing extreme anger, sat weakly on the saddle, feet resting on the pedals as Howard cycled to Om House Lodge. Newly painted, with a clean functioning loo and shower, English books, and the biggest surprise of all – a waste paper basket in our room – we'd struck lucky. The proprietor chatted when we initiated conversation, smiled discreetly for the rest of the time. We learnt that his retiring, beaming wife was a Nepali, which seemed to augur well.

We'd passed another thousand mile mark. When we saw Om's breakfast menu, we decided to have a celebration brunch right there. Anna tucked into 'cornflex', Howard into 'porridge and milk and food', we both had 'toaste plane', and chose between 'momlet', 'Egg Amlet (2 piece)', and 'egg scrumbled with round chips'. We felt it was too early for 'curry veg without spice'. It was all delicious until Anna decided to finish up with a 'lassi special'. Lassi is basically the same as Turkish *ayran*, yoghourt and water. They're fine usually, except the 'special' ingredient was a taste exactly the same as the sweet smell at the cremation *ghats*. Very rarely do either of us throw away food, and it seemed even worse in India, but this time the associations were too strong. Even Howard couldn't finish it. Fortunately Mr Om wasn't there to see our rejection of his 'special' by this stage. He'd gone for his fortnightly purge down by the Ganges, and wouldn't be back till he'd swallowed a handkerchief to clean himself out and meditated and fasted till sunset.

The day we left Benares was 'one of those days'. We zipped through twenty miles, then – *paff* – a blowout on a tube that had been fine a week ago when we'd checked it. We put on a new one and gave the old to the little boys who, as always, had begged for it. What they did with them we never knew. Five yards further on we had a flat. The bulky Pakistani valve had bitten into the tube. After we'd patched it, our pump gave out. Things were becoming farcical. We pushed the bike for a mile or so to a farm where a child was sent to pick up a pump from a couple of miles down the road. We pumped up and had tea with the farmer as the child disappeared into the distance to return the pump.

We thought we had got to the bottom of why we'd had so many punctures and blowouts. The subcontinental pumps – cumbersome, three-foot-long things on stands, operable with both hands – were so powerful compared with our little French one that we reckoned we were using them with rather too much gusto for the temperature. Because the tyres expand in the heat of the day, to avoid disaster you have to pump in much less air than at home and more frequently. The shoddiness of Subcontinental valves explains the plethora of pumps available on every street corner – in cities, that is.

When we came to get on again, however, the tyre was flat. As we mended this puncture, the tools in the heat almost too hot to handle, someone else went to catch the child, and someone else provided more water to replenish what we'd just thrown away. This time we were cautious enough to keep hold of the pump till we'd tested the tyre. After three minutes it went again. The patch was too close to the bulky valve to stay on. While Howard fitted an unused, month-old Pakistani tube, Anna mended the outstanding puncture on an old tube from under the saddle, our last one. We weren't taking any chances, though we didn't expect to have any problems with a brand new one. Howard pumped but there was no response. When we took it out we discovered that the tube was covered in hairline cracks where it had perished in the heat. We clearly remembered buying that Pakistani inner tube. The first man had asked thirty rupees, the second fifty, and the last the proper price of nine . . . In the end, it was the old tube Anna had been mending which got us going again.

In the morning we'd noticed that the mosquito bites on Howard's legs had begun to turn bright red. When we'd stopped at a medicine store, still sporting birth control posters from the Indira era with the perfect two child family grinning zanily at one another, all we'd managed to get was a rather expensive tube of antiseptic ointment. At least the fellow had been honest that he'd had no medical training whatsoever. And neither was 'M D (fail)' proudly displayed above the shop, as we saw more than once. We were rather worried. We were less than a week away from our destination. Howard had the perverse idea that we really couldn't get to Pokhara without a major mishap, and because the arrival date was getting closer, the likelihood of disaster was getting greater. We'd planned those last days down to the half mile. Our pride wouldn't let us be any later than the morning of Monday April 13th when we'd informed the INF we would arrive, and the last three days were going to see the end of the pancake flat plains. Howard couldn't afford to be shaky in the legs for the Himalayas, and our punctures had already used up one of our contingency days.

Our worry was unfounded. At the Christian hospital providentially just up the road, they said that the redness was simply because so much blood was being pumped round with the exertion of cycling, and that 'a few days' rest in Nepal' should put it right. It was so cool and overcast the next day that we covered a vast distance by early evening, making up for the previous day. Excitement at seeing our first Nepalis at Gorakhpur caused us to jump back on the bike early the next morning. That, in the light of forthcoming setbacks, was the best thing we could have done. The road we were misdirected out on was being resurfaced and was as stony as Brighton beach. We were so relieved to get back on to the saddle when we regained the tarmac that we didn't realise it was the wrong tarmac. We were going basically north, but on a road that finally took us seventy-three miles longer to get to the border.

The next day, when we tried to rectify our mistake, was even worse. Our error in the first place had been caused by a now familiar inability to get accurate directions. It was the same old problem as in Pakistan. When we asked,

'This road, or this one?'

'Yes,' would come the reply.

When we pushed, '*Which* one?' they'd nod happily.

'Acha, acha; teek, teek' (the all-purpose Urdu/Hindi for yes, OK, right on, I've got you). If we asked them to specify with a gesture, right or left or straight ahead, arms went out in a circular motion that encompassed all three. The most confusing thing of all, and the most crucial to get right, were the head movements for 'Yes' and 'No'. We just couldn't make out what was meant when, in response to our questions, the head would move diagonally from lower left to upper right, and perhaps back again. The final difficulty was a general reluctance about answering our questions at all. They were much more interested in asking us things.

We may therefore be excused for deciding that though nobody would own up to it, a small road we'd noticed was probably a short cut. Anna fought her way through the throng of people who'd closed in on her as she'd entered a shop to get directions, and we plunged off down it, ignoring their 'Nahi, nahi; jongol, jongol'. But for once, jongol indeed it was. We returned to the tarmac, tyres beginning to stick to the scorching, tacky, surface, forced to push on through our midday break, and much later into the evening too, than normal. Absolutely exhausted, and losing hope as dusk was turning to night, we turned into a *tana*. 'Desirable white damsels' notwithstanding, we asked the police for a cell for the night.

As if to wish us goodbye on our last night in India, the barking dogs that were the usual accompaniment to sleep were tonight intent on something unusual. To go for a brand new tent with foreign smelling bodies in it as they'd done in Greece was one thing. To attack a lit and walled compound of armed men was something much wilder and more desperate. They edged closer and closer. Lots of them. We listened in disbelief as the barking reached a pitch and they broke over the cacti planted along the top of the wall to deter intruders. We were so shattered we just lay there as the policemen had their evening's entertainment, lashing out at the yelping dogs with long staves and well aimed rocks. The battle raged for four or five minutes, and all of a sudden there was silence save for the chatting of men.

The next day we sped along, fuelled by the excitement of anticipation. We arrived at the Nepali border mid-afternoon.

We'd made it! We knew it was uncultural, but we held hands, the hairs rising on our necks, even a little bit tearful, as we passed through the border gate into our promised land. That night we got to the end of our six month study of the Exodus, with the moving account of Joshua crossing the Jordan. But then we sat on the bed in the little border town hotel, looking at one another, feeling rather empty. We were there. But not there yet. What were we going to do when we had nowhere else to go?

In actual fact the Terai, the plains which constitute southern Nepal, weren't much different from India. We kept straining to see these Himalayas that were meant to be so spectacular. At Butwal, seventeen miles in, there was still no sign of the mountains. Through the morning mist we wondered at a grey cloud, thousands of feet up, and feared a storm.

'Anna . . . that's not a cloud, you know.'

We stopped the bike and looked in disbelief.

It was the Himalayan wall we were going to have to scale before Pokhara. A quarter of an hour later there was no mistake. The sun was warming up, Butwal petered out, the road rose slightly, and once again we clicked into fifteenth gear and began to mount, reducing conversation to bare necessities. We hadn't even got as far as getting breathless, though, when we hit our first landslide. We really were in Nepal now. Luckily it wasn't impassable for us, and we heaved the bike over the freshly deposited mud and rubble to the envious interest of the bus passengers, snarled up either side of a huge chunk of rock that had just slipped down from hundreds of feet up.

There was a marked difference between Nepalis and Indians. Adults would simply beam a calm *namaste* greeting at us, hands raised in the traditional praying gesture, even though the children might rush out on seeing a *dweeta* (two piece) cycle and run after us shouting, 'Bye-bye, bye-bye' for half a mile or more, easily keeping pace up the one-in-threes. Even that was rather nice, for bye-bye to them also meant 'Hello', because their own *namaste* covered both options. We felt as if we were being welcomed to our new home at the same time as saying farewell to our itinerant life.

That first day left us in no doubt that this was indeed our promised land. Howard had studied the map of the last miles so often, fearing the hills, but now realised he hadn't been able to conceive just how impenetrable it really was. It was a real struggle up the precipitously winding road. None of our mountain riding – in the Alps, in the Pindos, or in the Zagros – had prepared us for this height, depth, and steepness. It was like coming on to the scene of a vast, geological accident and having to pick our way through the crumpled wreckage.

Our overwhelming impression however, was of cool and shade and moss and the trickling of water everywhere, after weeks of stagnant, glaring heat on the north Indian plain. Far off, waterfalls plunged down from under the pines and subsided into brooks running along the side of the road. The sun glistened off the vertiginous, terraced rice paddies. The river roared in the valley hundreds of feet below, giving into ultramarine pools.

'The Lord your God is bringing you into a good land – a land with streams and pools of water, with springs flowing in the valleys and hills' was how Deuteronomy (8:7) put it for us.

Our rose-tinted spectacles cleared somewhat when we met a Nepali teamaker prepared to defend her right to charge us 'tourist price' with her vegetable peeler – a nine inch long Gurkha knife. Dried rice flakes and potato curry was all that was available for supper that night in the little village before we set about the difficult task of looking for a camping spot with a cliff face constantly to one side of us and a gorge on the other. We finally wedged ourselves between two huge boulders right beside the road, and went to sleep to the drumming of a witch doctor way up the mountain side . When Anna got up in the night, she had to make sure she didn't step right into the chasm.

Opening the tent flap at first light, there were more wonders in store. There we were, thinking we were tackling the tallest mountains in the world, still marvelling at our surroundings, and there were they – the snowy trio from the centre of the Annapurna Himal. The legendary Fishtail was in the centre, flushed with the first pinks of dawn. They were the real, splendid, things, and we were only braving the foothills – mere tiddlers. In the afternoon the day before they'd been above the clouds. Now we were lucky enough to catch them before they were obscured again. More than Everest, more than Kathmandu, it was the Fishtail prong which we knew reared above Pokhara that symbolised 'Nepal' for us.

'That's going to be home, my love.'

The almost full moon was just setting as we shivered and got going in the delightful chill.

We were not the first up. Most of Nepal would have seen the sunrise and been at work for some while by the time we'd packed the tent into its bag for the last time. Barefooted women in bright *lungis* and sari tops and a length of cloth wrapped round and round their waists were already trudging up and down on the tracks crisscrossing the hillsides. They carried large, cone shaped baskets on their backs with a strap passed round their foreheads. Some were so bowed under such large bushels of buffalo fodder you could barely see the person underneath. It looked like Birnam wood coming to Dunsinane all over again. Anna washed her hair in a rivulet jetting out of a gully of poinsettias. We'd put on clean clothes that morning to arrive fresh, as if we'd not been on a journey at all.

We passed houses on stilts with slatted straw walls and mud floors the same brick red as the soil to which they clung, for all the world like the Normandy barns at the start of the journey. Women carded and spun wool on their verandahs or picked lice out of one another's hair. Sometimes the road was strewn with wheat for us to thresh, gratis, with our wheels. We went over a good few crests in the false hope that they were our last and finally, when we thought we could bear it no longer, the Pokhara valley appeared beneath us. 'You saw how the LORD your God carried you, as a father carries his son, all the way you went until you reached this place.' (Deut 1:31). It was down hill all the way now. Six months to the day after we'd begun, and mid-morning as we'd promised, we saw what we'd come for.

EPILOGUE

This is not the end.
It is not even the beginning of the end.
But it is, perhaps, the end of the beginning.
(Of the Victory in Egypt.
Churchill's speech at the Mansion House,
December 30th, 1941.)

'Howard, do please look at the road a bit more.'
It was true. We'd be over the edge if we weren't careful. Howard couldn't keep his eyes off the panoramic view beneath us. When we hit a second pothole rather painfully and it was obvious he hadn't been looking again, we thought we'd better stop the bike and get our fill of it. We drank it in, pointing downward into the spacious valley with the full extent of the Annapurnas displayed behind, guessing where the Shining Hospital might be. Back on the bike we fell to considering the last eventful six months.

How much had it changed us, we wondered? Maybe we were still our old selves. Then again, maybe we were like the bike. It had picked up a bit of each country it had been through. There were the water bottles from France we'd bought that day the old man had tapped our wheels with his stick and asked us whether we were just touring the region. Inside one tyre, a great deal the worse for wear, was an Italian inner tube, bought the day we had our first blowout on the outskirts of Bari, just before our happy stay in the Villa Squicciarini. Sparkling wines and *cappucinos* seemed a long way away now as we passed a farmer behind a single buffalo, scraping furrows into his terraced strips.

Our front wheel was still spinning, thanks to Mr Mario's skilful handiwork in Thessalonica: against all the odds, since once spokes begin to get out they're notoriously hard to maintain true. Our strip of Turkish leather was still wrapped round Howard's right handlebar, and the little screw at the right brake, the replacing of which had turned into a tea party with us as honoured guests. We sincerely hoped we'd picked up something of how to be hospitable from the Turks.

The heavy iron bolt from Isfahan, just before the bombs came down was still holding Howard's saddle and Anna's handlebars firmly in place. There was little chance of us forgetting that episode. We'd even kept the one they'd tried to weld together. It had been such a well-intentioned idea, we couldn't bear to throw it away. There was no doubt our Pakistani additions were still with us. The poor road surface had our harness bells jingling and our tassels tossing even though that perished inner tube had gone just a few days before. India was represented by neat patches on our panniers where the Delhi rats had gnawed them. And Nepal . . . ? Well, there was time enough for Nepal to make its contribution.

Our journey had stretched our senses in various directions. First had been our escape from the seasons: holding off the chill of autumn by our progress south – arresting it and then later turning our world order back to front and finding the 'summer' again in Greece. During our eastern passage through Turkey the earth's equatorial tilt caught up with us again, but we had only had a fortnight of mountainous 'winter' before slipping into a hot, sandy 'spring' in Iran. As we wrote our

January diary in our shirtsleeves, we felt quite disorientated and when, at the end of that month, we hit the
scathing, mirror-like heat of the Indian Subcontinent our
whole conception of the seasons broke down altogether.
It all seemed to us, out on the tarmac, a horrid abnor-
mality (and we were well aware that we had escaped the
worst of it).

As we travelled round the earth, like an ant walking
over the segments of an orange, we'd barely noticed the
half dozen time zones we'd crossed. But we had been
struck by a strong feeling, albeit a somewhat romantic
one, of going back in 'historical' time. Day by day our
experiences had reminded us of the history books or the
twentieth-century novels we had read, and as we went
on the associations seemed always of a remoter, more
curious past – much of it, as we've said, biblical.

The journey had also been a matchless education, not
just in the bookish sense – though we would have given
anything to have had an encyclopaedia to hand to
corroborate and clarify things – but also in the broadest
sense. It had challenged so many of our assumptions,
and pointed out within us intolerances we never knew
the existence of. It had taken a great deal of the mystique
and confusion out of our feelings about the world's poor
and replaced them with an outlook at one and the same
time more realistic and less hopeless. We immediately
identified with the sentiments of a nineteenth-century
Baptist minister from the Midlands, whose name has
subsequently become familiar in connection with
another side of his work.

It is delightful to see, as we travel on, the breaking
down of partition walls of prejudice, the subduing
of evil passions and unhappy tempers, the expan-
sion of the intellect, the grasping for information,
the desire for books and the eagerness of their
perusal, and the benevolent sympathies excited by

a more extended knowledge of the circumstances
and sufferings of fellow creatures.

That was how Thomas Cook put it in his pamphlet
*The Physical, Moral and Social Aspects of Excursions and
Tours*.

Most travel stories end with that singular combination
of pleasure and disappointment that characterise 'coming
home'. Ours didn't – couldn't – for as the road signs
trickled away to 'Pokhara 0 km' and we approached the
bustle of the bazaar, it began to dawn on us that another
phase in the adventure was really only just beginning.

Hinterland, village, animist Nepal certainly represented about as foreign a world as we could have
conceived, but now we could at last start learning
enough language to ask some of the hundreds of
questions we'd been unable to ask along the way. Now
we could begin really to identify with a society whose
way of life our own ancestors had lived centuries before.
Now, after so many months of simply observing, we had
the chance to get to the heart of a people – a nation who
daily placate petty spirits that inhabit stones and trees
and shrines upon its hills. Tomorrow was Nepal's New
Year's Day; the year 2044 Bikram Sumbhad. It was a
good day to start.

Full-faced above the valley stood the moon;
And like a downward smoke, the slender stream
Along the cliff to fall and pause and fall did seem.

A land of streams! some, like a downward smoke,
Slow-dropping veils of thinnest lawn, did go;
And some thro' wavering lights and shadows broke
. . . far off, three mountain-tops,
Three silent pinnacles of aged snow,
Stood sunset flush'd: and, dew'd with showery drops,
Up-clomb the shadowy pine above the woven copse.

The Lotos-Eaters
Alfred Lord Tennyson

Appendix 1

PERSONAL EFFECTS

In the Back Panniers

Anna's
1 Four Season Sleeping Bag
1 Shirt, 1 T-Shirt
2 Pairs Knickers, 1 Bra
4 Pairs Socks (from skimpy nylon to 'mountain')
3 Pairs Leggings (from skimpy to 'polarfleece')
2 Sweaters, 1 Sweatshirt
1 Pair Après-Ski Boots
1 Polarfleece Coat
1 'Sprayway' Gore-Tex Coat
1 Pair Thermal Inner Gloves and Ski Gloves
1 Pair Dark Glasses
1 Woollen Hat
1 Pair Waterproof Trousers

Howard's
1 Four Season Sleeping Bag
2 Shirts (dark to hide the dirt)
2 Pairs Underpants
2 Pairs Socks
2 Pairs Trousers
1 Sweater
1 Pair Cycling Shoes
1 Polarfleece Coat (both made by Anna)
1 'Sprayway' Gore-Tex Coat
1 Pair Mother-In-Law's Mittens
1 Pair Clip-on Shades
1 Spare Pair Glasses
2 Elasticated Bandages

In the army surplus Tote Bag
(Secured across the back panniers with bungy)

1 High-Tech Towel (dried in five minutes packed to size of handkerchief)
1 Ordinary Towel (much more bother, but much nicer when in need of a bit of comfort)
2 Karrimats
1 Phoenix Phreerunner Gore-Tex Tent

In the Front Panniers

Left: Food acquired daily, 1 Swiss Army Knife

Right: 1 Map of Every Country, Photocopy of Large Scale Map of the Baluchi Desert, Pocket Bible, 2 Biros, 1 Pencil (for the diary), 1 Pencil Sharpener, 1 Precious Diary, 1 Address Book (almost as precious), Photocopied Marriage Certificates (required for Iran), Spare Passport Photos, 2 International Certificates of Vaccinations, Press Cuttings – 'Totally in Tandem' Brochure – Laminated Ideogram (to explain ourselves), Photocopied Birth Certificates (a waste of space), Sponge Bag.

In the Sponge Bag

Soap Box, Flannel, Small Bottle of Shampoo, Ear Plugs
(for camping in unlikely places), Roll of Plaster, Eyebath
(thrust into Howard's hand by his mum as we set off
from the house), Nail Cutters (there wasn't absolute
agreement about taking these, either), Single Travelling
Toothbrush, Toothpaste (made you feel clean all over
even after a sweaty day in the sun), Nail Scissors
(actually very useful, and not just for nails, despite
Howard's protestations), Mosquito Repellent (brilliant,
used up all too soon), Dental Floss, Loo Roll (paper
inside as well as outside the cardboard tube), Brush and
Comb, Baby Tin of Nivea, Safety Pins, Antibiotics,
Aspirins, 'Bungers Up' (much better to let diarrhoea
out, but on the saddle . . .)

Sent ahead/acquired on the way

2 Turkish scarves (for the extreme cold), 1 Pakistani
Chaddr (donated), 1 pair of Light Canvas Shoes (to
replace ski boots), 1 pair of Glasses (to replace stolen
ones and which, with two safety pins and one can of oil
constituted all our thefts), 1 pair of Turkish *Sholvars* and
1 Baluchi *Cameez* (to maintain Anna's decency), Water
Purifiers, Vicks Inhalant (flu in Turkish monastery),
Dettol (to disinfect water bottles), Antiseptic Cream (a
week before the end of the journey), Indian Mosquito
Repellent (useless), Beard (but saved on shaving equipment), Back Block (sent to Izmir, changed well before
we needed to, to be on the safe side), Inner Tubes, Valve
Adapter (necessarily acquired in Italy when incompati-
ble inner tube had to be bought as replacement), Tyres.

Appendix 2

FOR THE BIKE

Expensive Milometer (speed, time, daily and total mileage)

Inner Tubes (stowed under each saddle, always kept two spare)

Tyre (in figure of eight behind front basket)

Five Specialised Gear and Brake Cables (to cover the possibility of them all breaking, strapped to the frame)

Block 'Bit' (to get Block off)

Sandpaper

One hundred Puncture Repair Patches (vast over-estimate based on the story of a couple who'd gone across the Sahara. Anybody want some?)

Square of Chalk

Big and Small Screwdrivers

Chain Link Remover

Four Spare Links of Chain

Two Top Quality Spanners

Cheap Multi-Purpose Spanner (for every conceivable little nut that might have come off)

Six Spare Spokes for Back and Front

Spoke Keys

Four Allen Keys

Insulating Tape (for electrics and spare cables)

One Foot of Electrical Wire

Wire Cutters (freed the bike after getting horribly ensnared on a French building site)

Pliers (to hold bolt while tightening nut)

Two Screws for Hub Brake Cable (not available from manufacturers, so engineered specially for us by the Royal Navy Workshops)

Valves (always needed in London when clever dicks remove them; needed from Pakistan onwards because local ones are notoriously useless)

Tiny Bottle of Meths (spectacularly useful one day in Pakistan to get speck of sand out of the valve adapter that was rendering it useless)

Tiny Bottle of Sewing Machine Oil (generally used after cleaning with the above; used on Howard's shoes too, before polisher wallah territory)

Bulbs for Front and Back Lights (wrapped in tissue in a film capsule)

Batteries (for milometer and Anna's watch, in with the bulbs)

Ancient toothbrush (from Howard's childhood, for cleaning and re-oiling)

Eyebath (transferred from sponge bag and brilliant for holding tiny screws when doing repairs)

Little Bag of Various Screws, Washers, Oddments (also spectacularly useful)

Very Large Padlock and Chain (defensive and offensive security)

Four one litre Water Bottles

Empty Wicker Basket (wired and soldered on to the front for anything and everything)

Travellers' Cheque Numbers (stuffed up one handlebar – never used)

String (stuffed up the other – often used)

A JOURNEY INTO GOD

Delia Smith

A *Journey into God* is a profound reflection on a subject of deep personal significance to Delia Smith: prayer. Written with the same spirit of simplicity and good sense which has characterised her approach to cookery, this book is ideal for personal use or as a gift.

'A spiritual classic for today.'

David Konstant, Bishop of Leeds

'A useful and practical guide.'

The Sunday Times

'It is like having a wise, practical friend on the same wavelength.'

Lionel Blue

'Welcome nourishment for a spiritual journey.'

Derek Worlock, Archbishop of Liverpool

'A book for the non-believer and, perhaps even more so, for the not-quite-believer — and this must include an awful lot of us.'

Barry Norman

'I cannot recommend this book highly enough to those who are hungry for God.'

Joyce Huggett

KHAKI PARISH

Helen and Bill Cook

Khaki Parish is a unique, personal view of wartime life seen through the eyes of young army padre Bill Cook and his fiancée Helen.

The pair exchanged an amazing 6,000 letters during their wartime separation, writing their way into The Guiness Book of Records.

After their marriage in 1946 the letters were stored in an old ammunition box, to be rediscovered forty years later. The resulting book is a testament to courage, humour and the joys of faithful marriage.

'May become the publishing event of the year.'

Daily Telegraph

'A marvellous record.'

The Universe

'This record is truly unique. Unlike records involved with being muscular or making a lot of money, here are two humans who cherished each other.'

Norris McWhirter, The Guiness Book of Records